CARDINAL LAVIGERIE

AND THE

AFRICAN SLAVE TRADE

CARDINAL LAVIGERIE

AND THE

AFRICAN SLAVE TRADE

EDITED BY

RICHARD F. CLARKE, S.J.

TRINITY COLLEGE, OXFORD

NEGRO UNIVERSITIES PRESS
NEW YORK

BX
4705
. L4
C5
1969

Originally published in 1889
by Longmans, Green, and Co.

Reprinted 1969 by
Negro Universities Press
A DIVISION OF GREENWOOD PUBLISHING CORP.
NEW YORK

SBN 8371-1283-4

PRINTED IN UNITED STATES OF AMERICA

PREFACE

ENGLAND has for a century and more taken her place in the forefront of the anti-slavery crusade. She has long since abolished slavery in all countries under her own sway. She has rejoiced over its abolition in the United States of America; her cruisers keep guard along the African coast to prevent, if possible, or at least to check, the export of slaves from thence : it is her earnest desire to penetrate into the heart of the African continent itself, and destroy the traffic in human flesh, with all its accompanying miseries.

Various circumstances have hitherto combined to defeat her designs of mercy. The conflicting interests of the European Powers and the mutual hostility of Continental nations have rendered impossible the united action which alone could produce a permanent effect. The complications of the Eastern Question have entangled the position in Northern Africa. But, above all, the fierce opposition of Mohammedanism to any European interference with its career of conquest and of crime has succeeded in frustrating the efforts of the liberator, even when nominally supported by a Mohammedan Government. One expedition after another has failed in the face of the deadly enmity of the Crescent to the Cross, and of the double-dealing, rapacity, and corruption of Egyptian officials in the Soudan and on the Upper Nile.

What has long been needed for the uprooting of the traffic which degrades and depopulates Africa, and inflicts on her children revolting cruelties and sufferings that call out to heaven for vengeance, is an Apostle. A man fired with the love of God and his fellow-men can work wonders and attain results that diplomacy and conferences and the action of the Powers can never accomplish. Such a man must, of necessity, have a difficult, it may be an apparently impossible, task. He can scarcely expect himself to witness the success of his work. He may pass to his reward with the end apparently as far off as ever. He is certain to meet with every sort of discouragement, opposition, abuse, and ridicule. He will be regarded as a visionary, an enthusiast, perhaps as a charlatan and an impostor. But if he himself is defeated, his cause will ultimately triumph. If he has to sacrifice himself for the cause of the slave, the sacrifice will be accepted as the condition of Africa's redemption from her present bondage.

Such an apostle, or one whom we may hope that God has chosen for the apostolate, is the subject of the following memoir. The name of Cardinal Lavigerie is already familiar to Englishmen. He has visited England and given a fresh stimulus to her zeal in the cause of the slave. He is at the present time struggling against difficulties enough to dishearten any ordinary man. Jealousy, animosity, suspicion, the accusation of political and self-interested motives, are doing their worst to ruin his work. His proposal of a Congress at Lucerne was unfortunately rendered impossible by the French elections, which were impending at the time. He has been accused of postponing it in order that France might dominate at its assemblies, and of being actuated by a desire to place other countries at a disadvantage to his own.

It is difficult to refute such charges as these; but the fact that the programme of his opponents is that which he had already determined upon, independently of the representations of his assailants, is the clearest proof of his disinterested motives, and of his devotion not to any national or political interests, but to the interests of our common humanity and to the cause of God.

Yet the following pages are perhaps the best evidence of what are the aims of Cardinal Lavigerie and the spirit that has actuated his life. His noble self-devotion is not the growth of a day or a year. It is the growth of a lifetime spent in the service of God and of his fellow-men. In his episcopate in France he was the apostle of his diocese. In Algeria he was the apostle of the Arabs, and that under circumstances which rendered his apostolate a most difficult one. At the present moment he is the apostle of the slaves of all Africa. Many may doubt the possibility of success in the crusade that he is preaching throughout Europe. Some may regard any sort of armed interference as likely to do more harm than good. Some there are whose practical acquaintance with Africa has led them to believe that it is from the English settlements on the Western Coast that the work must be begun; since there, and there alone, the power of Islam is not yet dominant.   But all must allow that there is no man living who has the power to effect the regeneration of Africa that is at present in the hands of Cardinal Lavigerie, and that, if the Congress of European Powers is to take any active steps for the suppression of slavery, they must listen to his counsels and avail themselves of his personal knowledge of the country and the people to whose cause he has devoted himself from the first day that he set foot upon the soil of Africa.

In presenting this account of Cardinal Lavigerie's life and labours, we have to acknowledge our indebtedness to Mgr. Grussenmeyer's interesting book, *Vingt-cinq années d'épiscopat en France et en Afrique.*

R. F. C.

CONTENTS

—◆◇◆—

PART I

CARDINAL LAVIGERIE

PART II

THE AFRICAN SLAVE TRADE

PART THE FIRST

CARDINAL LAVIGERIE

CARDINAL LAVIGERIE

CHAPTER I

LIFE IN FRANCE

CHARLES-MARTIAL ALLEMAND-LAVIGERIE was born at
Bayonne on October 31, 1825.   His father occupied a
good position in the Customs, and his mother, Laure-
Louise Latrilhe, was a daughter of the Director of the
Royal Mint at Bayonne.   Both parents were held in
general esteem on account of their high moral character
and strict religious principles.

From his earliest years the future Cardinal gave
unmistakable signs of a vocation to the ecclesiastical
state, those who were his companions still remembering
how he loved to give everything a religious colouring
and re-enact in his very games the ceremonies of the
Church which he had witnessed. As he was the eldest
son, his father had formed views of a different nature
in regard to his future career; yet when he saw how
decided was the boy's vocation, he had the good sense
not to oppose it: Charles was therefore sent at an early
age to a school in his native town, and subsequently
to the Diocesan Seminary at Larresorre, where he
remained until he was fifteen.

In regard to this period of his life we cannot do better than quote the words of the illustrious Cardinal himself, written on the occasion of the death of Monseigneur Lacroix, bishop of Bayonne :—

'The death of this memorable prelate has deeply touched me, and this for two reasons. First, because he was, in my eyes, the chief member of the French Episcopate, being moreover the bishop of my native diocese ; and, secondly, because he played a part in the most decisive actions of my life.

'I was about thirteen when I received from his hands the sacrament of confirmation. He had at that period been recently consecrated, and, looking back along the vista of years, I can in my mind's eye still see him entering the cathedral, his brow already whitened by the snows of age. I can see the place where I sat, in the nave just opposite the pulpit; I can hear his sermon ; nay, more, I believe that I could repeat it almost verbatim, were I to try to do so, for the sentiments with which his words inspired me thrilled to the very centre of my being, and have ever since remained deeply printed on my heart.

'But my reminiscences do not end here. In the course of the following year, as I felt an ever-growing certainty in regard to my vocation, my father presented me to the Bishop. With equal fidelity can my memory recall every circumstance connected with that first interview. Apparently so unimportant, it was to hold an important place in deciding my destiny. I can see with the utmost distinctness the reception-room of the episcopal palace, its ample proportions, magnified by my childish imagination, its furniture covered with gold-coloured velvet, the very sofa upon which the good bishop was seated. My heart beat loudly as I found myself for the first time in close proximity to a violet cassock. But the genial kindness of the bishop's manner soon set me at my ease.

' "So you have a vocation to the priesthood, my child," he said, as he drew me to his side and gently stroked my hair.

' "Yes, Monseigneur," I replied, emboldened by the encouraging tone of his voice, my resolution meanwhile getting the better of my self-distrust.

' "And what is your reason for wishing to be a priest?" he asked in the next place.

' "In order that I may have a country parish!" I exclaimed.

' My father stared at me, astonished to hear of these rural predilections, the secret of which had never been confided to him. The bishop smiled and said: "You shall first of all go to the Seminary at Larresorre, and then you shall be whatever God pleases."

' He saw more clearly than I could do what was to be my lot in life. I went to the Seminary, it is true; but whither have not my wandering footsteps led me since then? The country presbytery has never been anything more than the dream of my childhood, and sometimes, it must be confessed, one of the regrets of my later years, amid the varied turmoil and agitation which has fallen to my share. But God has led me hither and thither at His own good pleasure, according to the prophetic words of Monseigneur Lacroix, and thus it has come to pass that I am writing these lines amid the ruins of Carthage, and not in some quiet corner of my native province.

' Strange as it may sound, it is none the less true that the bishop, who, when he thus addressed me, more than forty years ago, seemed to me quite an old man,

has grown younger in my eyes, in proportion as I
have myself advanced in life, and have found my head
prematurely blanched by the scorching rays of an
Eastern sun. Indeed the day came at last when I found
myself quite as old as he.

'I told him this on the occasion of my last visit to
France, several years ago. I chanced to fall in with
him as he was walking on the beach one summer evening, accompanied by his faithful Vicar-General, M.
Franchistegny, and his devoted servant Ernest, his old-
fashioned carriage following slowly at a short distance.
If the bishop had confirmed me, it was M. Franchistegny
who had prepared me for my first communion, and,
finding myself thus unexpectedly thrown into their
company, it was only natural that a flood of bygone
memories should rush in upon me. I uttered my thoughts
aloud, and my two companions seemed equally interested with myself in thus recalling the past. "You
must own," I said in conclusion, "that it is a very un-
common thing for an archbishop, who can boast a snow-
white beard and has attained to my mature period of
life, to find himself strolling along with the bishop who
confirmed him on one side, and the priest who prepared him for his first communion on the other. The
strangest part of the story is that I look the oldest
of the three."

'Here Monseigneur Lacroix interrupted me. "Do
you forget that I am over eighty, while you have
scarcely passed your fiftieth birthday?"

'"What you say is perfectly true," I answered, with a
smile, "but permit me to remind your lordship that there
are various methods of computing the length of our existence in this world. One plan is to count the number
of years we have lived, and another to reckon up the

number of miles we have traversed. It is certain that incessant wanderings wear a man out as quickly as succeeding years can do. Therefore, if you are thirty years older than I am, I have assuredly traversed thousands of miles more than you have, so that after all we are much on a par." '

In 1840 M. Lavigerie placed his son under the care of M. l'Abbé Dupanloup, afterwards Bishop of Orleans, who was at that time Superior of the Lesser Seminary of St. Nicholas in Paris. It was there that he made his classical studies, having for companions and fellow-students many who subsequently filled high offices in the Church. But here let us once more listen to his Eminence, as he gives, in a letter written nearly half a century later to M. l'Abbé Lagrange, the biographer of Mgr. Dupanloup, his first impressions of the Seminary and its much-respected Superior.

'During the course of last year,' he wrote in 1883, 'I was on a visit to France, and it occurred to me that I should like to see my old Seminary once more. I never realised the wonderful genius of Mgr. Dupanloup as I did when I stood again within the walls of St. Nicholas. The gloomy old house, with its dusky corridors and its courtyard shut in by walls so high as to give it the look of a prison, joined to the shabby sordid air of the neighbourhood, is calculated to have a depressing influence. Yet, when I first beheld it, the dreary abode was inhabited by a bright, joyous, youthful band. Still the contrast struck me forcibly, coming, as I did, straight from the bright cloudless sky and clear mountain air of my southern home, where nature smiles its most bewitching smile. The leaden skies and damp fogs of Paris in October made my heart grow faint within me, until existence itself seemed barely

possible under such conditions. But ere long there
rose above the horizon another sun which warmed and
cheered my soul, awaking it from its torpor, and flood-
ing it with light. The beloved and honoured superior
of the house transformed all things around us by the
power of his intellect and the enthusiasm of his soul,
transporting us all, masters and pupils alike, to those
sublime mountain-tops which the clouds of earth can
never obscure. His bearing, his carriage, his looks,
his words, the deep and living faith betrayed by all
his utterances, completely overcame us, and awoke a
mingled feeling of awe, admiration, and respect, which
no other individual has ever succeeded in calling out,
at least in my own case. He used his influence as
powerful natures alone know how to do, and carried
us away with him, as it were, in a whirlwind of fire,
desiring to take entire possession of us in order that he
might offer us altogether to Jesus Christ according to
the words of St. Paul, " For all are yours, and you are
Christ's." [1]

In 1843 Charles Lavigerie exchanged the Seminary
of St. Nicholas for that of St. Sulpice. He went first of
all to the house at Issy where he made his philo-
sophical studies, and then to that in Paris of which
M. de Courson was Superior. Here his rare talents
attracted the notice of Mgr. Affre, who had just
founded a House of Studies where the monastery of the
Carmelite Fathers formerly was, and which still retained
the name of *Les Carmes*. He now proposed to Lavigerie that he should take up his abode there, in order
to prepare himself for taking an academical degree.
An offer like this, coming from such a quarter, virtually
constituted a command which left a seminarist no

[1] 1 Cor. iii. 23.

choice but to obey, and in October 1846, having just completed his first year of theology, the young Lavigerie removed to Les Carmes. Less than a twelvemonth later he took the degree of bachelor and licentiate of Arts, resuming almost immediately afterwards his theological studies, which had been temporarily suspended. He was ordained sub-deacon by Mgr. Affre in December 1846, deacon by Mgr. Sibour in December 1848, and priest by the same prelate on June 2, 1849, in virtue of a dispensation from the Holy See, as he had not attained the canonical age of twenty-four.

As soon as the time came for the re-opening of studies, he returned to Les Carmes at the express request of its superior, in order that he might go through the necessary preparation for his doctor's degree.

This he attained in as short a time and with the same marked distinction that had accompanied his previous efforts. Of the two essays he submitted to the examiners, the first was in French, entitled 'An Essay on the Christian School of Edessa,' and dedicated to Mgr. Sibour, the then Archbishop of Paris. The second was in Latin, and entitled 'De Hegesippo,' being dedicated to M. Victor le Clerc, President of the Faculty of Letters. Both essays met with the highest approval, and the youthful candidate received his doctor's degree without a single dissentient voice.

In the course of the following October, M. l'Abbé Lavigerie was appointed professor of Latin literature in the House of Studies mentioned above. The limited income of this establishment did not allow of its offering a sufficient stipend to its professors, and he was, therefore, appointed at the same time to be assistant chaplain to two convents situated in the immediate vicinity. These positions he continued to hold for about three years, during which he graduated in theology. By the express desire of Mgr. Sibour, he competed, in December 1853, for a chaplaincy which had fallen vacant in the Chapter of Ste. Geneviève and came out first among the candidates.

He was, however, destined never to fill the office he had thus won for himself. The impression he made upon the examiners was so great, that in the course of the same week the Archbishop of Paris introduced him to the Minister of Public Instruction with a view to his nomination to the Chair of Ecclesiastical History at the Sorbonne. The appointment was at once conferred upon him, and he entered upon his new duties in the early part of 1854. The professorship lasted over a term of seven years, but after his third year M. Lavigerie was made honorary professor.

It is foreign to the purpose of the present work to enter into a minute and detailed analysis of his lectures. Several of the courses delivered by him have been printed, amongst others a 'Study on Luther,' and some 'Lessons on Jansenism.' These latter are more especially worthy of mention, as having roused into fresh activity the slumbering animosities of the past century, and brought down upon the head of the young professor a shower of attacks on the part of a journal which, though Catholic in name, was Jansenist at heart. Then, as ever, he showed himself to be a staunch champion of the rights of the Holy See, and a firm upholder of Catholic doctrine in all its integrity.

But though his professorial duties left him free to engage in many good works, he felt that his powers were cramped. The tranquil and somewhat monotonous life of a lecturer, while it called into play his literary

talents and oratorical gifts, did not afford sufficient scope
for the exercise of his energy and activity. He was a
born missioner, and he needed a different and a wider
field of usefulness. He pined for freer air, and used, as
he said himself, to feel stifled and oppressed.

Ere long a new horizon opened out before him. A
Society had been formed among the leading Catholics
of Paris for the purpose of extending the religious and
political influence of France in the East by founding
Catholic schools there. M. Lavigerie shall himself tell
us how he became connected with it :—

'My confessor,' he writes, 'was at that time the
well-known Father de Ravignan, whose name, as I
inscribe it on these pages, awakens within me a feeling
of affectionate respect. From the outset I had been
strongly attracted to him by his eminent virtues, his
force of character, and in a measure also by the sympathy engendered by the early recollections we had in
common ; for he was like myself a native of Bayonne, so
that we had both spent our childhood under the shadow
of the same ancient cathedral, living in different houses
in the very same street.

'Father de Ravignan was a consummate master in
the art of guiding souls, and thoroughly understood my
difficulties and aspirations, though he never spoke
openly about the unsuitability of the life of study and
professorial duties in which obedience to my ecclesiastical superiors had induced me to engage. He merely
dropped vague hints from time to time in regard to his
own settled conviction that a more congenial career
was in store for me, doing this doubtless with a view to
sustaining my courage until the right time should
come.

'One day he told me that Father Gagarin had called

upon him the evening before in order to inform him that the members of the Society for the Promotion of Christian Education in the East had decided that the organisation and direction of the work ought to be placed in clerical hands. Then he suddenly added, with a significant smile, "These gentlemen all think that a certain professor at the Sorbonne is the very man they want, and they are anxious to secure him. What answer do you commission me to give them?" I was neither surprised nor disconcerted, but expressed my readiness to accept the proposal if Father de Ravignan thought it to be the Will of God that I should do so.

' "I do think it," he answered simply, and these words settled everything. Whither have not these four words led me since that day, during a period of nearly thirty years? For me the most important point is that the protracted voyage, which must ere long come to a close, should bring me at last to the haven of peace!

'The next morning Father Gagarin made his appearance at my lodgings, and carried me off with him in triumph to the room where the committee were holding a meeting under the presidency of Admiral Mathieu. The good father did not leave me time to speak, but explained that he had arranged everything, and I had merely come to receive the grateful thanks of the committee. They were duly expressed, and then the accounts were handed over to me, together with the cash-box, the latter being absolutely empty! As we left the house together, Father Gagarin looked at me with a droll smile, saying as he did so, " My dear Abbé, you are now afloat; it remains for you to show us how well you can swim!"'

This happened about the close of 1856, and from

that hour we may date the commencement of the apostolic career which Cardinal Lavigerie has pursued with untiring zeal and marvellous success until the present time. In order to make the work known, and raise funds for carrying it on, he used to go week by week, when his duties at the Sorbonne permitted, to some fresh town to preach and collect subscriptions, beginning with those in the neighbourhood and, gradually extending the circle until more distant spots were reached. But his own graphic words shall tell the tale : —

' What mingled reminiscences I have of those days ! and what an intense sympathy I have ever since felt for unfortunate individuals who have to go about begging as I did ! Nevertheless in my mendicant capacity I generally met with a kind reception, especially from the bishops. Nor were their flocks behindhand in generosity, and I could, did time permit, relate many touching incidents, many instances of heroic charity and unselfish liberality. But the roses were by no means free from thorns, and I was bowed out of houses not a few in a manner which was the reverse of flattering either to the cause I was advocating or to myself personally. People professed to be ignorant alike of the existence of the Society and of the Abbé Lavigerie—nay, more, of the very Sorbonne itself ! If I persisted and tried to make matters plainer, it was sometimes delicately insinuated that I must be the impostor who had been recently making the round of the neighbourhood attired in clerical garb, and who was "wanted" by the police.

' Others again went to work in a different way, and covered me with flowers, but with the charitable design of stifling me beneath the fragrant load. I remember

one diocese where the bishop, who is since dead, subsequently showed me much kindness; but I was
unknown to him at the period to which I allude.
He could not, indeed, for certain reasons, refuse me
permission to preach a sermon in his cathedral; but he
happened just then to be much interested in the erection
of a spacious church, and he not unnaturally feared
I should divert the stream of contributions which he
desired to see flowing into his own exchequer. He
therefore strove to effect a compromise, taking care to
be unavoidably absent when I arrived, and leaving to
his vicar-general the task of discouraging me and
arresting any undue outburst of enthusiasm on the
part of the faithful. I must say that he acquitted himself of his duty in the most careful and conscientious
manner.

' " I am so sincerely sorry," the vicar-general would
exclaim every other minute, " that you have come among
us at such an unfortunate time! We have really had
nothing but charity sermons in our cathedral during
the last few weeks, and besides this, our congregations
are very local in their interests, and the appeal of a
stranger never seems to make any impression on them.
Take my advice, and give up all idea of preaching."

' But I was young then, and all this cold water did
not succeed in extinguishing my enthusiasm. Moreover,
I could be very obstinate when I chose. So I quietly
answered that I had already had a good deal of practice
in the art of preaching to empty walls, as my hearers
were not always numerous at the Sorbonne, and I could,
like St. Francis of Sales, content myself with an audience
consisting of three individuals.

' When it became a question of calling upon the
principal inhabitants of the city, my friend changed his

tactics. He persisted in accompanying me everywhere, and no sooner were we fairly inside any house than he left me no time to speak, but introduced me to those present in the most flattering terms, always concluding his peroration by protesting that the bishop felt the impossibility of taking up a new society in a place where the local needs were so numerous and pressing.

'I patiently swallowed these doses of honey and vinegar as long as I could; but after a few specimens my patience gave way, and I unceremoniously broke into my companion's harangue. "I am perfectly certain," I said, "that the vicar-general is doing you an injustice. I have heard quite enough of you to know how ready you are to promote every good work."

'"Alas!" said the good vicar-general with a sigh. "you will soon find out your mistake!" But the following Sunday did not verify his forebodings. I felt thoroughly roused, and I made a more forcible appeal than I had ever done before. As I had been forbidden to make a collection at the church-door, I requested any who kindly desired to help the Society to come to me in the sacristy after the sermon. To my surprise, nearly the whole of the audience thronged in, displaying a liberality which exceeded my wildest expectations. The vicar-general stood by, not looking over-well pleased. I could not resist the temptation to turn the tables upon him.

'"Do you see," I exclaimed, "what a false impression you have given of your bishop and your diocese! I never met with such success before!"

'But there was worse in store for the poor man. Scarcely had we finished dinner, when the head priest of one of the churches in the town came in hot haste to entreat me to occupy his pulpit that evening. Upon this the vicar-general fairly lost his self-control. He took the priest by the shoulders and put him out of the room.

"His lordship the bishop positively forbids it!" he cried in his wrath.

' "How can his lordship forbid it," I suavely inquired, "since he knows nothing at all of the matter?"

' "I know that as well as you do," he answered, "and also I know that, if he could have foreseen what has happened here to-day, he would have forbidden you to set foot in the place!"

'A reception like this was, as I have already said, not a very frequent occurrence. But I can remember one instance in which the head priest of a cathedral fairly shut his door in my face. The incident has imprinted itself on my memory, because I was very near having the opportunity of revenging myself in a most unlooked-for manner.

'The bishop of this diocese died a few years subsequently, and the vacant see was offered to me. I could not repress a secret smile as I pictured to myself the discomfiture of the unlucky priest, should he find himself obliged solemnly to induct into his church the very man he had so unceremoniously thrust out of it. My appointment to the bishopric of Nancy prevented me from having an opportunity of proving to him that "the Kings of France do not avenge the wrongs of the Dukes of Orleans." '

Funds having been thus obtained, and the new Society fairly set on foot, the next step was to secure the approval of the Holy See. Cardinal Morlot kindly consented to accept the office of president, and also to solicit the approbation of the reigning Pontiff, Pius IX. This was graciously and readily granted by means of two Briefs, dated respectively December 13, 1857, and January 29, 1858, wherein every encouragement is given to the work, and numerous indulgences are granted both to the priests who direct the Society and the laity who assist in carrying it on. It was thus fairly embarked upon the current of Catholic life, and nothing now remained but for it to prove itself a real power for good.

This opportunity was not slow to make its appearance. In the latter part of 1859 and the early months of 1860 disturbances of a serious nature broke out in the Lebanon. The Druses and the Métualis, two of the wildest tribes among the inhabitants of Syria, made common cause with the Mohammedans, and executed a furious onslaught upon the Christians. Towns and villages were sacked and burnt, while their inhabitants were ruthlessly murdered. More than 50,000 Christians lost their lives, one of the leaders of the barbarian hordes having registered a solemn oath that his sword should never return to its scabbard until it had struck off the head of the last man who could make the sign of the Cross. The torrent of invasion left every kind of misery in its track, numberless widows and orphans stretched out beseeching hands, imploring in heart-breaking accents the sympathy and aid of the Catholic world. As the Lebanon was under her protectorate, France was specially bound to assist them. A military expedition was speedily organised, in order to save all that was left of the population of the Lebanon district. At the same time it was absolutely necessary to adopt measures of a different description. The Society of which we have been speaking felt that the task of succouring the victims of Moslem fury was one which specially devolved upon it to fulfil, and its director, M.

Lavigerie, issued an eloquent appeal to the clergy of France. This appeal was taken up and responded to with a ready warmth and large-hearted liberality. Not only did the entire Episcopate of France lend their support to the cause, but the bishops of England, Ireland, Spain, Italy, Germany, and Belgium showed themselves scarcely less ready to solicit aid from their flocks. The result was that in March 1860, M. Lavigerie had at his disposal, not only a sum of over two millions of francs, but a great number of contributions in kind, consisting of clothes, ecclesiastical vestments, church furniture, and other necessary articles.

The question now was how to distribute all these offerings in the most effective manner. No time was to be lost, and M. Lavigerie offered to go himself on the difficult and dangerous errand. He accordingly left Paris on September 27, accompanied by Dr. Jaulerry, a medical man of skill and experience. Early in October they reached Beyrout, where, in concert with the Eastern bishops, plans of relief on an extensive scale were immediately organised, committees being formed to superintend the distribution of supplies. Two orphanages were founded, one for girls under the care of the Sisters of Charity, another for boys under the charge of the Jesuit Fathers. But this was not enough. Beyrout had indeed served as a city of refuge, yet there remained the more hazardous duty of visiting those mountainous districts which had been the scene of the massacres, where the destructive action of the ruthless foe had made itself more especially felt. As soon as possible M. Lavigerie set out; his description of the horrors he witnessed and the utter wretchedness and destitution he beheld is forcible and touching in no common degree. He underwent a considerable share of personal suffering in the course of his journey. Upon one occasion the horse he was riding stumbled upon some loose stones, throwing him over its head down a rocky defile, and causing him to fracture his elbow-joint and dislocate his shoulder. Dr. Jaulerry did everything he could to relieve his companion's sufferings, and M. Lavigerie did not allow the accident to interfere with his work of mercy, but continued his journeyings in spite of the acute pain he was enduring and the swollen and inflamed condition of his arm.

In regard to the impression made upon him when he entered Damascus, he wrote as follows :—

'Hitherto it had never been my lot to witness a scene of such utter and terrible destruction. The Christian quarter, which was so separate as almost to constitute a distinct town, was formerly composed of 2,000 houses, containing 30,000 inhabitants. There were also various churches and religious houses, belonging to the Franciscans, the Lazarists, and the Sisters of Charity. Of these 30,000 Christians a large number had been either put to death in their own houses or else overtaken and killed as they were endeavouring to escape. Their dwellings had been all levelled to the ground, so that not even a shed was left standing. Everything that possessed the slightest value had been carried off, all the woodwork, the hinges of the doors, the very locks and bolts having disappeared. We ascended to the summit of a minaret which had been religiously spared by the fanatics, and we thus obtained a bird's-eye view of this picture of desolation. I should have imagined that the city had been visited by an earthquake, for it was impossible to make out even the direction of the streets. As to the innumerable and nameless atrocities which were perpetrated upon

helpless women, children, and aged men, they have been
dwelt upon at length in the pages of the public journals,
and it is unnecessary to repeat them here. Five or
six months after the massacres took place about six
hundred Christian women remained still imprisoned in
harems or in Bedouin tents, it being impossible to discover any definite trace of their whereabouts.'

Before finally quitting Damascus M. Lavigerie paid
a visit to Abd-el-Kader, the Emir, who had earned the
gratitude of France by taking the part of the Christians
during their days of severe trial. He thus describes
the interview : 'I shall not soon forget the impression
made upon me. The calm and gentle countenance,
the grave and moderate language, the firm and dignified
bearing of Abd-el-Kader, completely corresponded to
the idea I had formed of him. I was the first French
priest who had entered his presence—the first, indeed,
who had ventured within the walls of Damascus since
the massacres. One of the most distinguished members
of the Episcopate had charged me before I left my
native land to remind the Emir of his own sojourn upon
French soil, and to tell him that his noble conduct
could cause no surprise to those who knew him and
were aware of the high degree to which he carried the
practice of every natural virtue. I delivered this
message, together with several others of like import.
The Emir, striking his breast after the Arab fashion,
answered : "I have only done my duty and deserve no
praise on that account. I am truly pleased to hear
that my conduct has given satisfaction in France, for I
love your country, and shall never forget the obligations I am under to her."

'Our conversation next turned upon recent events
and the part we had played in them. I cannot express

the delight and admiration with which I listened whilst he, Mussulman though he was, gave utterance to sentiments which might well have fallen from Christian lips. When I rose to take leave he advanced towards me and held out his hand. Remembering that it was the hand which had saved and protected our unfortunate brethren, I attempted to carry it to my lips, in order thus to express my gratitude and respect. Abd-el-Kader, however, refused to receive this mark of homage, saying that though he allowed everyone else to kiss his hand he could not let me do so, because he beheld in my person a minister of God.'

Shortly afterwards M. l'Abbé Lavigerie brought to a close his six months' sojourn in the East, and returned home, followed by the thanks and blessings of those whose sufferings and privations he had done so much to alleviate, if not altogether to remove. On his arrival in France, the recognition accorded to his work was of the most flattering nature. It would manifestly be impossible to specify in detail all the addresses which were presented to him, and the appreciative paragraphs which appeared in the journals of the day. Yet we cannot but mention the address forwarded by all the Catholic bishops of the East to his Holiness Pius IX., and that sent to the episcopate, clergy, and people of France by the Orthodox Greek bishops, in both of which the self-denying and indefatigable exertions of M. Lavigerie are spoken of in terms of the most unqualified admiration. Nor was this all. M. Rouher, the Minister of Public Worship, drew up and laid before the Emperor Napoleon III. an official report, in which, after enumerating the services of the Abbé Lavigerie, he requested that the Cross of the Legion of Honour might be conferred upon him.

Demonstrations such as these could not fail to attract to him who was the subject of them the notice alike of the Holy See and of the French Government. The office of Auditor of the Rota for France having become vacant, the Minister for Foreign Affairs, who had received from his subordinates in the East a detailed and eulogistic account of the labours of M. Lavigerie, mentioned him to the Court of Rome as being in every way qualified for the discharge of these important functions. The proposal was favourably received, the Holy Father sending in due course to the newly elected prelate a brief embodying his decision. As on a former occasion, M. Lavigerie had no room left for deliberation, his duty being simply to obey. His new office constituted him Domestic Prelate to his Holiness and a member of the highest tribunal of the Roman Court, and he took his departure for Rome in October 1861. In accepting his new dignities he had expressly stipulated that he should be allowed to retain the direction of the Society for Promoting Education in the East, and to found in Rome a council in connection with it in order that this Society should thenceforth have two centres or headquarters—one in Paris, and the other in the capital of Christendom. This council was established without delay, with Cardinal Reisach as its president, and included among its members some of the most distinguished prelates of the Roman Court.

Mgr. Lavigerie discharged his new duties in a manner worthy of the highest praise, but his apostolic vocation swept him onward with resistless force, and in less than two years caused him to leave Rome. The French Government agreed with the Holy See in thinking that the active duties of a bishop would suit him

better than either diplomatic functions or the seden-
tary occupations connected with a judicial post. The
see of Nancy was therefore offered to him in 1863 by
M. Rouland, Minister of Public Worship. The Supreme
Pontiff having signified his approval, Mgr. Lavigerie
was consecrated at Rome on March 22, in the Church
of St. Louis des Français.

The pastoral letter he addressed from Rôme to his
future flock is dated Easter Sunday, April 5, 1863, and
expresses the feelings with which he was animated in
taking possession of his episcopal dignity. Although
worthy of being quoted *in extenso*, its length forbids us
to give more than a few brief extracts.

' The day is close at hand, my dear brethren, when
I shall appear for the first time in your midst. As yet
I have never beheld you face to face, nor has the sound
of your voice ever fallen upon my ear; but I love you
with that charity of which religion alone possesses the
secret—that charity which knows neither time nor
space, because its source is in the omnipresent God.'

' My mission is to teach you three things—the most
important, the most sacred, the most indispensable
which can be taught on earth—faith, which sustains
and guides the life of man; hope, which consoles and
cheers him; charity, which renders his existence a
source of happiness to himself and a benefit to others.'

On Sunday, May 10, 1863, Mgr. Lavigerie made his
solemn entry into his cathedral church of Nancy.

Seldom, if ever, has a new bishop found his diocese in a more satisfactory condition: the clergy were
numerous and devoted; good works met with ready support and generous sympathy from the laity; the education of the poorer classes was carried on with zeal and
efficiency. All this rejoiced the heart of Mgr. Lavigerie,

and he thus expresses his thankfulness in this regard in a letter addressed to Pius IX. :—

' These things, and many more which I might enumerate, are the result of the wise influence and active charity of my venerated predecessors in this see. They worked in the vineyard, Holy Father, they bore the burden of the day and the heats, in order that I, the last and the least of them, might reap the fruit of their toil. " Others have laboured, and we have entered unto their labours." ' [1]

But there was still much to be done, and the four years during which Mgr. Lavigerie occupied the see of Nancy were years filled with untiring efforts on behalf of the flock committed to his care, and productive of great and permanent results for good. This first episcopate was a training-school in which he qualified himself for his labours in Africa ; and in the narrower, as afterwards in the wider sphere, he gave constant proof that he possessed the soul of an apostle. His increasing and many-sided activity never degenerated into restlessness or love of making changes; his zeal was tempered by prudence ; the measures he proposed were put forward with moderation and carried out with tact.

His first undertaking was a work of charity and justice. On entering upon the administration of the diocese the new bishop at once turned his attention to the circumstances in which those members of the priesthood found themselves who, bowed down beneath the weight of years or incapacitated by sickness, were obliged to give up the exercise of their sacred functions. It is well known how scanty is the yearly stipend of the parochial clergy in France, and

[1] St. John iv. 38.

how impossible it consequently is for them to lay aside
a provision for their declining years.

'We are poor, my dear fellow-labourers,' Mgr. Lavigerie wrote to his clergy on September 6, 1863; 'we are
poor in all ranks of the hierarchy; for if some of us
have more their burden is also greater, and at the end
of the year we all, bishop and priests, invariably find
ourselves, by the grace of God, without funds, whether
it be that we have only what is barely necessary for our
daily bread, or whether we have (as is our bounden
duty) given to the poor what might appear a super-
fluity.

'I thank God for this poverty of the Church in
France. To it she owes her virtuous and zealous
priests, her brave missioners—a body of clergy, in a
word, whose self-denial, courage, faith, good works are
the glory of our land, and an example to the whole
world.

'But the day comes when this poverty, which by
dint of sacrifices is made a sufficiency, becomes absolute
indigence; when the priest, after having for many
long years borne the burden of the day and the heats,
prematurely aged by his strenuous labours, or overtaken by the infirmities of advancing years, is deprived
of the slender income appertaining to the functions he
is no longer able to fulfil. What is to be done in this
case, when he finds himself reduced to the straits described in the Gospel—I cannot dig; and to beg I am
ashamed? for this the law of the land, the dress I
wear, the dignity of the priesthood alike prohibit.

'To provide for these circumstances of destitution, I
have determined to found in the diocese of Nancy a
fund for sick and superannuated priests. I enclose a
prospectus giving the rules &c. of the proposed Fund.'

The liberal manner in which the clergy responded to the appeal made to them proved the confidence they felt in their bishop. Aid was also obtained from the Government, and the new Fund was placed on a sound and satisfactory basis, enabling it fully to meet the demands made on it. When the time came for Mgr. Lavigerie to leave Nancy it possessed a capital of more than 70,000 francs, which was still increasing, and was the means of relieving the aged members of the clergy from want.

Nor did the fatherly care of the bishop rest content with providing for the temporal wants of his clergy. He knew how to be firm as well as kind, and he next applied himself to alter and improve the existing mode of dealing with charges brought against any of the priests over whom he was placed. These charges had up to that time been exclusively dealt with by the bishop, with whom alone it rested to pronounce judgment according to the information he received. Such a method of procedure was open to many objections, among which that of possible partiality or prejudice on the part of the bishop was one of the foremost; and Mgr. Lavigerie resolved to establish a diocesan tribunal, composed of members of the higher clergy, whose duty it should be to examine into all charges made against ecclesiastics. He drew up a scheme which met with the approval alike of the Holy See and the French Government, and which was found to work admirably, ensuring to priests, on the one hand, a fair and impartial hearing, and giving to the laity, on the other, a full and thorough guarantee that no dereliction of duty on the part of their pastors would be suffered to pass unreproved or unpunished.

Another matter that occupied Mgr. Lavigerie's attention was the formation of a body of professors for the public schools and colleges of his diocese.

It had long been an acknowledged fact that in the diocese of Nancy, and indeed all over France, the educational establishments under the management of ecclesiastics were, in regard to moral and religious training, far superior to those which were directed by laymen; the surveillance exercised over the pupils was more satisfactory, and temptations more carefully removed from their path. But with regard to secular instruction the reverse was unhappily the case; as far as science and classics were concerned, the schools taught by priests enjoyed a very poor reputation, and on this account many Christian parents were deterred from placing their sons under their charge. The reason of this inferiority was, that whereas the University professors went through a special course of study, and were examined for their degree by examiners appointed by the Department of Public Instruction, the young clerics who desired to devote themselves to teaching had no such means of qualifying themselves for their career. To remedy this evil Mgr. Lavigerie saw at first no alternative but to send the future professors to the House of Higher Studies in Paris, where he had himself been first a student, then a teacher. But this plan had serious drawbacks, and was at the best uncertain, on account of the difficulty of finding a sufficient number of vacancies in an institution under the jurisdiction of another bishop. In addition to this, Mgr. Lavigerie was fully alive to the advantage of having under his immediate control and surveillance the young men who were destined for so important a work as that of education. He therefore determined to found at Nancy a house of studies where they could prepare for their degree. This design was productive of the happiest results. Owing to Mgr. Lavigerie's energetic action and power of administration, the standard of attainment in secular studies for the clergy in the diocese of Nancy is still higher perhaps than in any other diocese of France, and the schools and colleges under clerical direction are in a most flourishing condition. But he was not satisfied with providing a more efficient staff of teachers. He also caused the course of studies in all the diocesan schools and seminaries to undergo thorough revision and reform under his personal superintendence. He also reorganised the financial arrangements of these institutions ; all the diocesan educational establishments were obliged to pay a tenth part of their income into a common fund, destined for the help of any which should happen to be in temporary difficulties, and for the maintenance of the older professors, who after twenty-five years of work became entitled to a fixed pension.

Mgr. Lavigerie also paid great attention to the extension and improvement of several religious communities of women. One of these had for its object to teach and care for the children of the poor in country districts, and to nurse the sick. Another had been specially established in view of opening workrooms for young girls. Several of these communities were called upon at a later period to form a house in Algeria, and devote themselves to missionary work, under the direction of Mgr. Lavigerie.

While the ties which united the Bishop of Nancy to his flock grew and strengthened month by month and year by year, the hour was rapidly approaching when those ties were to be severed in a sudden and unexpected manner.

Mgr. Pavy, the Bishop of Algiers, having died on

November 16, 1866, on the 18th of the same month
Mgr. Lavigerie received from Marshal MacMahon, who
was then Governor-General of Algeria, a letter offering
him the vacant see. The marshal had made his acquaintance since his appointment as Bishop of Nancy,
and friendly intercourse had ever since been kept up
between them. Mgr. Lavigerie's answer is couched in
the following terms :—

'Having carefully considered the most unlooked-for
proposal contained in the letter I received a day or two
ago from your Excellency, and having asked God to
enlighten me in regard to the matter, I am about to
tell you quite frankly what I think and feel on the
subject.

'As far as I am personally concerned, I should never
have thought of leaving a diocese to which I am deeply
attached, and in which I have set on foot many good
works ; so that if your Excellency had offered me a see
of greater importance than that of Nancy my answer
would certainly have been in the negative. But when
I took upon myself the duties of a bishop, I did so in a
spirit of self-devotion and self-sacrifice. You now place
before me a trying and laborious mission, an episcopal
throne in every respect inferior to my own, and one the
acceptance of which involves exile from all I hold dear.
Yet since you seem to be of opinion that I am the man
best suited for the post, a Catholic bishop can return
but one answer to your request. I therefore accept the
painful sacrifice without hesitation, and am prepared to
make it, be the cost what it may.'

It was no motive of worldly ambition that determined Mgr. Lavigerie to accept the see of Algiers. He
was already marked out by public opinion as destined
to fill the highest positions in the Church in France

itself. Yet at the call of duty he went into exile, giving up, as far as all human probabilities were concerned, the splendid career which opened out to him at home.

By a decree dated January 12, 1867, Mgr. Lavigerie was nominated to the see of Algiers, which had been recently raised by Pius IX. into an archbishopric, with two suffragan sees, those of Oran and Constantine. He was preconised on the 27th of the following March.

It will now be our task to follow him to a new scene of action, where a wider horizon will open before him— one in every respect worthy of the apostolic zeal which inspired him.

CHAPTER II

THE ARCHBISHOP OF ALGIERS

THE new Archbishop reached Algiers on May 16, 1867, accompanied by M. l'Abbé Bourret, a friend of many years' standing, who is at the present time Bishop of Rodez.

Mgr. Lavigerie took possession of his see with the customary ceremonial, the effect of which was heightened by the brilliant African sun and the picturesque appearance of the native population. It would be no difficult matter to imagine what were his feelings on that important occasion, even if he had not given them eloquent and characteristic expression in his first pastoral letter, addressed to the clergy and faithful under his care. Nothing could give a more just idea of the sentiments which led him to the shores of Africa and of the plan of action he had sketched out beforehand for himself. The energy and fidelity with which he carried out that plan and adhered to that line of action will appear later on. At present we will allow him to speak for himself by means of some extracts from the letter to which we have just referred. After a few introductory phrases in regard to the circumstances attendant upon his landing on African soil, he thus continues :—

'I should only be deceiving you, dearest brethren, were I to attempt to conceal from you the fact that my

weakness at first recoiled from the thought of the
difficult and laborious task now lying before me, and
that the idea of all that is involved in exile from my
native land was deeply painful to me. But the sacrifice has now been consummated, the tender ties have
been broken. To you alone I belong, and the sole
delight for which I crave is that of seeing you accept
those heavenly gifts it is my duty to offer you.

'Well may the heart of your Bishop tremble at so
responsible a mission, but it may also beat high with
joyous hope; and whether I gaze into the past, inter-
rogate the future, or contemplate the present, I can
perceive no undertaking among all those at present
being carried on throughout the length and breadth of
Christendom preferable to the one which has fallen to
my share.'

Mgr. Lavigerie next proceeds to sketch with a
master's hand the outlines of the history of Northern
Africa, and goes on in the following terms :—

'Observe the ruins which everywhere strew the
ground. You will discover in them, lying one above
the other, the traces of three great historic races; the
remains of the highest and most varied civilisation; the
graves, the monuments, and the memories of the most
illustrious men; the scattered stones of world-famed
cities. What names are those of Carthage, Hippo, and
Utica; of Scipio, Hannibal, Marius, Cato, Jugurtha,
and Cæsar!

'But for us who are Christians, there exist memories
of a far more hallowed nature, sacred memories of the
heroes of our Faith—of their courage, their genius, and
their sanctity.

'Grand indeed was the Church of Africa with her
seven hundred bishops, her innumerable churches, her

monasteries, her doctors! Her soil was saturated with
the blood of martyrs; the whole Church rejoiced to
listen while a Cyprian and an Augustine unfolded
dogmas and doctrines; in the hour of persecution the
courage of her delicate maidens surpassed that of hardy
and intrepid men; the grottos of her mountains and
the oases of her deserts were perfumed by the virtues
of her solitaries, and she stirred up the admiration and
excited the holy envy of the entire universe.

'Too soon, alas! were these days of triumph to be
followed by days of mourning, since Christian Africa
was destined to be as celebrated for her misfortunes as
she had been for the virtues and talents of her children.

'Why hast thou fallen, great and illustrious Church?
Wherefore have the stones of thy sanctuaries been
scattered and dispersed? In what manner hast thou
incurred the wrath and vengeance of Heaven, and
become an object of compassion to the whole Christian
world?'

A brief account is then given of the barbarian in-
vasions, their lamentable consequences, and the savage
persecutions they initiated. The Archbishop further
tells us how, when the Christians of Africa had enjoyed
upwards of a century of repose under the sway of the
emperors, the fierce disciples of the Prophet swooped
down upon them, conquering their lands and driving
them from their homes into the rocky fastnesses of the
desert, where they gradually lost their faith, though in
some parts traces of it have ever remained.

'Several melancholy centuries,' he proceeds, 'passed
over their head, while the greatest monarchs of Christian
Europe from time to time vainly essayed to destroy the
lair of the pirates and restore to Africa the liberty of
her ancient faith. St. Louis, Charles V., the illustrious

Cardinal Ximenes, John of Portugal, Louis XIV. were in turn compelled to acknowledge the impotence of their efforts, and to confess that on these shores the courage of their best and bravest soldiers had been displayed in vain. Throughout the gloomy record of this depressing period, the virtue and devotion of the heroic priests who dared to land on these inhospitable shores alone stands out in bright relief. And among the names of the devoted band those of Vincent of Paul and of his sons glow here as everywhere with the lustre of the purest charity.

'Is, then, I ask, the death of this unhappy nation to last for ever? Will no breath of life pass over the dry bones and awaken them, even in the depths of the grave?

'France is calling to thee, O Africa! For the last thirty years she has been summoning thee to come forth from the tomb! Gather together, then, the fragments scattered over thy mountain-sides, strewn along thy trackless deserts; take once again thy place among the nations united to thee by a common faith and a common civilisation. Teach thy children that we have come among them only to restore to them the light, the greatness, and the glory which were theirs in the past, and that we will make thy former conquerors to understand that our sole wish is to avenge thy wrongs by loading thy enemies with deeds of charity and Christian love.'

Mgr. Lavigerie proceeds to depict, in language glowing with sanguine enthusiasm and ardent hope, the Africa of the future as he even then beheld her in his mind's eye, risen again from her ashes, purified, regenerated, endued with fresh life and renewed vigour. Then turning to the practical side of the subject :—

' In his providence God has chosen France to make of Algeria the cradle of a great and Christian nation, a nation like unto herself, her sister and her child, happy to walk by her side in the paths of honour and justice. He is calling upon us to use those gifts which are especially our own in order to shed around us the light of that true civilisation which has its source and its spring in the Gospel ; to carry that light beyond the desert, to the centre of the continent which is still enshrouded in the densest darkness, thus uniting Central and Northern Africa to the common life of Christendom. Such, I repeat, is our destiny ; and God expects us to fulfil it, our country is watching to see whether we show ourselves worthy of it—nay, more, the eyes of the whole Church are fixed upon us ! Could any task be higher, any duty more honourable, than that which lies before us ?

' And it is to my weak hands that God has entrusted the direction of this great work ! By my teaching and example I am to lead my brethren to believe, respect, and love the precepts and commandments of His holy religion ! Like the great bishops whose names make illustrious the early annals of our story, I am to make myself all things to all men, shrinking neither from toil nor from suffering in order to prepare the way for the complete resurrection of a land still sitting in the shadow of death !

' Yes, dear brethren, this is what I have to do as far as my weakness allows ; nay, more, this is what, with the help of God, I must succeed in accomplishing.'

After paying a suitable tribute to the memory of the two distinguished prelates who had preceded him on the archiepiscopal throne, he expresses the feelings with which he had taken into his own hands the crozier they had wielded so worthily, and winds up by entreating the prayers of the Supreme Pontiff, of the bishops of France, as well as of the clergy and faithful of his archdiocese, and by bestowing his benediction.

The first care of the Archbishop was to settle some internal affairs which claimed his urgent attention, more especially to arrange some differences which had unfortunately arisen between the members of the chapter and the clergy at large. He took the administration of ecclesiastical matters as much as possible into his own hands, no matter at what cost of time and trouble, being fully aware that if union is strength, with division, on the other hand, weakness must inevitably come. Pacific and conciliatory as he was, he knew, like everyone qualified to rule, how to be firm as well as kind, and how to put forth, when the occasion arose, an indomitable strength of will. Before long he discovered that it was necessary for him to go first to Rome in order to have an interview with the Pope, and then to France in order to confer with the heads of the Government.

Accordingly he left Algiers on June 11, reaching Rome towards the close of the same month. There he kept the feasts attendant upon the centenary of the apostle St. Peter, and afterwards proceeded to Paris. In that city he was detained longer than he had anticipated, owing to a serious illness ; indeed, a period of more than three months elapsed before he was able to return to Algiers, where his presence was nevertheless imperatively demanded.

He embarked at Marseilles on September 22, accompanied by several priests, among whom was the superior of the monastery of La Trappe at Staouëli, and by some nuns belonging to various communities. The

passage was protracted to the unusual length of six
days, and during the course of it the Archbishop had
the opportunity of proving himself a true apostle, by
encountering those dangers mentioned by St. Paul in
the catalogue of his own sufferings, where he describes
himself as having been ' in perils in the sea.'[1]

It was the season of the year when the equinoctial
gales are to be dreaded; and scarcely had the vessel
which carried the prelate been many hours at sea when
a furious storm arose. So fierce was the rage of the
tempest that the sailors belonging to the ports of
Marseilles and Algiers subsequently declared that its
equal had not been known for years. The steamer,
which was named the ' Hermus,' was one of the smallest
among those belonging to the Compagnie des Messageries
employed to carry the mails between France and
Algeria. Upon this occasion it unfortunately happened
to be more heavily laden than was customary. In
addition to the passengers, who numbered over seven
hundred, the greater part of them being soldiers, it
carried a considerable cargo. Ere long the danger
became imminent, and the captain endeavoured to make
for the land. It was too late, however, since the wind,
which blew a hurricane from the north-west, compelled
the vessel to proceed on its way, tossed hither and
thither at the mercy of the raging waters. The waves
ran mountains high, and one more powerful than the
rest struck the little steamer with such force as to unship its helm and place it *en perdition*, as French
sailors say. The engine-fires were extinguished by the
water which gradually rose in the hold, and officers,
passengers, and crew every moment expected the ship
to founder.

[1] 2 Cor. xi. 26.

Those only who have been witnesses of such a scene as now presented itself can attempt to realise it. Some of the passengers seemed dazed with terror, others grew wild with delirium, while others again gave way to hopeless despair. The officer who was second in command loaded his revolver, declaring aloud his intention of blowing out his brains as soon as death became inevitable. This foolish act completed the panic. It appeared as if no boat could live for an instant in such a sea. Amid the general confusion, faith alone rose triumphant. In a clear ringing voice Mgr. Lavigerie called upon all present to repent of their sins and to trust in God. After himself receiving the absolution from one of the priests on board, he absolved the other passengers, exhorting them to make a vow of a pilgrimage of thanksgiving should they be delivered from the danger which hung over them; and his suggestion was complied with by the greater number.

Shortly afterwards the wind suddenly lulled, and the sea became so much calmer that it was possible to improvise a temporary rudder. On the sixth day after leaving Marseilles the 'Hermus' reached its destination. Mgr. Lavigerie was not slow in fulfilling the promises he had made in his hour of need; in less than a month after landing he sent out a pastoral letter, wherein the faithful were urged to visit the Church of Our Lady Star of the Sea in thanksgiving, numerous spiritual privileges being attached to the pilgrimage. Some years later he also caused an obelisk bearing a suitable inscription to be erected on the edge of a cliff, which can be seen far out at sea.

To return to the affairs of the archdiocese. During the absence of Mgr. Lavigerie that terrible scourge, the cholera, had broken out in Algeria. We may

imagine how he longed to be able at once to take his
place in the midst of his stricken flock, to cheer, aid,
and encourage them ; but illness, as we have seen,
detained him in Paris, so that when he was at length fit
to travel the epidemic had begun to diminish in severity. By the time he once more landed on African soil
there remained little for him to do except to thank the
clergy, as well as the nursing sisters, for the heroic
devotion they had displayed in tending, at the risk of
their own lives, the victims of the fell disease, and to
arrange for the maintenance of the widows and orphans
who had been left destitute.

About six months after Mgr. Lavigerie had taken
possession of the see of Algiers, the obstacles presented
by the timid policy of the Government to the evangelisation of the Arabs, which was the work that he proposed
to himself, were removed, in a great measure, by the
direct interposition of Providence. In the year 1868,
close upon the footsteps of the cholera followed a second
and yet more terrible scourge, a severe famine, the
result of two years of excessive drought and the ravages
of a swarm of locusts. It was also partly due, it must
be owned, to the improvidence and inefficiency of the
native authorities. The unhappy Arabs, destitute of
any provision against this visitation, were reduced to
pitiable straits. Official statistics, published at a subsequent date, attest that no less than 500,000 succumbed
to famine and fever ; for an outbreak of typhus, the
plague attendant on famine, came to complete the
misery. But the colonial government, instead of taking
prompt measures for the relief of the people under
its rule, through fear of public opinion, which was
already strongly adverse to the system of policy pursued in Algeria, studiously suppressed all details of their

sufferings; and drove the famished wretches away from the towns, not suffering them to approach the dwellings of the European residents. The country was consequently covered with troops of starving wanderers, clothed in rags, resembling skeletons rather than human beings, who might be seen rooting up and eating the very grass of the fields to stay the pangs of hunger. No offal or refuse was too filthy to be greedily devoured, and even the carcases of animals which had died of disease were disinterred to serve as human food. The roadside was daily strewn with the corpses of those who perished from want and exhaustion; and in the course of a few months thousands of unhappy children were left orphans by the death or abandonment of their relatives, and were found straying from house to house in search of food, or dying of fever and starvation in the desolate huts which contained the putrefying corpses of their parents. The natives met their fate with the patient resignation, or rather apathy, engendered by Moslem fatalism: when they felt their forces fail, and when they could no longer avert death—the slow and terrible death of starvation—they would uncomplainingly lay down by the wayside, and, drawing their tattered garments over their face, await its approach, murmuring the name of Allah.

In the midst of this dire calamity, the zealous Archbishop, having tried in vain to arouse the authorities to a sense of humanity, lifted up his voice, and in a heart-stirring appeal called on all Christians to hasten to the rescue of their famishing fellow-creatures. At his words a stream of charity poured forth from all parts of Christendom, which enabled him to relieve the most pressing wants of the afflicted. Not pecuniary aid alone, but personal assistance also, was freely offered; priests and laymen, religious of various orders, ladies of rank, physicians, soldiers, all lent their hand to the work. Food and clothing were plentifully distributed, the sick and dying were gathered into hospitals, and committees formed in various parts of the province for the systematic distribution of relief. The wished-for opportunity of reaching the soul of the Arab through the bodily assistance afforded him by Christian charity had now arrived, and the power of the truth was, it was hoped, to be brought home to him by the unselfish devotion which nursed and succoured him in his time of need. But it was to the poor orphans of the famine, whose minds were not yet obscured by pride and prejudice, that the Archbishop looked with special confidence as supplying the good soil wherein the Word of God might be sown with the well-founded hope of obtaining a plentiful return. These without exception found a place in his paternal heart, and he directed that they should be forwarded to him from every part of the province, since he had determined to treat them as his adopted children.

'First of all,' he writes, 'I took in one, then ten, then all who either came of their own accord or whom the priests of the diocese had by my orders picked up by the wayside; at last I found that I had two thousand on my hands.

'I know I have been much blamed, and laughed at too, for what people were pleased to call my imprudence; but despite all the disagreeables and difficulties of the past, and all the anxieties of a future which, it must be confessed, does not always wear the most brilliant aspect, I cannot say that I regret doing as I have done. One thing compensates to me for the cares, the trials, the disappointments I have met with, and that is the pleasure of thinking that throughout the whole of that calamitous period not one unhappy outcast has ever been turned away; not a single child has knocked at my door or that of any other Christian priest without finding admittance—nay, more, without finding in me a father and a friend.

'I seem still to see the poor little things, coming to us covered with rags and dirt, pitiable to behold, frightfully emaciated, their hollow eyes unnaturally large, bright with the weird lustre of the famine fever. I remember what they said, and how it touched me to the heart; and I say again I am far from regretting what I then did.

'It was in November 1867 that the first one presented himself—a boy about ten years old. He was worn to a skeleton.

' " Where do you come from, my child ? " I asked.

' " From the mountains, a long, long way off."

' " What has become of your parents ? "

' " My father is dead.   My mother is in her *gourbi* " (a kind of hut, formed of branches).

' " Why did you leave her ? "

' " She told me there was no more bread for me there—that I must go away to the Christian villages; so I came here."

' " What did you do on the way ? "

' " In the day-time I ate the grass in the fields, and at night I hid in some hole lest the Arabs should see me ; for people said that they killed children and ate them."

' " And now where are you going ? "

' " I do not know."

' " Would you like to go to an Arab marabout ? "

' " Oh, no, no.   When I went to them they drove

me away, and if I did not go off fast enough they set
their dogs at me."

'"Would you like to stay here with me?"

'"Oh, yes, I should like that."

'"Well, then, come with me and I will take you
into the house where my children are; you shall be one
of them, and you shall be called by my name, Charles."

'That same day I took him to the Lesser Seminary.
He proved to be a charming child, docile and intelligent. The answer he made me when, after the famine
was over, I one day asked him whether he would not
like to go and look for his mother, was worthy of the
tact and warmheartedness that are so strangely blended
in the Arab character. He negatived my proposal most
decidedly, and I inquired the reason.

'"Because," he replied, "I have found a father
here who is both father and mother to me."

'This child's story is a fair sample of all the rest.
All who came to us were equally homeless, equally
friendless; and some of them told us tales so terrible as
to make us shudder.

'Unhappily help came too late for a large proportion
of these unfortunate outcasts. Typhus fever, the plague
that follows in the track of starvation, broke out among
them, and despite the care lavished on them, and the
best of nursing on the part of the kind sisters, of whom
several succumbed to the disease, we lost, for about two
months, as many as ten, twelve, or even twenty in a
day.'

The number of children received into the two large
orphanages, one (for boys) founded first at Ben-Aknoun
and afterwards transferred to the Maison Carrée in the
vicinity of Algiers, and the other at Kouba (for girls),
from November 1867 until June 1868, when a fresh

harvest put an end to the famine, was no less than 1,800.
Of these about 500 died ; others, but not so many, were
claimed by their relatives as soon as the distribution of
relief afforded them the means of subsistence. About
1,000 remained, and for these the Archbishop was
enabled to provide, thanks to the liberal aid he received
from the charity of Christians.

Such was the origin of the Arab orphanages. A
year later Mgr. Lavigerie gives the following account
of the results obtained :—

' To rescue these children from an untimely grave
was the primary but not the principal object we had in
view ; to rescue them from the fatal fanaticism of the
Moslem creed, to enlighten their minds by religious and
moral training, to form them to habits of industry and
thrift, to furnish them with the means of earning their
daily bread, was the higher and less easy task we proposed to ourselves.

' We bring them all up, both boys and girls, to industrial pursuits. To till the ground and gather in the
fruits of the earth seems to me the best employment we
can give them. Country life and agricultural labour is,
in my opinion, far preferable for the children of the
lower orders, especially the waifs and strays of the
world, than life in towns, where they too often yield to
the temptations which beset them. Country life, the
life of nature, undeniably possesses the double advantage of promoting the health of the soul as well as of
the body.

' And if in the older countries of Europe, to withdraw
the sturdy sons of the soil from agricultural labours is
a fatal mistake, and generally leads to their hopeless
demoralisation, how much more will this be the case in
Algeria, where the produce of the ground is, and long

will be, the sole and the true source of wealth to the population, to a race of so childish a character as the Arabs.

'This persuasion decided me as to the choice of a life for my children. They may be seen at work in the fields under the guidance of the brothers and sisters who have undertaken their training, tilling the ground, planting vineyards, making pastures, sowing cornfields, reclaiming to the best of their ability the uncultivated lands amongst which their houses are situated. People told me I was attempting an impossible task—that it was not in the power of man to implant habits of industry and toil in children bred and brought up to the vagrant life of the Arab.

'You will not keep one of them, my friends told me; they will every one make off to their respective tribes. But I had too firm a belief in the power of kindness to give ear to these discouraging prognostications; and the event proved me right. Though we gave them full liberty, having no locks to the doors, or rather no doors to the houses, only a very few children left us; the rest remained of their own free will, and displayed no disinclination to work. . . .

'In many cases,' he says later on, 'we met with what we least expected, namely gratitude. Here is an instance which occurred quite recently—I confess I was deeply touched by it. To others it may appear hardly worth telling; but it must be remembered that I go by the name of "Grandpapa Bishop."

'Yesterday I had a visit from one of my boys, who is settled in Algiers. He is named Charles, as so many of them are, for they mostly want to add my name to that which is given to them by the sponsors I find for them. The poor lad is lame, so we had to choose a trade for him in which this infirmity would not be a drawback, and he learnt shoemaking.

' When he left the orphanage, nearly three years ago, he began in a very humble way as a journeyman. As time went on he managed, by practising great economy, to save out of his wages enough to buy blocks, tools, and a small stock of leather ; then he set up business on his own account in an obscure lodging in the Arab quarter of Algiers.

' At first he was sadly unsuccessful. Being utterly inexperienced, he worked for customers who did not pay him ; but he did not allow himself to be discouraged. He set to work again, and contrived to induce some of his former comrades and the fathers of the orphanage to employ him, getting on so well that about three months ago he was able to take a man to work under him. He came on purpose to tell all this to me, doing it with a curious mixture of modesty and self-confidence ; telling me how careful he was to act uprightly, how regularly he went to mass, and how he had defended his religion in discussions with the French and Arabs. I could not but admire his fervent faith and Christian conduct in all that he related. At last, kneeling down before me, he said he wanted to ask a favour of me.

' " It would please my fellow-orphans so much, and me most of all, if your lordship would let me make you a pair of shoes."

' " What ! A pair of shoes ! "

' " Yes, if you would allow me to make you a pair of shoes as a New Year's gift—a beautiful pair, of the best varnished leather."

' It will readily be believed that the *étrennes* this poor youth wished to present me with caused me more genuine gratification than the richest gifts which could have been offered me. He laid hold of my foot to take the necessary measurements without awaiting my reply, and indeed no reply was forthcoming, for I did not wish to show the emotion my voice would have betrayed. When he had done he sprang to his feet in triumph, exclaiming, " Oh, how delighted they will all be when they hear that Monseigneur has really consented to accept a pair of shoes of my making ! "

'Let those who have no children laugh at me if they will. At any rate, many a father and mother will, I am sure, envy me my Arab son, with his homely pair of shoes.'

All the children displayed a marvellous aptitude for apprehending and appreciating the divine truths and practices of religion. Mgr. Lavigerie mentions one child who appeared to be taught of God in a most remarkable manner.

'Last May one of our orphans at Ben-Aknoun, a boy of about twelve, who had given proof of an intelligence far beyond his years, fell seriously ill. He was soon unable to leave his bed, his poor body being literally covered with sores.

'The sisters who nursed him were delighted with his gentleness ; one day when I went, as was my custom, to visit the sick, they pointed him out to me. I approached his bedside, and he laid hold of my arm to draw me closer, and make me bend down over him, for he could not speak above a whisper.

' " Father," he said, laying his hand upon his breast, " I am all black inside here."

' " What do you mean by that, my child ? "

' " I mean my heart is black, because I am not a child of God. I want you to give me the water."

' " What water is it you speak of ? "

' " The water of baptism which makes the soul white in God's sight . . . and then one will go to heaven."

' Whilst saying these words he fixed his wistful eyes on me and raised my hand to his lips.

' " As you wish it," I replied, " I will send to you the father, who will teach you more about it, and then will baptise you."

' The following day the sacrament of baptism was administered to him ; he received it in the happiest dispositions.

' On visiting the infirmary again, the next day but one, I asked my little friend : " Well, you have been baptised ? "

' " I have, father," he replied ; " and now I want you to give me the *bread of God*."

' " He means holy communion," the sister said in explanation. " The priest spoke to him about it, and now he can talk of nothing else but receiving it at once."

' " Do you know what this *bread of God* is ? " I inquired of the child.

' " Yes, father, it is *Sidna-Issa* " (the Lord Jesus).

' As may be imagined, I readily consented to the fulfilment of his pious desire, and a few days later, as he was sinking fast, the priest who had baptised him brought him the Holy Eucharist. The effect produced upon the child was so marvellous that it will never be forgotten by those who witnessed it. At the sight of the Sacred Host, the countenance of this poor little Arab —but yesterday a savage, to-day the prey of a terrible and fatal disease—beamed with the celestial brightness of faith and love. The beauty of his soul seemed to illuminate and transform his wasted features ; he stretched out his poor thin arms towards the Heavenly

Guest whom he was about to receive, and when his lips had closed upon the bread of angels he lay still, looking upwards, apparently unconscious of all around him. A feeling of awe fell upon the by-standers, priest, sisters, and children, as with tearful eyes they gazed on this solemn and touching sight.

'I arrived a few minutes later. As soon as the children in the infirmary caught sight of me they ran to meet me, and, clustering round me, begged that they too might be baptised like Jerome—that was the name given to the little neophyte in baptism.

'I went to the bedside of the dying child ; his face was indeed transfigured.

' "I am going to heaven to see *Sidna-Issa*," he said to me. A short time after he breathed his last.'

Consoling as were instances such as these, there were yet many and great difficulties in training these wild children of the desert, some of whom, even in their earliest years, exhibited the evil habits and characteristic vices of their race in a striking degree. In such cases it was only by the powerful grace of God, with long and watchful care on the part of their kind teachers, that the weeds were uprooted, and sterling qualities were discovered, which, like fair flowers, blossomed and made the barren land bright. Then were the hearts of their foster-parents rejoiced at the sight of their perseverance in combating their passions, and their rapid advance in religious and secular know-ledge—a progress due not merely to their natural in-telligence, but also to the ardour wherewith they pro-secuted their studies. And with a glad and grateful heart did the good Archbishop discern in some the germs of a priestly vocation, of a desire to make their

fellow-countrymen partakers in that great treasure of
the faith with which the hand of Providence had enriched themselves. A number were accordingly placed
in the diocesan seminary, to be prepared by a course of
prayer and study to become one day the apostles of
the numerous tribes scattered over the neighbouring
deserts.

Five years having elapsed since the scourge of
famine swept the land, many of the orphans had arrived
at an age at which it became necessary to consider
the question of their future settlement. Were they to
be restored to the tribes from which they had been
taken, and allowed to resume their former savage habits
of life, or to be launched forth amid the dangers of towns,
peopled, as is often the case with newly-established
colonies, by a class drawn mostly from the dregs of
society? Mgr. Lavigerie had long meditated upon and
matured a plan by which all these dangers might be
avoided, and the foundations permanently laid of a
settled native population. He determined upon the
establishment of Christian villages, the inhabitants of
which should be principally employed in the cultivation
of the soil. They were to be taken in the first instance,
and afterwards recruited, from the youths and maidens
who had grown up under his own eye in habits of
industry, and with the advantage of Christian training.
With this view he had already purchased large tracts
of fertile land and laid out the plan of a new agricultural settlement, to be placed under the patronage of
the great African martyr St. Cyprian. The land
having been divided into allotments, and streets laid
out, cottages were built to receive the newly married
couples. A chapel was also erected in the midst of
the village, with a presbytery intended for the residence

of the priest, who was to be the temporal guide as
well as the spiritual father of the infant colony. It
was in the year 1873 that the first married couples,
having plighted their vows and received a fervent
blessing on their union from the good Archbishop,
came to take possession of their new homes. Thus
was the Christian colony of St. Cyprian formally inaugurated; an event which Mgr. Lavigerie hoped would
be regarded with approval by the Government, since,
should the result be successful, no surer means could
be found to bring about the fusion of races and prevent the gradual retreat or eventual extinction of the
conquered people in presence of the powerful and
prosperous invader.

Mgr. Lavigerie, who knew the Arab nature, had
correctly judged that the example of Christians of their
own race and kindred, leading a settled and laborious
but happy and tranquil life, would exercise a beneficial
influence on the wandering tribes who peopled the
neighbouring plains. Such an exemplification of the
practical working of Christianity could not fail, he
thought, to remove prejudices, and in due time to open
the hearts of the Arabs to receive Divine truth. He
was not disappointed. Numbers of their countrymen
visited the young settlers, some to have their sores
dressed or their maladies prescribed for by the Christian
marabout; all went away full of amazement at the
order and peace that prevailed in these homesteads,
and of admiration at the tender charity with which
these poor orphans had been cherished, educated, and
settled in life. 'Your own fathers,' they said to the
young housekeepers, 'could never have done for you
what the great marabout of the Christians has done.'
And when they saw the missioners and the sisters

kneeling to dress the loathsome wounds of the sufferers who were brought to them from far and near, they would show their appreciation of the spirit of self-sacrificing charity by such remarks as these : ' It is certain that all Christians will be damned, but you will not : you are true believers, you know the one true God.' Or again they would ask, ' Why is it that you do all this for us ?—our own fathers and mothers would not do as much.' Thus it was that some among them were led to know and love the Incarnate God, whose charity to man was so well shown forth in the devoted lives of His servants.

It might be imagined that the hostility of the fanatical followers of the Prophet would be aroused on finding that the young people of this colony had for the most part abandoned the creed of Islam and embraced Christianity. This was, however, by no means the case. The Arabs regarded the change of faith of their countrymen with the indifference peculiar to the Moslem; they were, besides, well aware that perfect liberty of action had been left to the children in this respect, as well as in the option whether they would remain with the Christians or not.

' The marabout has every right to teach them his observances,' was the opinion generally expressed. ' Their life belongs to him, for he it was who preserved it for them.'

' It was written,' was the reply made by others.

A few years later the foundation of this first village was followed by that of a second on the same model, situated at the distance of a few miles, and dedicated to that admirable model of wives and mothers, St. Monica. It was the delight of the Archbishop to visit his adopted children, to counsel and encourage them, to witness their growing numbers, their increasing prosperity, their steady perseverance.

Writing on this subject some years later, he says :—

' The villages are the salvation of our children. There, gathered together under the eye of the missioner, encouraging and helping one another by mutual example, they are sheltered from the dangers to which they would be exposed in any other part of the colony. The Christian village is an oasis in the desert; all around is sadly desolate and parched up by human passions. Here grow up not only my children but my grandchildren, for I have been for some years a grandfather, the greater part of the cottages being now enlivened with the presence of one or two, or even three, little ones. I wish you could come with me to visit the village of St. Cyprian, and see me surrounded by a crowd of little folk who call me "Grandpapa Bishop," pull me by my cassock, and climb up on my knees to see if I have any goodies to distribute. I submit to all with joy, and thank God who has made use of the charity of the faithful to give life to so many innocent creatures, destined to be one day the instruments of His wise designs. It is only in church that these little ones sometimes give a small amount of trouble; for one cannot induce the mothers to leave them behind nor can we induce the children, when there, to cease from their spontaneous cries of joy and wonder. But no matter, they give to God their unconscious homage, like the birds that chirp around us, and celebrate in their own way the infinite providence of their Creator.

' But come now and let us visit the village. The houses stand apart, and are arranged in regular streets. They are humble, it is true, but they are bright with cleanliness—one of the most attractive signs of civilisa-

tion. Young plants of the eucalyptus display their
verdure. A church—poor, indeed, but clean and spot-
less like the other buildings which it overlooks—is surmounted by that sign of peaceful conquest, the cross,
which is destined to give spiritual life to this land, so
long bent under the yoke of death. In front of the
village there stretches a long garden, divided into lots
apportioned to the different families, and watered by
two wells sunk in the soil. At the back there is a field,
surrounded by a double mound of earth, within which
are enclosed at night-time the oxen employed in tillage,
and the goats and sheep which supply the inhabitants
with milk and clothing. All around, the sterile bram-
bles and coarse dwarf palms are giving place to luxuriant fields of wheat. Everywhere are to be seen
signs of useful labour and of active life.

'If you ask a European the name of the new
village, he will answer, "It is St. Cyprian of the Atafs."
But if you go to any of the Arab tribes that are encamped on the neighbouring mountains, and point out
the white cottages afar off on the distant plains, they
will say at once, "It is the village of the sons of the
marabout." The marabout is myself, for in their
language they give this name alike to Catholic priests
and to the ministers of the false Prophet. The sons of
the marabout are the orphans who were rescued in the
great famine, and whom the Arabs regard as my
adopted children.'

.   .   .   .

In this manner a public scourge of a terrible and
calamitous nature became, thanks to the far-seeing eye,
the tender heart, and the able hand of the Archbishop,
a source of incalculable and lasting benefit. The
desolation and death which overshadowed the land

became the principle of a new life; a new light rose out of the darkness; the famine and the famine-fever, that mowed down their victims by thousands, opened the way for the foundation of Christian villages, the foundation of a society of African missioners, and finally for the evangelisation of Africa. The curse was changed into a blessing, and the bolt which struck the rock caused a stream of living water to flow forth and fertilise the whole land.

CHAPTER III

THE ARCHBISHOP AND THE ALGERIAN GOVERNMENT

WE must here say a few words on the existing relations
between the French and the Arabs at the time when
Mgr. Lavigerie entered on his episcopate. The French
administration in Algiers had always been marked by
an unjustifiable opposition to any attempt to christian-
ise the country. The government seemed to imagine
that the policy of non-interference would do more to
conciliate the natives than the heroic devotion of the
Catholic missioners; the clergy, so far from being supported by those in authority in their attempts to establish schools and orphanages and to spread the religion
of Jesus Christ, had been discouraged in their zealous
and self-denying efforts; the Sisters of Charity and other
religious institutions had been established there rather
in spite of the French authorities than with their
sanction and aid. Even the Archbishop and those
around him met with but cold courtesy at the hands of
a government which was at best but half-Christian. Its
policy was to divide the country into two nationalities,
the French and the Arab, and to keep them entirely
apart. This had been the system pursued ever since
Algeria passed into French hands. One of the leading
newspapers, 'Le Royaume Arabe,' openly advocated it.
It was the representative of a number of generals who
were all-powerful at the French Court, and who were

opposed to colonisation and the assimilation of the two races, and to the spread of Christianity.

The success of Mgr. Lavigerie in his apostolic labours roused the bitter enmity of this party. They determined that as soon as the famine was over they would undo his work among the natives, and procure the return of the hundreds of little orphans whom he had gathered into his schools to the Arab tribes to which they belonged. Mussulman fanaticism, they thought, would soon efface the influence of Christian teaching. They hoped thus to discourage the Archbishop, and prevent for the future the education which threatened to reverse their own anti-Christian policy, which had almost become traditional in the colony. The dominant party had not been merely neutral in their action. This would have been bad enough. They had not merely offered no encouragement or countenance to the assimilation of the races and the conversion to Christianity of the natives, but they had persuaded the government to aid with material and moral influence Mussulman institutions and the religion of the Prophet. Through them Catholic and Christian France had been the supporter of the Crescent against the Cross. They had rendered every facility to the pilgrimage to Mecca, and had actually spent the public funds in propagating Islamism in the outlying provinces and in teaching their inhabitants the Koran. They had, moreover, persuaded the French Government to contribute to the repair of the mosques and the building of new ones, and to vote a certain sum of money to be spent on schools, where the Arab children were taught a creed of which an essential element is hatred and contempt of Christianity. Nor was this all. When some of the French missioners had gathered into a

Catholic home the waifs and strays of the city, children
deserted by their parents, or orphans who had no one
to befriend them, they were threatened with fines and
imprisonment if they did not desist from their work of
charity.

What had been the result of this policy? It had
been regarded by the Arabs as a sign of weakness;
far from conciliating them, it had made them conscious
of their power. They regarded the French occupation
with feelings of bitter hostility; the separation between
the two nations was complete—their interests were dia-
metrically opposed; and they regarded the assistance
given to their religion as a spoil won from the enemy,
not as a boon coming from the hand of a friend. All
that they had learned of French civilisation was the
lesson that so many races have unhappily learned from
the presence of Europeans among them—the lesson of
vice. So far from the moral tone of Algiers being
raised by the presence of the French colonists, it was
quite the reverse.

When the famine came this party wisely held their
peace. The separation which they had promoted between
Christian France and Algeria left the poor Arabs isolated in their distress. The anti-Christian faction did
their best to conceal from France the misery that prevailed. The magnificent efforts of the Archbishop were
regarded by them with suspicion and dislike, and his
appeal to France incited them still the more. When
the time of want had passed, they determined to undo
his work if possible, and to ruin him if they could.
But they had not his courage, and the foes of Mgr.
Lavigerie soon found that they had encountered a
more formidable adversary than they had expected.
But we cannot do better than reproduce the letter of

Mgr. Lavigerie to the governor general, in which he defends himself against the charges brought against him.

'You, M. le Maréchal, know better than anyone else what the malicious insinuations of the anti-Christian newspapers are worth. They accuse me of making these poor Arabs pay, by the sacrifice of their religion, for the bread that Christian charity distributes to them by my hands.

'This has not been, and could not be, the conduct of a Christian bishop. I have not said, or allowed others to say, a single word of the kind to any adult Arab whom I have relieved. I did not wish, as I openly announced, that a single one of the 1,200 children I collected together should be baptised, except at the hour of death, and even then those only were baptised who had not attained the age of reason.

'In that respect I wish each one to retain full liberty to do as he pleases. If they prefer to remain Mussulmans when they are of an age to decide for themselves, I shall not on that account withdraw from them my protection and support.

'I shall, it is true, teach them—for I can only teach them what I myself believe—that it is better to provide by the labour of their hands against the vicissitudes of fortune than passively to resign themselves to die, saying it is their fate; that it is better to have a family than to live, under the pretext of divorce or polygamy, in a state of shameful and continual debauchery; that it is better to love and aid their fellow-men, to whatever race they belong, than to kill *those dogs of Christians*; that France and her rulers are greater, in the eyes of God and men, than Turkey and her sultans.

'This is what I shall teach them. Who will venture to find fault with it?

'You too, M. le Maréchal, know better than anyone else the solitude, the complete seclusion, in which I live—-how I shun society and only occupy myself with my episcopal duties and work. If, then, as you tell me, the population of Algeria gathers more closely round me, it is because they consider that the ideas and principles I maintain will prove a harbour of refuge to them after so many storms. . . .

'But I will not enter further upon these details, since your letter evidently alludes to matters of higher importance. It is, in fact, an outcome of the system unhappily pursued up to the present day in Algeria in regard to the natives. The object seems to be to shut them out of every man's sight; and the thing most dreaded, as most calculated to break down the barriers which have been set up, is the action of the Church.

'The system I refer to dates back to the conquest of the country. The first bishop of Algiers was abandoned by those in power, and obliged to fly from the land which he had watered with his tears and the sweat of his brow; and had it not been for the generous interference of the prince who is now on the throne of France he would have died a prisoner. Everyone knows that in handing over Mgr. Dupuch to the tender mercies of his greedy creditors they were handing over in his person the apostle who stood in the way of the anti-religious schemes which had long since been formed, and were being carried into execution.

'His successor, Mgr. Pavy, had no better success. He was forbidden to enter into any relations with the Arabs.

'The venerated superior of the Grand Séminaire, too, was publicly threatened with imprisonment, and

even the galleys, for having picked up in the gutters
of Algiers some little orphan boys of whom he wanted
to make useful members of society.

'And yet, while all liberty was denied to them,
my two venerable predecessors saw mosques which
were not really wanted, erected at a great expense;
schools assisted, and religious assemblies encouraged
where fanaticism was fostered in the natives; facilities
afforded for the pilgrimage to Mecca; nay, more, that
pilgrimage accomplished by the Mussulmans of Algeria
at the cost of the State; finally—a thing almost incredible—the doctrines of the Koran taught, in the name
of France, to a people who were unacquainted with
them, such as the inhabitants of Kabylia.

'The same trials were in store for me. Despite the
authorisation I had obtained from the kindness of those
in high places, I could not succeed, in face of the
determined opposition I encountered, in establishing
at my own expense in Kabylia some unpretending
houses of sisters, to distribute medicines or alms to
any of the natives who might apply for them.

'When the famine was devastating Algeria, I wished
to use my right and do my duty as bishop, by rescuing
the native orphan children, and so I did; but ere long
I heard around me murmurs which augured ill for the
future of my undertaking. All doubt on this point was
at an end, when I heard that you had stated, on the
occasion of the establishment of the brothers at Ben-
Aknoun, that the orphans would, after the harvest was
over, be claimed by their respective tribes; and that
since it was impossible to refuse to give them up, in
the space of a few months the orphanage would be
closed. In other words, M. le Maréchal, these children,
without father or mother, forsaken by everyone and

left to die, but whom I gathered together and supported, thanks to the liberality of the bishops, priests, and Christian laity of France; who were watched over and tended, at the risk of their own lives, by religious of both sexes, more than twenty of whom caught the typhus fever from them, and several of whom have fallen victims to their charity—these children, I say, whom we had rescued at the cost of so much sacrifice, were, after a few months, to be given over, boys and girls alike, without protection, without defence, without friends, to the demoralising influence of their co-religionists. Better a thousand times to have left them to perish!

'And this is what people are pleased to represent as necessary! But it shall not be done till I have protested so loudly that all the world shall hear.

'I would of course have given them up unhesitatingly to their fathers and mothers, or their natural guardians; but I have constituted myself the father and protector of all those children who have no longer parents or guardians; they belong to me, for it is I who have preserved their lives for them. Nothing but force shall wrest them from me; and if they are wrested from me by force, I shall utter cries that will draw down upon the perpetrators of such deeds the indignation of everyone who deserves the name of a man and a Christian.

'To sum up all, M. le Maréchal, two accusations are brought against me, and of both I have the greatest reason to be proud. One is, that I have been the first to raise—somewhat roughly, perhaps—the sombre veil which shrouded from the eyes of France the sufferings of Algeria.

'If this is a crime, I certainly plead guilty to it. As a bishop, I could not, I would not, remain a spectator of the agonised throes of so many unhappy sufferers without imploring for them the aid which charity was so ready to supply.

'The other charge laid at my door is that of having first exercised, and afterwards publicly claimed, in my last letter, a right which certainly belongs to me, because it is that of the Church and that of truth. It is inscribed in our National Code of laws, and will be in the future essential to the salvation of Algeria. This right is liberty for the Christian apostolate such as I have defined it; it is liberty for the exercise of the devoted charity of the Christian priest towards the Arabs, apart from all coercion, and guided by the rules of wisdom and prudence.

' If this is a fault, M. le Maréchal, I have committed it, and I shall commit it again, for I shall demand freedom of action in Algeria; though, if needs be, I shall only demand such freedom as is enjoyed in infidel lands, and at the risk of those who exercise it, without asking protection from anyone.

'I am aware that in asking this I am asking for the abolition of the system pursued up to the present day by the Bureaux Arabes; that I am asking for the removal of those impassable barriers which separate us from the natives, for release from the pressure which from the first has been brought to bear on them.

' And what,' he asks in conclusion, ' has been the result of the pernicious system which it is my desire to see abolished? I am ready to pay my willing tribute to the army, and to acknowledge the good effected by the prowess of our soldiers; but it is not of them that I now desire to speak, nor of the military authorities in general. I am alluding to the administrative system which regulates our relations with the Arabs.

' *From a political point of view*, our enemies are as

numerous as they were on the day the conquest was made. When your Excellency was upon one occasion, before the outbreak of the famine, explaining to me your reasons for opposing in so decided a manner every attempt at evangelisation, you asserted as a principal one among those reasons your dread of exciting the fanaticism of the Arabs, telling me at the same time that, were a European war to occur, we could, in presence of a local insurrection, scarcely venture to reckon on the fidelity of even a mere handful of the native population.

'*From an economical point of view*, the Arabs belonging to the various tribes have been ruined for several years to come by the famine which has prevailed for the past five months.

'*From a moral point of view*, they have acquired our vices without learning our virtues, and have shown themselves obstinately opposed to everything in the shape of progress or amelioration. Such is the result of the rule of Christian France during a period of eight-and-thirty years! Is it not high time to have done with a system so fatal in its consequences, so absolutely condemned by the voice both of God and man?

'Fresh efforts, new exertions, may perhaps be demanded of us. But is it not a hundred times better to make these efforts, even should they amount to sacrifices, for a few years, rather than to see France condemned to the fruitless toil of rolling perpetually the rock of Sisyphus, until at last it falls on her and crushes her, as it must infallibly do, unless she finds for it a more stable resting-place? And what can that resting-place be, if not the basis upon which she herself reposes, the sure footing of Christian civilisation?'

The Emperor was then in power, and liberty of the press did not exist in Algeria, and bold speaking was not looked upon with favour. The letter from which we have just quoted was sent round to the clergy, accompanied by one addressed especially to themselves; and the effect was that of a thunderbolt. The colonists at once understood its import, and perceived that what the Archbishop required was the definite cessation of the system which separated the country into two castes—the one Arab, the other French—and the inauguration of that fusion of races which could alone ensure their own future.

From various parts of Algeria addresses breathing gratitude and affection came from the colonists. We will give one or two of them as a sample of the rest.

' To Mgr. Lavigerie, Archbishop of Algiers.

'Monseigneur,—We, the undersigned colonists of Aïn-Tedlès, have the honour to pray your Grace to receive the expression of our most lively gratitude for the noble and courageous devotion you have manifested in serving the cause of Algerian civilisation and colonisation by making known to the Emperor and the country the critical situation of our fair colony, which ought to be one of the glories of France, its mothercountry. We salute you with all respect as the Saviour of Algiers.'

(Here follow the signatures.)

' To Mgr. Lavigerie, Archbishop of the Diocese of Algiers.

'We, Monseigneur, the inhabitants of Misserghin, urged by the heartfelt admiration we feel for the noble courage and perseverance with which your Grace defends the truth against falsehoods equally incredible and absurd, which barbarism persists in maintaining in

Algeria, to the prejudice of civilisation, desire to lay at your feet our most sincere sentiments of sympathy and gratitude.

'If the firm conviction of a sacred duty to be performed did not sufficiently sustain the courage of your Grace in the struggle, you would derive fresh strength from the knowledge that the whole of Algeria is with you.

'Deign to accept, Monseigneur, the assurance of our respectful affection.'

Mgr. Brossais-Saint-Marc, Archbishop of Rennes, afterwards created Cardinal, wrote as follows :—

'The interests which are at stake in Algeria are too sacred, and the struggle which you are sustaining in order to uphold them is too noble, not to give you every right to the support of all your brethren in the episcopate. The Archbishop of Rennes begs you to reckon upon his support, and at the same time to accept his most sincere testimony of the admiration with which your firm and courageous conduct inspires him. It is, in a word, worthy of the great bishops of the primitive Church in Africa, of whom you are a successor : '—

Mgr. de la Bouillerie, bishop of Carcassonne, subsequently coadjutor of the Cardinal-Archbishop of Bordeaux, uses similar language.

'Your letter to the Governor of Algeria is a splendid specimen of episcopal firmness. There is not a single bishop who would not be proud to have written it. The principles you defend are absolutely above all attack. *You cannot yield one of them—liberty of speech, devotion and charity, are the first rights of the Church.*'

Other bishops and archbishops wrote in the same strain, and the most distinguished Catholics echoed the sentiments of their pastors. Thus M. de Montalembert wrote in the *Correspondant* of May 25, 1868 :—

'At the moment that I write these lines Mgr. Lavigerie, a prelate who is French to his heart's core, is making the hearts of all Catholics throughout Europe thrill with admiration, and is acquiring for himself an enviable place in history.'

Lastly, the Sovereign Pontiff addressed to him a long Brief, which contains the following paragraphs :—

' If We are deeply touched at the numerous afflictions that have fallen on your diocese, and if We grieve over the fate of your people, and the troubles and fatigues you have to endure, We have nevertheless the great consolation of beholding how, in the midst of all your adversities, the light and power of Christian charity shine forth brightly; of seeing the immense benefits that will accrue both to religion and society through your pastoral zeal, your generosity and courage.

' We cannot doubt that your actions are approved of by all those who desire the advancement of religion and the true glory of your country. As for Ourselves, We congratulate you with all our heart, and this all the more because of the serious difficulties you have had to contend with, and the courage with which you have overcome them. We think also that We ought to bestow special praise on all those who assisted you so liberally with their alms, and all who shall hereafter assist you in your noble undertaking.

' With the help of God, neither grace nor strength, nor material aid for accomplishing your work, will be wanting to you and yours.

'We wish all these things for you with our whole heart as a mark of the Divine favour, and our especial good will. We give our apostolic benediction to you, Venerable Brother, to all who support your excellent work, and to your whole diocese.'

Meanwhile the hostile party left not a single stone unturned in order to gain influence with the Emperor, and to induce him to put down ' this episcopal insurrection,' as they were pleased to term it. The Pope was cautiously sounded, with a view to discovering whether he could be prevailed upon to remove the obnoxious prelate. But he stood firm, and upheld in every possible way a bishop who gave proof of such dauntless courage in the fulfilment of his duty.

Mgr. Lavigerie now felt that the time had come for him to plead his cause in person at the Tuileries. He had already written a letter to the Emperor, in which, refusing to play the part assigned to him, of appearing in the character of accused, he turned the tables on his enemies, by assuming that of accuser.

' An endeavour, Sire,' he says in this letter, ' is being made to conceal the miseries of the Arabs as far as possible from the eyes of Europeans; they are in reality greater than is generally thought, or than report in France commonly describes them to be.

'These miseries, and the incredible inertia of the native population, are opening the eyes of many prejudiced persons. On all sides it is beginning to be understood and openly stated that there remains in the present day but one only chance of saving the native races—their rapid and complete assimilation.

'This is the opinion of all the civilians of the colony, *without exception*, to whatever creed they may belong. It is also my opinion, Sire; and I believe, myself that the moment has now come to allow us, at our own risk and peril, to begin to exercise over the Arabs, by the means of charity, at least a moral and religous influence.'

He then explains his views in regard to the Apostolate, and continues as follows :—

'The State cannot undertake a work like this; but we, the clergy of Algeria, can do so, without compromising anything, provided we act with discretion, prudence, and charity.

'This liberty, so long asked for, but hitherto asked for in vain, on account of the obstinate opposition of the Bureaux Arabes, can no longer be confronted with the bugbear with which these officials invariably resist every measure that does not commend itself to them. I mean the prospect of an insurrection in the West and South. It is this with which they threaten us. But such a thing is impossible, now that the Arabs have lost all power of revolt for a long time. I venture, therefore, Sire, to hope that we shall soon see these obstacles disappear which have hitherto always been opposed to our charitable action, and that, after having rescued from death so many native children at the risk of our own lives, we shall no longer be forbidden to strive to save, by the force of example and charity, a people which has unfortunately fallen so low.'

In May 1868 he went to Paris for the purpose of seeing the Emperor. On the 17th, after his interview with him, he wrote him a second letter, of which we give the greater portion, as it will throw light upon the point at issue :—

'I have the honour of forwarding to your Majesty the letter in which I announced my intention of writing to his Excellency the Minister of War, in order that he might send me an official reply addressed directly to myself.

'I venture to hope that your Majesty will vouchsafe to give the necessary orders in respect to the answer which I am to receive, so that it may be such as will enable me to terminate, to the satisfaction of all parties concerned, the unfortunate dispute which appears daily to assume new and more formidable proportions.

'During seven years of my life I exercised, as Director of the Society for Promoting Education in the East, the liberty of action I now claim in Algeria, without being challenged by anyone, under the protection of the Mussulman authorities, in every part of the Turkish Empire. I founded or supported orphanages, refuges, and hospices at Cairo, Beyrout, Damascus, Smyrna, and Constantinople—wherever, in fact, I saw fit. In these orphanages and refuges children and persons in distress were received without distinction of creed. Mussulman orphans were adopted, baptised, and educated, without opposition or interference.

'These facts will be confirmed by the testimony of our former ambassadors at Constantinople.

'How can a right which I have freely exercised in a land essentially Mussulman be refused to me on French territory? Will not the question be set at rest if we confine ourselves to demanding for the Church, in that part of Africa which belongs to France, *the same liberty as in Turkey?*

'Nothing, Sire, could be simpler than for your representatives to say to the Mussulmans of Algeria: The French marabouts will open charitable asylums for your sick, for your orphans and widows in this country, wherever you wish them to do so, *as they do in Turkey, under the protection of the Sultan.* You can avail your-

selves of them or not, as you choose, and in no case
will the marabouts interfere with your liberty or with
the exercise of your religion. They will content themselves with doing you all the good they can, and praying for you.

'It is a strange thing, and one which posterity
will find difficulty in believing, that in Turkey I was
publicly rewarded by the Sultan for doing these things.
Fuad Pasha came in person to my residence in Beyrout
in order to bestow on me, on behalf of his sovereign, the
decoration of the Medjidji. Your Majesty is aware
what has befallen me, and to what treatment I have
been exposed for desiring to begin the same work on
French territory.

'The same applies to all our foreign missions. When
our French bishops and priests out there are persecuted,
not merely on account of works of charity such as I am
carrying on, but even for openly preaching the Gospel,
your Majesty demands for them, by the voice of your
ambassadors, and, if need be, by the sword of your
soldiers, the free exercise of their ministry.

'What is the reason of the strange inconsistency
through which we alone, the clergy of Algeria, are
directly opposed in the fulfilment of our mission,
especially when we desire to limit it to the unfettered
practice of Christian charity, deeming that this charity
is in itself sufficient gradually to win for us all hearts?

'Finally, through another and no less strange inconsistency, the scrupulous regard for the Mussulmans is
pushed to such an extreme that we are prohibited from
doing them good under the pretext of not alarming
their religious susceptibilities. Meanwhile, we who are
Frenchmen and Christians are debarred from the exercise of one of our most sacred religious duties, that

of benevolence! In a word, we are deprived of our liberty of conscience on the plea of respecting that of the Arabs.

'And why is this? It is, I am not afraid to say, solely to be attributed to prejudice and a love of opposition, as well as to the influence of those who are enemies of religion.

'All these things, therefore, combine to solicit from your Majesty a solution of the question favourable to our wishes. We base our request—

'(1) On our right as Christians and missioners, which cannot be contested, and which we exercise all over the world under the protectorate of France.

'(2) On the true interests of our colony, where our charitable work will, if not impeded, hasten the fusion, so much to be desired, of the various races which people it.

'(3) And, finally, on the religious welfare of all those who, witnessing our practical charity, will, I hope, be gradually and gently drawn towards the Christian faith.

'It is, therefore, with the confident hope that we shall have for the future full freedom to carry on and develop the various good works which we have set on foot for the benefit of the poor Arabs, and that these undertakings will be the object of your Majesty's royal favour, that I venture to express my heartfelt gratitude, and have the honour to remain, with the deepest respect, &c.

'CHARLES, Archbishop of Algiers.'

This dignified and unflinching letter met with unlooked-for success. The Emperor, who was timid at heart, and was alarmed at the commotion that was made, declared that he would listen to no more complaints against the Archbishop. He even offered him a much more distinguished see in France. Mgr. Lavigerie replied, with all the respect due to his sovereign, that he was very grateful to the Emperor for his kindness, but that to accept his offer would be to disgrace himself and the Church. It was, therefore, agreed that he should remain at Algiers, and carry on his works of benevolence ; and the Emperor gave orders to Marshal Niel, the Minister of War, to give him a formal assurance that he would be in no way interfered with. The letter to this effect was published in the ' Official Journal,' May 28, 1868. The following passages are taken from it:—

' I am happy to state that the differences which have arisen between the Governor-General of Algeria and your lordship are caused by a misunderstanding rather than by any real and fundamental divergence of opinion upon the questions in debate. . . .

' Be assured, Monseigneur, that it was never the intention of the Government to restrict your rights as archbishop, and that every latitude will be granted you for the extension and improvement of the refuges where you rejoice to lavish on outcast children, widows and old men, the kindly aid of Christian charity. . . .

' I cannot close this letter without thanking your lordship for the conciliatory spirit in which you have put an end to a dispute much to be regretted from every point of view, and the existence of which is not easy to understand, since it has arisen between distinguished men who are the greatest credit to their country, and a prelate who, in his anxiety for the welfare of his good works, only feared one thing—that a sufficiently wide field would not be left to him for the exercise of his charity.'

Upon the receipt of this letter, in which the minister

strove to conciliate alike the military authorities and the Archbishop, the latter, shortly afterwards, published, in a letter addressed to Mgr. Soubiranne, the Director of the Society for Education in the East, the true account of the conclusion of the contest.

'I am writing again, to make a fresh appeal to your charity. I have delayed doing so for nearly two months on account of the opposition which was suddenly stirred up in Algeria, and which seemed to threaten, and that at no distant date, the very existence of the refuges where I have gathered together the native orphans and widows.

'Now, thanks be to God, my anxiety is fully set at rest on that point in consequence of mutual explanations. I have received from the Imperial Government the most positive assurance that my charitable institutions will not be interfered with, and full liberty is granted me to add to their number. Besides this, I know now that the orphans will not be taken from me, and that if any questions arise in regard to them, they will be laid before a court of law. I made this a special stipulation, as I am sure beforehand that the court will only confirm our rights.

'These are concessions worth having. There is not a single person in Algeria who would not, only six months ago, have declared them to be completely unattainable, and I can only acknowledge myself deeply grateful to the government for them. Everyone knows what obstacles have hitherto always been put in the way of any intercourse, even on the footing of simple charity, between the Catholic clergy and the native population.

'In regard to foundations on Arab soil, the same liberty is, in principle, granted me. Such foundations would be subject to the legal conditions which apply to institutions of the same nature, whether in France or Algeria. Such are the terms of the declaration I have received.

'This is the dawn of a new era for Algeria, and for the work of Catholic charity the augury of a happy future. The most important thing to be done now is to set to work in good earnest to improve and develop our refuges, and this cannot be done without substantial aid from the Catholics of France. . . .'

Such was the end of the first act of the drama, the military stage, if we may so call it, of the contest between the Archbishop and the faction that opposed him.

The fall of the Third Empire took place just at this time, and shortly afterwards civil government superseded military rule in Algeria. The first representative of the government was Admiral Gueydon. The appointment was a happy one. No man was better fitted to cope than he with the difficult task before him. He recognised the errors committed in the past, and saw how they were to be repaired. He entered at once and thoroughly into the scheme for the assimilation and christianisation of the province. Cardinal Lavigerie bore witness to this quite recently in a letter which he published, and which is a tribute to the memory of the quondam governor.

He begins by recalling the situation of affairs when the admiral first came to Algeria.

' At that juncture we felt our vessel was sinking fast, and we did not know what might happen from day to day. France was occupied by our foes, the Commune was triumphant in Paris, the government had been put to flight, our soldiers were either taken prisoners or engaged in a fresh and a more terrible warfare. Algeria, whose only thought had been to hasten to the aid of her mother-country, was left without any regular troops, and at the same time Kabylia, trembling in the gust of revolt which swept through the country, seemed as if it would fall upon and overwhelm us.

' The disaffection had assumed a definite shape from the moment when we had allowed the natives to perceive that we were disunited amongst ourselves. . . .'

The Cardinal proceeds to show how ably Admiral Gueydon, to whom was given the difficult task of upholding his country's honour, succeeded in arresting and suppressing the insurrection, and to what good account he turned his victory in order to resume and promote the work of civilisation. He continues:—

' To no less an extent did he further the assimilation of the natives. I remember how one day, very soon after he was made governor, he came by his own desire to see our missioners at the Maison Carrée. It was not an easy thing to do, but on that account it showed all the more what was his character and what were his views. " Gentlemen," he said, addressing to them a few straightforward, manly, and sensible words, " there are people who oppose you; but I, as an old French sailor, can say that I approve of you and shall always praise you, provided you follow the rules of caution and prudence that your Superior has given you. I approve of you because, by endeavouring to draw the natives nearer to us by instructing their children and showing kindness to them, you are doing the work France wants to see done. You are doing it, too, without offending the prejudices or rousing the fanaticism of the people, and thus you are preparing a future for the colony. France has not enough men to people Algeria ; she must

supply the want by making Frenchmen of our two millions of Berber Arabs. Again I say, you can reckon
on my support so long as you continue to act with the
prudence you have hitherto shown." '

Unhappily the admiral's term of office was of short
duration, and in losing him Algeria lost the most intelligent and energetic friend she had had until then.
Then a fresh storm arose, stirred up this time, as has
been said, by those among the colonists (and amongst
the French they are only too numerous) who had run
up the flag of radicalism and atheism, ever since the
convicts had in 1848 been brought to the country.

These persons took advantage of the goodwill with
which Admiral Gueydon regarded the Archbishop's
various undertakings to make a direct attack upon them.
It was just the time when the religious schools were
established in Kabylia, and the second Christian village
founded in the plain of Kheliff. Mgr. Lavigerie was
accused of aspiring to supreme political power in Algeria.
No accusation could be more unfounded, for never was
there a man who had less desire to mix in politics. However, some pretext had to be sought ; and in lack of any
better proof, an expression made use of by the Rector of
the Algerian Academy, when reporting to the Council the
success of the schools of Kabylia, served the purpose.

' If he is allowed to continue his work, in ten years'
time the Archbishop will be undisputed master of
Kabylia.' The press took up these words, and thence
drew the conclusion that when the naturalisation of the
native converts had been effected (quick work if done in
that time) Mgr. Lavigerie would be in the position of
Dictator of Algeria.

Thus the onslaught began. It soon gathered strength.
Malicious insinuations, fictitious statements were set

afloat, above all anti-religious and anti-christian hatred was stirred up.

The Archbishop, faithful to the plan he had traced out from the first, having given an example of what could be done by founding his two villages and native schools, intimated to the State that he had now done his part. It was by his own private means, and the sums he and his clergy had collected, that the various orphanages had been founded and kept up; now other works on a larger scale in the interior of Africa drained his resources. He accordingly appealed to the Government for a grant to help carry on what was already set on foot, and the Assembly voted a subsidy of 90,000 francs annually for two years, to finish building the villages and support his eight hundred orphans.

Upon this the atheists of the colony could no longer contain their rage. Efforts were made to rouse the jealousy of the colonists just as if the grant had been made to the Archbishop for his private purposes. Misleading tables of figures were published in the newspapers, representing that he received 1,300 francs a year for every child, whereas in reality he did not receive as much as 130 francs, not more than half of what each cost. Last of all a weapon was resorted to which had always proved effectual in the hands of the Bureaux Arabes. It was alleged that the public safety was endangered by the existence of villages peopled by Christian Arabs in localities where Moslem fanaticism raged fiercely.

One of the deputies, formerly Prefect of Algiers, took upon himself to sum up all the charges against Mgr. Lavigerie in a speech delivered in the National Assembly asking that State help should be denied to him. All the stories invented by the adversaries of the Archbishop and opposers of his good works were brought forward to gain this end; besides pretended confidences, said to have been made to the speaker himself by former Archbishops, as well as untruths and garbled accounts of the utterances of the prelate himself and his missioners respecting the future of the Arab orphans, and predictions as to the fate reserved for them at the hands of the unscrupulous Moslems. The object of all this was to induce the Assembly to withdraw the vote which had just been added to the Budget.

Up to that time Mgr. Lavigerie had held his peace; but when he found himself publicly attacked by a man who had once professed himself decidedly friendly to his views, he felt bound to speak. The following extracts form part of a letter addressed to the deputy in question, a copy of which was given to each member of the Chamber, and which forms a sequel to the letter addressed to Marshal McMahon :—

'Permit me to express the surprise I felt on reading your speech delivered in the National Assembly on July 22 last, attacking the work of Arab villages.

'Had you confined yourself, as others have done, to asking, in the name of liberalism and freethought, for the abolition of Christian liberty—I mean the liberty of ministering to the needs of the native population of Algeria—I could have kept silence. The answer to such a demand must suggest itself to the mind of any honest reader. But you put forward facts which appear authentic, and I cannot let pass unchallenged fabrications to which you have given such wide publicity—I doubt not in good faith, though your memory has assuredly played you false.

'With regard to the communications which you allege were made to you in confidence by the three prelates who have filled the see of Algiers, I simply ask,

is it likely that men to whom discretion is all-import-
ant and habitual should have chosen to confide their
supposed failures to a man who was so little their friend
as to be unable to refrain from betraying their confidence in a public speech? My predecessors are dead,
and cannot contradict you; but I am alive, and I can
affirm that never until the present moment did I say a
single word to you respecting the conversion of the
Mussulmans. . . . I could not possibly have told you
that during my episcopate "all or nearly all the converts
had relapsed into Islamism under circumstances of a
scandal most disgraceful to ourselves." For my part I
never met with a case of the kind, nor do I believe that
you, sir, could mention a single instance which has
occurred since I have been archbishop. . . .

'It is no secret that my two predecessors complained
bitterly of the manner in which their efforts were
frustrated by political intrigues or exigencies; but the
apostasy over which they had to grieve was not that of
the Mussulmans whom they could not convert, but that
of Christians and Frenchmen, who openly disavowed the
religion of their country, and were afterwards raised to
the highest posts in the Algerian government. . . .

'You have, moreover, in speaking of the future of
our orphan settlement, made use of an admission which
you state—with what truth I will proceed to show—to
have been made to you by the missioner in charge
of it.

'It is impossible that he can have said that our
orphans would become Moslems again, for the excellent
reason that they never were Moslems. When we
received them, they had, like other native children of
their age, no possible idea of religion except the vague
notion of a Supreme Being, and not one of them could

have told us who Mohammed was.   All that the father in question told you was that, uneasy as to the influences they would be exposed to, alarmed at the ill-will displayed towards them, and fearful of the effect that the example of bad Christians would have on them, we were not without fear as to the perseverance of our children in the way of virtue. . . .

'But you are not content with raising gratuitous doubts as to the future good conduct of our children; you oppose their settlement in villages on the plea that it is unsafe to place them so far from a Christian centre, in the midst of Mussulmans.   This we do not do.   The settlements are made on land set apart for the purpose, it is true, but it is surrounded by the residences of Europeans, either already built or in the course of construction.'

Mgr. Lavigerie proceeds in the course of this letter, which is too long to quote in full, to remonstrate with his opponent, and refute the specious arguments and fallacious assertions wherewith he sought to ruin a work which was acknowledged by all good men to be the first practical successful attempt at the fusion of races.   He cites the testimony of the various governors of Algeria, beginning with the words uttered in public by Admiral Gueydon, the inaugurator of the new era of things :—

'"I have passed my life," he said, "in protecting Catholic missioners on all the seas, and I will not see them persecuted on French soil.   Great caution, immense tact, kind deeds rather than words, are needed in order gradually to impart Christian civilisation to the people we have conquered; but, undoubtedly, the time for this has now come."'

Amongst others, Mgr. Lavigerie gives the witness of

one of the most eminent officers who have taken part in the government of Algeria.

'"Take good care of yourself," he wrote to me when I was lying dangerously ill at Karlsbad. "What would become of your undertakings without you? What above all would become of the Christian villages? As we had reason to foresee, the Algerian deputies wanted to get the vote of 75,000 francs withdrawn. This work, important alike to Christianity and to France, will have a struggle to maintain with the partisans of the Crescent and 'Le Royaume Arabe.' One never saw so plainly how blind some of these Algerians are! Their hatred to Christianity makes them sacrifice even their safety and their prosperity."'

This courageous and outspoken defence of his principles had its effect, and the subsidy the Archbishop had petitioned for was granted that year. But so-called Liberalism was in the ascendant, both in France and in Algeria, and the next year the vote was not passed. This was a fatal blow for the *Œuvres*. No new settlement could be made, and the native orphans had to be placed out as domestic servants. Some of the girls were married by the Archbishop, and became good Christian mothers; the steady conduct of these, and indeed all for whom suitable employment had been found, did credit to the care bestowed on their training. Others, alas! both boys and girls, exposed to temptation and led away by bad example, fell away from the right path, thanks to those who refused to the institutions where they were guarded from evil, the support necessary for their maintenance.

Such were the many vexations and trials, followed by pecuniary embarrassment, by which the Archbishop was disquieted, but not discouraged, while carrying on the work of the Apostolate. Far from giving up what he had already set on foot, he desired to give his work a new and extensive development; to begin again, as we shall see, in a wider sphere, where he would have full freedom of action. But in order to show how unfounded were the charges brought against him, and how invariably his burning zeal was tempered by extreme moderation and prudence, it may be well to state that he inculcated, in regard to the conversion of the heathen, the greatest caution upon his priests. They were strictly forbidden by the diocesan statutes to baptize any child whatsoever without the express consent of his parents, unless he were known certainly to be an orphan and abandoned by his relatives. And in the case of adults—of those, that is to say, who have attained the age when the law permits them to choose a religion for themselves, and for whom the authorisation of their parents is consequently not necessary—the special permission of the bishop, so a further statute decreed, had to be obtained for their baptism.

'No one,' he writes to his clergy, ' desires the conversion of the heathen in Africa more earnestly than myself; it is, in fact, the object of my life; but I know how essential it is not to transgress the rules dictated by wisdom and prudence, as would be done were we to receive anyone whose motives for a change of creed were open to suspicion. It is not by individual conversions, or any conversions which are not the result of deliberate conviction, that we can hope to procure the return of the natives of Algeria to the faith which for the large majority may be said to be the faith of their forefathers, since most tribes are of

Berber descent. We must influence the masses, and for this I have already pointed out to you the most efficacious means to be employed. The first and foremost is the instruction of the children, that thus the rising generation may be liberated from the fanaticism which in the creed of Islam takes the place of faith; the second is the practice of charity; the third, good example; the fourth, prayer.'

It has, we hope, been made sufficiently plain that the hope of evangelising, not Algeria alone, but the whole of the African continent, was the motive which principally attracted the Bishop of Nancy to Algiers. It cannot, therefore, seem surprising that he should make the fulfilment of this hope the primary object of his efforts, although it would have ill accorded with his strict sense of duty to have neglected the internal affairs of his diocese. We have already said that they occupied his attention upon his first landing in Africa ; and now that a temporary lull had come in the storm of vexatious opposition to which of late he had been exposed, he embraced the opportunity of providing for various wants which he had long felt, but which he had not as yet clearly seen his way to cure.

He had long been sensible of the grievous deficiency of suitable church accommodation, a large number of parishes being unprovided with any becoming place of worship. Hence mass was said in barns, in private houses, sometimes even in outbuildings little better than sheds. To remedy so deplorable a state of things, the Archbishop made an energetic appeal to the colonists and their pastors. This appeal met with a hearty response ; clergy and laity did their utmost, while the Government willingly came forward to aid in the good work, so that, in a comparatively short time, no fewer than sixty-nine new churches and chapels were built in various parts of the diocese.

Mgr. Lavigerie also took in hand the improvement of the tone of the public press. Deeply conscious, as every right-minded man must be, of the immense and incalculable amount of mischief done by pernicious literature, he tried in the first place to raise the character of one of the leading journals of Algiers. Failing in this, he established a Review, the management of which he confided to a priest whom he had brought over from France, and who possessed great literary ability. This periodical had, unfortunately, to be given up three years later, on the outbreak of the Franco-German war and the insurrection in Algeria. But the mere fact of its establishment serves to show that Mgr. Lavigerie neglected nothing which could benefit the land of his adoption. He did everything in his power, too, to further and promote the interests of agriculture, which is the very soul and spirit of colonial life in Algeria, since it is only by a careful and enlightened system of cultivation that the fertile soil can become a means of subsistence to the settlers. His efforts in this direction were greatly aided by the Trappist Fathers belonging to the extensive monastic establishment at Staouëli, who proved by their own example what industry and economy can do. The Archbishop purchased large tracts of barren soil in the neighbourhood of Kouba, where was situated the Maison Carrée or Square House, of which mention has already been made in the preceding chapter. These tracts when cultivated by the orphans, under the direction of the religious who had charge of them, were speedily transformed into fruitful vineyards and fertile fields. When the change had been effected, he made the land over to the charitable institutions in due legal form, so that it should become their own absolute possession, and assure to them a source of support in the time to come. The Algerian Government, which too often showed itself hostile to his views, did him full justice in regard to the subject of which we have just been speaking. On one occasion it publicly entitled him ' The head farmer of Algeria ' (*le premier colon de l'Algérie*), a name of which he was justly proud, as he proved by referring to it at several subsequent periods.

We must not forget to mention that his thoughtful care for those over whom Providence had placed him extended to the days when they would be obliged by age and infirmity to cease from toil. With this view he availed himself of an opportunity which came in his way, and bought an estate situated in a most advantageous position on the slope of the Bouzaréah range. Here he established a sort of almshouse or hospice, where the aged poor might spend in peace the evening of their days under the care of the Little Sisters of the Poor. He also drew up a set of admirable regulations in regard to the admission of suitable candidates, and sent them round, in the form of a letter, to each of his clergy.

Cardinal Lavigerie is justly regarded in France as a true and ardent patriot ; but to show that the appreciation of his merits in this respect is not confined to his native land, we may quote the following sentence from an Italian Review, published in 1887.[1] ' We are convinced that the Archbishop of Algiers, Primate of Africa, possesses in the land of his adoption more authority and influence than any other agent of France,

[1] *Corriere mercantile di Genova.*

and has rendered to the French power in Africa greater services than anyone else.'

The eventful history of the Franco-German war now called out the patriotism of Mgr. Lavigerie in a new but not less practical direction. As a matter of course his sympathies were enlisted on behalf of his suffering country; he ordered public prayers to be offered up for the success of her armies, and alms to be everywhere collected for the relief of the sick and wounded. A considerable number of priests and seminarists entreated his permission to proceed to the seat of war, in order that they might act as army chaplains, or serve as attendants in the ambulances. Three priests only were selected for the coveted posts; they all distinguished themselves by signal services and heroic bravery. One of their number, M. l'Abbé Gillard, was severely wounded on the field of Reichshoffen by the bursting of a shell, whilst engaged in administering the last consolations of religion to the wounded and dying. In order to mark his appreciation of his noble conduct, Mgr. Lavigerie went in person to meet him on his again landing at Algiers, and at once appointed him to the office of vicar-general; the whole of the clergy, too, belonging to the city assembled at the archiepiscopal residence in order to welcome his return to their midst, and to offer him their heartfelt congratulations on his providential escape. Mgr. Lavigerie further wrote to M. Warnier, at that time Prefect of Algiers, placing at his disposal the two seminaries of the diocese, in order that they might be used as hospitals for those among the wounded who had been required to leave their homes in Algeria and serve under the banner of their native France.

At the same time, imitating the example of St.

Cyprian, who during a period of public calamity hesitated not to order even the sacred vessels belonging to the Church of Carthage to be sold, the Archbishop wrote to M. Dusserre, at that time his vicar-general, now his coadjutor, authorising him to permit the heads of factories to offer to the Government the bells which summoned the workpeople to their daily toil, that they might be converted into cannon. On the conclusion of peace, a solemn service of requiem was celebrated in the cathedral, and, by command of the Archbishop, in all churches of the diocese, for the repose of the souls of those who had fallen in battle.

Charitas is the motto on the armorial bearings of the Archbishops of Algiers, and well did it become Mgr. Lavigerie, whose large-hearted charity embraced the country of his adoption with scarcely less warmth, and certainly with not less devotion, than it did the land of his birth. Of this fact he gave ample proof on occasion of the insurrection in Kabylia, which threatened the safety of the colonists, and imperilled, for a season at least, the very existence of the colony. As on a former occasion, the priests of the diocese, stimulated by the example of their chief pastor, volunteered to accompany the troops who were proceeding to the besieged localities, and one parish priest fell a victim to his courageous devotion.

We must now quit the sphere of politics, and turn our attention for a while to the Œcumenical Council which was being held at the Vatican. Mgr. Lavigerie had scarcely been a priest four years when, in the course of his Lectures on Jansenism, he formally declared his belief in the Infallibility of the Pope. But he always entertained a deep-seated aversion for theological controversy, and was frequently heard to say,

'St. Martin is an excellent example for a missionary bishop to follow, for he made a vow never to attend any council, having found that through such attendance he partially forfeited his miraculous powers. I have taken a similar vow in regard to theological discussions.' For this reason, when he had to draw up a rule for his missioners, he made it binding on them to avoid controversy. 'In all questions,' he says, 'touching faith and morals, it is for us to follow implicitly the decisions of the Holy See; and devotion to the Supreme Pontiff, who is the corner-stone on which rests the edifice of Faith, should be our one distinguishing characteristic, our chief pride.'

Summoned by the Holy Father to Rome, in order to take part in the Œcumenical Council, he could not do otherwise than obey. Before leaving he expressed his determination to hold aloof from all discussions concerning the opportuneness of the definition of Papal Infallibility. 'It is of primary importance,' he said in his farewell address to his clergy, 'in these days of strife and contention, when we have to sustain the attacks of many adversaries of God and His Church, that Catholics should offer to the world an example of unity, that they should be one heart and one soul with their Head. For my part, I only desire to be on the side of the Pope and the majority of bishops.' On his arrival in Rome he could not be persuaded to depart from his resolution, though strenuous efforts were made to induce him to identify himself with one or the other party. This attitude was all the more difficult to maintain, as he had to resist the solicitations of his two suffragans, who entered hotly into the debate, and were both adverse to the definition of the dogma. Most painful of all was it to him—one of the greatest griefs, he affirmed, of his whole life—to be compelled to separate himself from some of his best and oldest friends, especially Mgr. Maret, who, on the occasion of his exchanging the see of Nancy for that of Algiers, was almost the only one who understood and appreciated his motives. This prelate published, on the eve of the Council, a work in which he defended the Gallican theses, and argued against Papal Infallibility. Mgr. Lavigerie thought it his duty to remonstrate with him, but his words failed to make any impression. In justice to Mgr. Maret it must be added that immediately upon the definition of the dogma he withdrew the book from circulation, at considerable pecuniary loss to himself.

As the affairs of his diocese urgently required his presence in Algeria, the Archbishop sought and obtained permission from Pius IX. to return thither before the close of the Council, so that he was absent when the dogma was proclaimed. On the tidings of its proclamation reaching him, he instantly telegraphed to the Archbishop of Bourges, who was in Rome, to lay his submission at the feet of the Sovereign Pontiff; not content with this, he assembled all the clergy of the diocese, read aloud the Acts of the Council, and called on them not only to declare their adhesion and loyal acceptance of them *vivâ voce*, but to sign an address to the Pope expressing the same sentiments. Nor could he be satisfied without including all the dioceses of the province in this act of adhesion ; a Provincial Council was accordingly convoked to promulgate in the first place the Vatican decrees, and in the second place to deliberate on the affairs of the diocese. This Council was opened with great solemnity, and in a long and eloquent discourse the Archbishop spoke of the authority of the Church, of the necessity of maintaining purity of doctrine and strictness of discipline, of the evils and errors of the day, and the weapons wherewith they are to be combated.

This formal profession of faith was followed by the discussion and arrangement of various local matters, an account of which could have no interest for the general reader. It may, however, be well to state that by means of tact and management the Archbishop succeeded in maintaining a spirit of peace and harmony throughout the proceedings, so that the result of the Council was eminently satisfactory both to himself and to all who had taken part in it.

To close it, a solemn service was held in the Cathedral Church of Algiers. Mgr. Lavigerie delivered on this occasion a powerful and appropriate address, in the course of which he expressed his thankfulness for the spirit of fraternal charity which prevailed among the members of the Assembly now about to separate, enabling them practically to experience the truth of the Psalmist's words when he says : ' Behold, how good and how pleasant it is for brethren to dwell together in unity.' [1]

[1] Ps. cxxxii. 1.

CHAPTER IV

THE ALGERIAN MISSIONS

It is now necessary for us to acquaint the reader with what Mgr. Lavigerie did for the work he had so much at heart—the evangelisation of Africa itself, and of the lands which lay beyond the bounds of the colony. Here, as we have seen, his freedom of action was too often hampered, and the execution of his plans retarded, by popular prejudice and official opposition. Already, five years previously, in 1868, when casting his eye over the fields white for the harvest, and looking round for labourers whom he could send to gather it in, he had felt the necessity of founding a congregation of priests who should devote themselves exclusively to the work of the Apostolate. The clergy under his rule barely sufficed for the needs of the colony. Impressed as they had been from their youth up with the idea that to hold any intercourse, or establish any relations, even those of simple charity, with the natives, would draw down on them the displeasure of the authorities, they had never attempted to acquire such mastery of their language as would render intercourse with them possible. In fact, after the famine of 1867, Mgr. Lavigerie was unable to find a single priest in his diocese who was able and willing to take the direction of the Arab orphanages. No wonder, then, that he sighed for a band of men specially trained to aid him in his

work. One day, when he had been thinking over the
steps to be taken for the attainment of this end, the
Superior of the Seminary at Kouba entered, accompanied by three young men. This ecclesiastic, generally
known amongst the Algerian clergy, all of whom had
been trained under his care, by the name of *the Ancient
Father*, on account of his great age and venerable
appearance, had, for nearly forty years, been longing
for the moment when France, by whose arms the gates
of the vast continent had already been opened, should
carry into its dark interior the Gospel of Peace. Knowing that the Archbishop cherished the same wishes as
himself, that it was in fact the hope of realising those
wishes which had induced him to exchange the see of
Nancy for that of Algiers, this aged son of St. Vincent
of Paul now conducted to him three of his seminarists,
who offered themselves for the African missions. 'With
God's help,' he said, ' this will be the commencement
of the work that both you and I so ardently desire.'
Then the old man knelt down, together with his three
seminarists, and bent his snowy head to receive the
episcopal blessing. It was given with mingled feelings of wonder and emotion, for the visit was quite
unexpected, and the offer, coinciding as it did so
singularly with the subject of his thoughts, seemed
to the Archbishop to have been directly inspired by
Heaven.

But it was not enough to find young men desirous
of devoting themselves to the African missions ; the next
thing was to provide the means of training them for
the work. Here, again, Providence appeared to inter-
pose, for at this juncture two good priests, the one a
Jesuit, the other a Saint-Sulpician, both since dead,
came to Algiers for the benefit of the climate, and asked

Mgr. Lavigerie for some employment suited to their enfeebled health. A house was hired, and to their charge the three aspirants were confided, to be carefully prepared for their future career.

Such was the first noviciate of the Society of African Missions founded by Mgr. Lavigerie, and he rejoiced to see typified in the three men who were, so to speak, the nursing-fathers of the work in its infancy, the three virtues most necessary for the Apostolate: the charity of St. Vincent of Paul, the faith of St. Ignatius, the sacerdotal sanctity of M. Olier.

The course of training extended over five years; during that time the number of novices increased continually, and the shabby little house they at first occupied soon became too small to accommodate them. The noviciate was accordingly removed elsewhere; a year later it was transferred to the Maison Carrée, or Square House, for which Mgr. Lavigerie had given a high price, and where he had already installed his orphans.

In 1873 the Provincial Council published a decree, afterwards ratified by the Holy See, giving formal sanction to the new society. Its constitutions and rules were drawn up, and received the Archbishop's canonical approval. There were now several missioners ready to go forth on the perilous but glorious enterprise to which they were called. Those who truly love souls count no sacrifice too costly, no labour too great, if they can but serve them and save them, and Mgr. Lavigerie did not conceal from his missioners the difficulties, the hardships, the sufferings they were about to encounter.

'That which encourages me to hope,' he says in addressing them, 'that you are indeed chosen as instru-

ments to kindle the light of truth amid the dense
darkness which covers the land once cursed of God
for Ham's sake—to make known to the unhappy African
race, who have so long experienced the effects of the
Divine anger, the greatness of the Divine mercy—is the
spirit of renunciation and self-sacrifice wherewith I rejoice to see you animated. No ordinary measure of
zeal and heroism is required to secure success in your
enterprise. In this mission you will have much to
suffer—more, perhaps, than in any other on the face of
the earth—from poverty and fatigue, from hunger and
thirst, from scorching heat and fatal fever; and, as you
penetrate farther into those heathen lands, from the
barbarous cruelty of their savage inhabitants. But
these things, calculated, one would imagine, to repel
you, are precisely what attracts you to this work. I
will tell you what I inscribed as the future motto of our
Society on the papers presented to me by one of your
number, a priest from one of the most tranquil and
well-ordered dioceses of France, in order to obtain my
authorisation to say mass. Instead of the usual formula, I wrote across them the words, " Endorsed for
martyrdom " (*Vu pour le martyre*); and returned them
to him, saying, " Read that; are you prepared for it ? "
" It is for this that I have come here," was his reply.
And you too, each and all, have in one way or another heard the same inquiry and made the same
answer.'

The Society being now established, Mgr. Lavigerie
proceeded to organise a definite form of government.
Although the mother-house was situated in the diocese
of Algiers, the Society was to be exempt from the authority of the Archbishop of that see, and subject only to
the jurisdiction of the Apostolic Delegate of the Sahara, a

title recently conferred on Mgr. Lavigerie by the Sacred Congregation of the Propaganda. A chapter was convoked for the purpose of electing a Superior and the members of the council. The newly formed congregation would fain have had for their first Superior-general their venerated founder; but, though gratified by the proof of filial affection thus afforded him, he decisively declined the office on account of the multifarious and pressing duties already resting upon him, as well as the somewhat precarious state of his health. Choice was then made of the Rev. Fr. Deguerry, nephew to the martyred Curé of the Madeleine, at that time head of one of the missionary stations. He could not, however, be Superior-general, since he had not been ten years in the Society, a condition indispensable for holding the post; but he fulfilled the duties attached to it under the title of vicar. To him was committed the management of the funds and the government of the work, the general superintendence and direction remaining in the hands of the founder.

Shortly after, a ceremony took place which brought the Society of African Missions before the notice of the public. This was the consecration of a handsome church, erected to replace the modest chapel, or rather room in the house, which up to that time had been the only sanctuary of the seminary at the Maison Carrée. The ceremony was performed by Mgr. Lavigerie, assisted by two bishops, before a large gathering of clergy from Algiers and the environs, as well as the principal Government officials, members of the magistracy, and officers of the army, who, with the governor, General Chanzy, at their head, had accepted the invitation of the Archbishop to be present on the occasion. Almost all the missioners who had come from the mountain-

heights of the Djurjura and the Atlas, from the remote
oases of the Sahara for their annual retreat, were there
too. It was a touching sight to see this army of
apostles, their bronzed faces testifying to a hard life
and constant exposure, meeting together for one brief
moment to reanimate their courage and renew their
zeal by the contemplation of the Divine heart of Him
who loved us unto death ; and close by their side were
the orphans of the African Seminary, whose astonishing
progress in knowledge and piety was their greatest consolation, the most valuable fruit of their labours. After
the Mass, Mgr. Lavigerie, in a touching and eloquent
discourse, announced his intention of giving the charge
of all the various works he had set on foot in the archdiocese to the Society he had founded, to the men who
had co-operated with him from the first, who had
shared his anxieties, seconded his efforts, sustained with
him the insults and opposition of the unjust and en-
vious. He knew that institutions which depend upon
an individual too often die with him, and he felt a grave
responsibility weighed upon him, and that he would be
justly blamed should the hand of death remove him
before he had assured the future of the charitable
works he had called into being.

'But now,' he said, addressing his spiritual sons,
'my conscience will be at rest. My works will not
perish, for I have placed them in your hands ; you will
continue them ; nay, more, they will grow and multiply,
for they no longer depend for support on the frail force
of one whom a few steps may carry to the grave, but
on the stalwart shoulders of a young and flourishing
community. I can depart in peace, certain that the
children we have received will not again become outcasts, that the poor we have befriended will not be

forsaken, that the souls who cried to me for help will not cry to you in vain.

'. . . Ever keep in view the spirit and distinctive character of your Society ; lose sight of that, and the peculiar object of its creation disappears. Our vocation is the conversion of the unbelievers of Africa, and nothing that does not directly promote this end can or ought to be undertaken. This special end must be accomplished by special means ; we must assume as much as possible the manners of the natives, we must speak their language, wear their garments, eat their food, in conformity to the example of the Apostle : " I became all things to all men, that I might save all."

'But mission work in Algeria is far from being the chief, still less is it the exclusive, object of your ambition. The aim and end of our Apostolate is the evangelisation of Africa, of the whole of Africa, of that almost impenetrable interior whose dark depths are the last hiding places of a brutal barbarism where cannibalism still prevails, and slavery in its most degrading forms. To this work you have pledged yourselves by a solemn vow and promise, and I see you now, waiting with impatience to enter the field of battle, your weapons deeds of charity, your shield gentleness and patience, your teaching that of example, your triumph the heroic sacrifice of your life.'

Some years previously, the Sacred Congregation of the Propaganda had created two new African missions. The one, bounded on the north by Tripoli and on the west by Egypt, included the Eastern Sahara, and was subject to the Vicar Apostolic of Alexandria ; the other comprised the territories which lie between the Atlantic on the west, Morocco, Algiers, and Tunis on the north, Fezzan on the east, Senegal and Guinea on the south.

The ecclesiastical government of this latter, a vast tract of country, was given to the Archbishop of Algiers, with the title of Apostolic Delegate. To the south of Algeria stretches an immense sea of sand, on whose arid surface oases of greater or less extent are scattered like islands on the bosom of the ocean. It was in the outposts of Algeria which lay on the borders of the wide expanse of territory which comprised the Libya and Ethiopia of the ancients, and is now known to us as the Sahara, that the missioners first established a footing, and chose as their stations Biskra, Géryville, Laghouat, Metlili. Conformably to the injunctions of their founder, who was aware that by hasty and premature action not only would no good be effected, but much harm done, and that a single imprudent proceeding on the part of one of the missioners might not merely retard but indefinitely postpone the conversion of the people, they observed extreme caution, and abstained from preaching openly, only endeavouring by acts of kindness to win the confidence of the natives, and, by teaching the children, to remove the prejudices of the parents and prepare their minds for the reception of the truth.

'Our school and pharmacy,' wrote one of the missioners, 'are our great strongholds. Whenever we can, whilst administering remedies for physical ills, we think of the sickness of the soul. Too often the maladies from which our poor Moslems suffer are brought on by their reckless vices. When this is the case we never fail to speak to them of an offended God, of the chastisement sin deserves, of the efforts they ought to make to conquer themselves in order to avoid those faults which even in this world bring upon us the penalty of disease and suffering. The result of our little homily is always the same : " O marabout, truth speaks by your lips, God himself inspires you with wisdom. But the sons of Adam are weak and sinful. May God have mercy on us!" To this we invariably rejoin in the Saviour's words: "Go, and now sin no more." Oftentimes the Arab is not satisfied with expressing his gratitude in words; he kisses the missioner's hands effusively, and would, were he not prevented, prostrate himself at his feet. And on returning to his own people he proclaims loudly the benefits he has received from the Christian marabout. Our influence is rapidly extending; our *clientèle* not unfrequently come from a great distance.'

After this manner did the far-seeing Mgr. Lavigerie endeavour gradually to overcome by kindness and conciliation the great and various difficulties which opposed his labours for the evangelisation of the natives, difficulties arising not only from the peculiar principles of their religion, their aversion to the French as their conquerors, but also from the jealous and suspicious disposition characteristic of their race. But the time soon arrived when the soil of Africa, so prolific during past ages in Christian heroes, was again to be watered by the blood of martyrs. In the month of December 1875, Mgr. Lavigerie authorised the departure of an expedition to Timbuktu, that great emporium of the Soudan, which so few European travellers have ever visited, but which so many have lost their lives in attempting to reach. It was not, however, in the cause of science or of commerce that Father Paulmier, the writer of the letter quoted above, with two of his fellow-workers, entered on so perilous a journey. They burned to break through the barrier erected against the progress of the Gospel by Moslem fanaticism, and to carry the glad tidings of salvation to the pagan

nations which peopled the Western Soudan. During
the time that they had been living in the northern part
of the Algerian Sahara, they had made themselves
familiar with the habits and language of the principal
nomad tribes; and, encouraged by the assurances of
certain Touaregs, whose sores they had dressed and
healed, and who had invited them to visit their desert
home, the fathers presently determined to take the road
which led to the negro nations of the south. In vain did
the Arabs in whose tribe they had been dwelling, and
who had become devotedly attached to the Christian
marabouts, seek to dissuade them from the enterprise.
Finding their entreaties of no avail, they at length
suffered them to depart, but not without first exacting
from them a written attestation to the effect that they
had undertaken the journey of their own free will and in
spite of the efforts made to detain them. The missioners
were deeply touched by these signs of affection, but
they would not be diverted from their generous purpose,
and under the escort of five Touaregs the little caravan
set out, resolved either to establish themselves in the
capital of the Soudan, or lay down their lives in the
attempt. The latter part of this heroic programme was
carried out. From the day of departure the most complete mystery shrouded the events of their journey, no
letter or communication of any kind ever reaching their
friends in Algeria. At length a vague rumour began
to be current among the tribes of the Northern Sahara
that the three missioners had been murdered in the
desert when almost within reach of their destination.
This report was soon after confirmed by the testimony
of a party of ostrich hunters, who had discovered their
remains amid the sandy wastes within a short distance
of Timbuktu. As to the particulars of their death, all

we know is that they were beheaded ; their bodies were found lying side by side, as if they had drawn near to each other for mutual support and absolution, and had knelt down together to receive the fatal stroke.

The news of this triple martyrdom, far from daunting or discouraging the comrades of the deceased missioners, filled them with holy envy and a generous ardour to follow in their footsteps. The attempt to penetrate into the Soudan from the north having failed, the White Fathers—a name given to the Algerian missioners on account of their wearing the long white robe of the Arab—essayed to gain access from another point, and open communication with the negro nations by another route. They accordingly established a depôt in the Province of Tripoli, and a mission station in the little town of Ghadames, which is situated in one of the oases of the Tripolitan Sahara. There, as elsewhere, they confined themselves in the commencement to the practice of the corporal works of mercy, and, whilst awaiting a favourable moment for the enterprise they had at heart, devoted themselves to the study of the manners and language of the neighbouring tribes, and lost no opportunity of making the acquaintance and gaining the confidence of the wild children of the desert, who were deeply impressed by the charity of the missioners in tending the sick, and in a time of scarcity distributing food to the famishing. Experience having shown the uselessness of individual conversions, since were a native to be baptized the surroundings in which he would find himself would make perseverance almost a matter of impossibility, the fathers set themselves with persevering kindness and patience to win the hearts of the Moslems, in the hope that by influencing the masses some permanent good might be effected. In this they succeeded so well that the principal inhabitants of the town expressed their desire to the French Consul at Tripoli, that the fathers might be replaced by others of the same congregation, should they depart, as was known to be their intention, on an expedition into the interior. This projected expedition had been postponed by Mgr. Lavigerie's express command, on account of the excitement into which the population of the Sahara was thrown on hearing of the campaign in Tunis, which made the name of Christian and Frenchman more hateful than ever to Mussulman ears. On tranquillity being restored, however, the missioners thought themselves authorised to set out, having received solemn assurances from the natives that travelling would be attended by no danger. But hardly had they got a day's march from Ghadames, when they too, three in number, fell victims to the treachery of their guides.

It was not only in the direction of the Sahara that the White Fathers had turned their steps. They had painfully scaled the steep mountains of Kabylia, carrying with them little more than their breviaries, and a case containing the requisites for offering the Holy Sacrifice, and pitched their tent in the first village they came to. Here was formed a basis of operations for apostolic work amid the native population of the mountain ranges, who had once been Christian ; the conversion of these tribes seemed more hopeful than that of their Arab neighbours, whose rule they had long resisted, and whose creed they had reluctantly embraced. Soon after his arrival in Algiers, Mgr. Lavigerie had visited the mountain fastnesses where the Kabyles had entrenched themselves centuries ago, in order as long as possible to avert the dreaded moment when they must stoop their neck under the Moslem yoke. He thus relates his

introduction to a people who in time past suffered much
for the faith they ultimately lost :—

'We went through several villages, passing sometimes below, sometimes above the houses, as our zigzag
path led us. Ever and anon the women's faces would
peep out from behind the walls of their dwellings, regarding us half with alarm, half with curiosity. Some
of the boldest children ventured a little way towards
us, but if we took a single step in their direction, they
instantly took to their heels, screaming at the top of
their voices. We held out some *sous* to them from
afar, as an enticement. This was a sore temptation. I
remember one little fellow about four or five years old,
less timid than the rest, a very bundle of rags, one eye
already gone, the other soon to disappear in its turn
beneath the crust of dirt and the repulsive sores which
covered his face; he longed for our *sous*, but still kept
at a respectful distance.

'"Come along, then," one of our party said to him;
"if you want them, come and get them."

'The boy, whose single eye had in it all the cunning
of the savage, stretched out his tiny hand, and pointing
with his finger, said:

'"Ah! I know why you want me to come for the
sous; you want to catch me and carry me off; throw
them down on the road, and then I will pick them up."

'We burst out laughing, as may be imagined, and
threw him the coins, which he gathered up in a moment,
and then sped away like an arrow from a bow, scaling
with marvellous agility the precipitous rocks over-
hanging the village. The reason of the terror we excited
was afterwards explained to us. In order to prevent
the boys and girls of their villages from holding any
intercourse with the French, the Kabyles give them the

most alarming accounts of the way in which we treat
children. According to them, the French are a race of
ogres who live on raw flesh, and greedily devour all the
unfortunate children on whom they can lay hands. Our
overtures of friendship, in the eyes of my little urchin,
were a diabolical trap, laid for the purpose of providing
a fresh dish for our breakfast. We could not help
laughing at the fright the poor little fellow had been in ;
but it was sad to think that the child, who had been
taught to consider Christians as objects of terror, was
himself a descendant of Christians who had loved the
faith and had suffered for it.'

One of those who accompanied Mgr. Lavigerie on
this journey, thus describes his reception in a village:—
' We went thither on foot, for the steep mountain
paths are, as may well be imagined, quite impassable
for carriages. After interminable windings among rocks,
valleys, and trees, we came in sight of the village
whither we were bound, standing on a slight eminence.
' The Archbishop had announced his visit beforehand, and at the entrance of the village all the men,
headed by its venerable patriarch, were assembled to
receive him in a house entirely open on the side which
looked on to the road. The women and children were
perched on all imaginable places, the ledges of the
rocks, the roofs of the houses, every spot which afforded
standing-room, where human feet could climb or human
limbs could rest. Mgr. Lavigerie was in full canoni-
cals, and was surrounded by the priests belonging to his
suite. When he arrived within a short distance of the
village, the men advanced in a body solemnly to meet
him and bid him welcome. The aged patriarch who
preceded them was the *amin* or mayor, the others

were his council; for the Kabyles have retained a
municipal form of government, after the model of the
Roman, with public assemblies and popular elections.
The building mentioned above was the forum, or, as
they call it here, the *djemmâa*, a kind of town hall, the
meeting-place of all the male inhabitants of an age to
carry arms. There affairs of local or general interest
are discussed, transfer of land is effected, and all business of a civic or political nature transacted.

'The *amin* approached the Archbishop, and with a
stately and dignified gesture laid his hand lightly
on his vestment, and then raised it respectfully to his
lips.

'"May the blessing of God be with you all!" the
Archbishop said; and with one voice they all responded, "May it be also with thee!"

'We then proceeded to the *djemmâa*, the first house,
as we have said, at the entrance to the village; being
completely open on two sides, it looked more like a shed
than anything else. Against the two walls on the right
and on the left were rows of stone seats rising one
above another like the tiers of an amphitheatre. The
place of honour was assigned to Mgr. Lavigerie, then
each one took a seat where he pleased.

'"I have come to see you," the Archbishop began,
addressing the *amin*, "to show my affection for you.
(Here all present simultaneously laid their hands, first
on their heart, and then on their forehead.) I have
reason to love you, for we French are related to you;
the same blood runs in our veins. Our forefathers
were Romans, in part at least, as were yours; we are
Christians, as you too once were. Look at me. I am a
Christian bishop. Well, in days gone by, there were more
than five hundred bishops like me in Africa, all Kabyles,

many of them illustrious men, distinguished for their learning. All of your race were originally Christians, but the Arabs came and ruthlessly slaughtered your bishops and priests, and compelled your ancestors to adopt their creed. Do you know all this?"

'A very voluble consultation took place among the audience, then the *amin* replied :—

"" Yes, we know it; but you speak of a time long past. Our grandfathers have told us these things; but as for ourselves, we have seen nothing of them."'

It was on the past history of these Berber tribes that Mgr. Lavigerie grounded his hopes of their future regeneration. He judged that a land that had once been Christian, where the sign of the Cross was not un-known, whose inhabitants, a thrifty, brave, and laborious race, were possessed by no fierce fanaticism for the re-ligion their conquerors had forced on them, was likely to prove a more grateful field for missionary effort than one where the creed of Islam had long held undisputed sway. From the first he had interested himself on behalf of these mountainous regions, having aided and encouraged the Jesuit Fathers, who founded, and managed with singular skill and success, two missions, the one at Djemma-Saharidj and the other amongst the Beni-Yenni. Unfortunately the small number of subjects in the Jesuit province of Lyons, in which Algeria was included, prevented this work from being developed as the circumstances of the case required; and it was to supply the want that, in 1873, Mgr. Lavigerie sent, as we have seen, three of his Algerian missioners to Kabylia, one of them being the Rev. Father Deguerry, afterwards chosen to be the Superior of the congre-gation. The privations and hardships endured by these generous apostles were most severe; but for God's sake they were gladly borne. For three months the White Fathers had no bed but the bare earth, no shelter from the inclemency of a rigorous winter but the open vault of heaven. At last, one of the natives, more kindly disposed than the others, gave them permission to build a house; this they did, constructing it with their own hands. Before long, their patient courage was rewarded with success, and, as time went on, one station after another was made in the vicinity, until a little group had formed itself around the first one.

Under the shadow, as it were, of the seminary of the Society of African Missions, Mgr. Lavigerie laid the foundations of another and a humbler institution, a house for the training of missionary sisters, who should supplement the exertions of the fathers by labouring for the evangelisation of the female portion of the population. In Mohammedan and heathen countries, as is well known, the restrictions which custom imposes on the appearance in public of women, and the utterly degraded position they occupy, debar them from profiting by the ministrations of teachers who are not of their own sex. It was, therefore, only by women that the moral regeneration and Christian conversion of the wives and mothers, and through them the reform of family life, could be accomplished; by women, who could approach them freely, penetrate the strict seclusion wherein they are shrouded, relieve the monotony of their tedious existence, sympathise in their sorrows, and succour them in sickness. Thus only could their hearts be reached, or the glad tidings of Christianity brought to them. Thus only could they be raised from their debased condition, or taught the true dignity of Christian womanhood. Mgr. Lavigerie did not look in vain for women willing to devote them-

selves to this work. From his former diocese of
Nancy, the Sisters of St. Charles, a community founded
some three centuries ago, and resembling in many
respects the Sisters of Charity of St. Vincent of Paul,
responded to his call. They took up their abode in
1868 at Kouba, where a noviciate was formed, in a
house of modest proportions, at that time serving as a
refuge for Arab girls rescued from starvation during
the period of the famine. Shortly after, these religious
were joined by the Sisters of the Assumption, who
also came from Nancy ; but it was not until nearly ten
years had passed by that the Archbishop formed them
into a congregation of missionary sisters, under the title
of Sisters of Our Lady of African Missions, giving them
an independent existence and system of self-government.

That the growth of this congregation was slow, and
its development very gradual, is not to be wondered at.
Vocations were not wanting, for an order distinctly
and exclusively destined for missions to the heathen
would naturally attract to itself many an ardent spirit,
eager to spend and be spent in the service of the souls
for whom Christ died, now perishing in ignorance and
error. But this prospect of danger and even death in
foreign lands, though alluring to the postulant, would
be the greatest objection to her parents and friends.
Few would consent to allow a young girl to take a long
journey and cross the seas to enter the noviciate in a
distant, unknown country, uncertain whether she might
not after all be mistaken as to the choice she had made,
and her own qualifications for so arduous and difficult
an enterprise.

But the tiny seed sprang up, and the community
lived and grew, at first, as their Founder wished, in
obscurity and humble circumstances, until the time for

action came. Ordinary prudence forbade them to follow the footsteps of the messengers of the Gospel into barbarous regions, where they might be exposed to perils worse than death; they must wait until the way was cleared and the ground prepared before they could pitch their tent among the savage natives of Africa. Meanwhile they carried on the work of mercy in native orphanages and schools, ministering to the sick, teaching the elements of religion to the women, offering up fervent prayers for the conversion of Africa. Houses were founded in Kabylia and in several Moslem territories; and so greatly did God bless the efforts of the humble and hardworking sisters, that the results obtained by them surpassed, it was said, what the fathers had been able to effect. The moral superiority of these women, their self-denying kindness, their courage and devotion, deeply impressed the unbelievers; they gazed at them with astonishment and admiration, as if they belonged to a different order of beings, and were something more than human. On one occasion, when pleading the cause of missions, Mgr. Lavigerie speaks thus of the sisters :—

'I have seen them in the midst of their work; I have seen them surrounded by a motley crowd of men and children, both Christians and Mohammedans, all clamouring to them for succour, begging them to cure their ailments, to relieve their poverty, kissing with the utmost veneration the habit they wear. I remember hearing one of our sisters say that once, while passing through the streets of a populous Eastern city, she was accosted by an old man, a Turk, who asked her with a mixture of curiosity and respect : "Tell me, sister, when you came down from heaven, did you wear the same dress in which we now see you ?"'

CHAPTER V

MONSEIGNEUR LAVIGERIE'S ADMINISTRATION OF HIS DIOCESE

THE accumulation of labour attendant on the creation and direction of the missions, in addition to the regular work of the diocese, proved too heavy a burden even for Mgr. Lavigerie's resolute will and untiring energy. The necessity of providing funds for the expenses of the missionary work in heathen countries, and the support of the various training institutions for missioners and sisters of charity, involved an amount of travelling and correspondence that absorbed a large portion of his time, not to speak of the mental strain inseparable from the grave anxieties and responsibilities which weighed upon him. Feeling that he had more work than any one man could do, or at any rate do well, since the office of Apostolic Delegate, which he had recently accepted, required him to absent himself from Algiers more frequently and for a longer period than was compatible with his duties as Archbishop, he resolved upon taking a coadjutor, who should, at least for a time, assist him in the discharge of his episcopal functions. He accordingly obtained permission from the Holy Father to consecrate as Bishop-auxiliary Mgr. Soubiranne, at that time director of the Society for Promoting Education in the East. But unfortunately the climate of Algiers did not suit the new

Bishop. In the course of two or three years he was compelled to return to France, and eventually, so completely was his health shattered, to resign the bishopric of Belley, which had been assigned to him.

About the same time Mgr. Lavigerie, in order to insure the proper government and superintendence of the several parishes, divided the archdiocese into districts, and appointed over them the most experienced of the parochial clergy as rural deans, delegating to them his authority for the control and management of the districts respectively assigned them. And it was well that he made this provision when he did for the due administration of the diocese in his absence, since the precarious state of his health—the principal motive that induced him to take steps for the appointment of a bishop and vicars auxiliary—began in 1874 to give cause for serious apprehension. An hereditary malady, from which from his youth up he had never been entirely free, had of late entered upon a fresh stage of development, threatening to affect the heart and the chief centres of the nervous system, producing acute neuralgic pains and other alarming symptoms. The disease, having been aggravated by overwork and exposure to the inclemency of a more than usually severe winter, had gained ground so rapidly as to necessitate a change of air and a period of complete rest; and Mgr. Lavigerie, acting on the urgent and repeated advice of his physicians, decided upon spending a winter in Rome. Before leaving he addressed a pastoral letter to his clergy, expressing the regret he felt at being compelled to suspend his labours for a while, and temporarily absent himself from his diocese.

The winter of the year 1874–5 was accordingly spent in Rome. It pleased God to hear the prayers

offered on his behalf; and the Archbishop returned to
Algiers in the spring with recovered health and renewed
vigour.

It will be remembered that when Mgr. Lavigerie,
acting always with the full consent, if not at the direct
request, of the village communes, established schools and
other works of mercy in view of gradually lessening,
by means of kindly influence and civilising intercourse,
the inveterate hatred and hostility entertained by the
conquered for their conquerors—by the sons of the
Prophet for ' Christian dogs '—and thus bringing about
the fusion of races, his efforts met with determined
resistance on the part of the French Government. The
policy persistently pursued during a period of thirty-eight
years had been one of complete separation of races, the
drawing of a hard and fast line between the French
colonists and the native population; and a struggle
ensued in which the Archbishop did not give way, as
his predecessors had done, but justified his conduct and
maintained his course of action. In consequence of this,
there was for some time considerable tension in his relations with Marshal MacMahon, who, as military governor,
represented the French Government in Algeria. This
state of affairs subsisted in a greater or less degree until
after the fall of the Third Empire, when the situation
was changed, and the two authorities stood once more
on the most cordial footing with one another. Mgr.
Lavigerie had always taken the liveliest interest in all
matters appertaining to the army, and had from the
first been on the best of terms with the generals who
were not in any way officially connected with the
government of Algiers; they too, in their turn, had at
the time of the famine seconded and supported in the
kindest manner his exertions for the relief of the

suffering natives. The testimony of General Wimpffen, who was at that time Commandant of the Province of Algiers, to the beneficial results of the Archbishop's work is too valuable to be omitted here, the more so because the General was well known for his liberal sentiments. In a letter to the Archbishop, dated February 24, 1868, he writes :—

'I cannot thank you sufficiently, Monseigneur, for the services you are rendering to our poor orphans and to the colony in general. Your work well deserves to be supported not only by public benevolence, but by the State. Whether the children remain for a longer or shorter time under your care, they will assuredly never forget the kindness to which they owe the preservation of their lives, and the new ideas they will have imbibed will be a sure guarantee of a future good understanding between the two races.

'. . . The right moment has now come for us to make of the people we have conquered good Christians and loyal subjects of France. I do not think our Government is to blame for not having attempted, either in the first flush of victory or at a subsequent period, what we are now attempting. The lessons of history teach us that a people struggling to maintain its independence, to defend its homes, is naturally ill-disposed to adopt the creed of the invader. You, Monseigneur, have perceived that the recent disasters afforded a favourable opportunity to inaugurate the much-desired social change, and you have availed yourself of it to the utmost. Your orphanages and refuges, open to the outcast and the afflicted, will prove a potent factor in the dissolution of Arab society, and the most efficacious means of leading the Mussulman to accept our faith.

'I am proud to be permitted to associate myself

with you in this work, the most remarkable of the present time which your energy and vigour has initiated.'

After peace was made in 1871, the command of the army in Algiers was assumed by General Wolff, an upright and energetic man, well acquainted with the character of the native population. For twenty-five years he had been associated with the Arabs in an official capacity, and had had the good fortune to win their respect, esteem, and affection. Knowing them so well, and liking them as he did, and feeling that it was incumbent on France to draw closer to herself the people she had subjugated, it will be readily imagined that the efforts of the Archbishop met with his fullest appreciation and sympathy ; he admired the courage and zeal of the prelate, and his prudence in prohibiting all direct attempts at proselytising. Accordingly he rendered him every assistance within his power, and, perceiving how great an influence the missioners acquired through their tender charity in visiting and tending the sick, and how eagerly they were sought after by the Mussulmans in their character of physician of the body rather than of the soul, he one day proposed to Mgr. Lavigerie to found a permanent hospital for the exclusive use of the natives, not far from Algiers. ' It would not only be a work of Christian charity,' he said, ' but a wise stroke of policy, a means of attracting the people to ourselves without offending national prejudices.'

Mgr. Lavigerie gladly fell in with a suggestion that coincided so completely with his own wishes, though it was perhaps prompted by different motives. He replied that he would gladly give a plot of land for a hospital, were it not that the most essential thing was lacking : funds for its construction. Even for a single wing, a

portion of the entire building, no less than 100,000
francs (4,000*l.*) would be required.

'If that is the only objection,' rejoined the General,
'I can furnish you with enough to start with. In the
exchequer of our department, the sum of 38,000 francs,
subscribed on the occasion of the Emperor's visit to
Algeria, has for fifteen years been lying idle. It was
collected for the purpose of founding some charitable institution for the benefit of the native population, but no
one has yet been able to hit on a scheme for employing it.
If it were given over to you, the charity of Catholics
would make up the remainder.'

So it was agreed upon. General Chanzy, the
Governor-General at the time, who was always willing
to promote the interests of the natives, gave his consent,
and Mgr. Lavigerie at once set to work. Trusting that
Providence would not fail him, he determined to do the
thing well, as was his wont. The new hospital was a
handsome building in Byzantine style, fitted up with
every convenience; nothing was wanting to the comfort
of the inmates, or even to the elegance of the structure.
The Archbishop's object in this was to show the natives
with what respect and affection he regarded the poor.
It was not lost on them. The Arabs gazed in wonder-
ment at the building as it rose from the ground; they
admired the handsome colonnades, the rich colouring
of the corridors, the commodious bath-rooms, the extensive gardens.

'All this must be intended for a prince,' they
said.

'On the contrary,' they were told, 'it is for the
Arabs when struck down with poverty and sickness.'

'Will not the Arabs pay in that house?' they further
inquired.

' They will pay nothing at all.'

' Can that really be true ? ' they exclaimed ; and when repeated affirmations convinced them that so it was, they lifted up their hands and eyes to heaven in bewilderment and stupefaction.

In about two years' time the hospital was finished. On the occasion of the opening an Arab *fête* was held in the neighbouring plains. A large and distinguished company was invited, comprising the chief Government officials, the magistrates, the officers of the army, all the notabilities of Algiers and the vicinity, the principal residents and visitors. It was a solemn and beautiful scene when Mgr. Lavigerie, in full pontificals, attended by fifty priests, having ascended the hill on which the hospital stood, gave his benediction to the building, which bore the inscription *Bit-Allah* (God's House). It was like an episode out of the past, recalling to the minds of all who witnessed it the glories of the early Church of Africa. The English Consul, Colonel Playfair, kept repeating to everybody : ' We have St. Augustine amongst us again ! '

While the Archbishop thus won all hearts by his benevolent charity, and with active zeal organised one good work after another, a severe blow was unexpectedly struck at the institutions he had set on foot. At the close of 1876, the French Chamber of Deputies, in voting the Budget, diminished by more than half the grants of Government aid for the support of the diocesan orphanages and seminaries, and for the requirements of public worship in Algeria. A report circulated in France that large territorial grants had been made to the clergy, and that the seminaries had been richly endowed, although false, had served as a pretext for the enemies of the Church thus to curtail the subsidies

voted for her support in the colony. Nor was this all :
in the following year the Council of Algiers, infected by
the Radical principles of the day, suppressed the accustomed grant for the maintenance of the religious communities engaged in active work in the department.
Mgr. Lavigerie protested against this measure, but to
no purpose ; the only alternative was to appeal to the
liberality of his flock to cover the deficit. He did not
appeal in vain, and private charity supplied what public
prejudice withheld. But a further blow was struck ;
under the influence of ' modern liberalism ' the teaching
of the catechism in the public schools was opposed, and
even prohibited, the teachers being first not required,
then not allowed, to impart any kind of religious instruction to their scholars. Unable to prevent this
innovation, the Archbishop could do no more than
address a letter to his clergy, reminding them of the
danger to which the faith of the children was exposed
by the absence of religious teaching in the schools, and
urging upon them the sacred duty of compensating as
far as possible for this privation by themselves teaching
and explaining the catechism to the children of their
flock.

A few quotations from this pastoral will allow him
to explain his views in his own words.

' . . . In order to fulfil aright this portion of your
sacred ministry, mere intellectual ability and learning
are not enough. You must have zeal for souls, active and
practical love for the souls of the children under your
care, the lambs of the flock whose pastor you are.
Do not allow yourselves to be discouraged and dis-
heartened by the indifference of the parents, the ill-will
and opposition of the schoolmasters, the inattention and
dulness of the children, for those who love souls count

all labour light for their salvation. This is what the great African Bishop teaches us, and not us alone, but all servants of God throughout the world : *Ubi amatur, non laboratur; aut si laboratur, labor amatur.* (Where there is love, there is no toil; or if there is toil, the toil is loved.) St. Augustine in his diocese of Hippo had to contend with the same ignorance, the same evils, as you have ; on his arrival the whole of the inhabitants were either heathen or heretics. It was by means of his catechetical lectures, delivered almost daily, delivered in spite of disappointments, calumny, insults, and threats that he changed and christianised his flock, and made himself the model of a Christian pastor to all time. Imitate him, then, my brethren, imitate his painstaking, persevering zeal ; imitate his patience and piety, for these are qualities essential to the teacher of religion, and which go far, as I said above, to compensate for the want of all else.

' We need not, however, look back to past ages ; in our own day, too, we have a striking example set before us, in the person of the parish priest of an obscure French village, who never for one single day omitted the teaching of the catechism. He thus attracted to himself in a short time an audience consisting, not of a few simple rustics, but of crowds from every part of Christendom. His plain instructions were the means of converting more sinners, sanctifying more souls, than the most persuasive rhetoric of celebrated orators. The Curé d'Ars was neither learned nor eloquent, yet few hearts could resist the simple faith, the heartfelt piety, which inspired his words.'

' Our enemies themselves teach us a lesson,' he continues further on. ' They spare no pains to remove the children from all religious influences ; they neglect no

opportunity of attaining their end by open attack or
covert calumny; they deem themselves sure of victory,
for they hope that, having banished the name of God
from the school, they will be able to banish all thought
of Him from the domestic circle, from social life.

'Remember, too, that by kindling the light of the
truth in the hearts of the young, you will not only
further the cause of religion, but also promote the
interests of France, the interests of society, and
especially of this colony in which you are placed; for
on the training of the rising generation the whole
future depends for evil or for good. If they reject
the authority of their Father in heaven, will they acknowledge the authority of the rulers His providence
has set over them on earth? If they are not to be responsible for their actions to the Great Judge of all
men, what motive will they have for acting uprightly,
restraining their passions, respecting the rights of their
fellow-men?'

Meanwhile the state of Mgr. Lavigerie's health,
which, though improved, was far from robust, again
warned him that he was overtaxing his powers, and
that the weight of care and responsibility resting upon
him was too heavy for him to bear. Unfortunately,
Mgr. Soubiranne, who had administered the affairs of
the diocese during the Archbishop's illness and consequent absence from Algiers, had, before the time of
which we are speaking, been compelled, on account of
his inability to bear the climate of Africa, to resign his
post and return to France. Thus Mgr. Lavigerie stood
alone; and, as the reader is aware, two important
charges were united in his person. Independently of
the arduous and ever-increasing labours of the archi-
episcopate, which he had already discharged during ten

years, the title of Apostolic Delegate for Sahara and the
Soudan, conferred on him by the Propaganda, involved
the care and responsibility of the missionary work
throughout the vast provinces stretching from the
south of Algeria to the very centre of the African continent. He therefore determined upon relinquishing
one of these dignities; and judging, after due deliberation and earnest prayer, that it would be easier to find
some one to take his place as Archbishop of Algiers
than as superior of the work he had himself originated
and organised, he wrote to the reigning Pontiff requesting that he might be permitted, since he found himself
unequal to the conscientious performance of the duties
of the twofold charge, to resign the archiepiscopal
functions and dignity, whilst he retained those of Apostolic Delegate. He proposed furthermore to withdraw,
with the consent of his Holiness, to the House of the
Society of African Missions, and take up his abode with
and among his spiritual sons.

The congregation he had founded already numbered three hundred members, and had sent some
martyrs to heaven. Mgr. Lavigerie felt that, at this
early stage of its existence, the hand of its Founder
was still needed to sustain and direct it; the work of
the Apostolate was besides the work to which of all
others he was most strongly attracted, and he desired
to consecrate himself exclusively from that time forward to the development of the missions to Central
Africa, which were the great object he had at heart,
and the aim of his lifelong toil. He announced his
intention to the Society of Missioners in the following
words :—

' I cannot, my children, any longer reconcile it with
my conscience to allow you to contend alone in this

perilous arena. You can already count some martyrs in your congregation; I sent those heroes to the distant battle-field, and it is for me to appoint others to fill the gaps left by the fallen. I cannot, I ought not to do so any longer without marching with you to the battle. You have left all things to come hither at my call, you have abandoned your country and your friends; I have left nothing, I still sit on my episcopal throne. This thought is a misery to me, for what sort of a captain is he who does not march with his company—what shepherd is he who appears to dread an encounter with the wolves? I have laid the matter before God in prayer, and the failure of my health seems to me a sufficient indication of His will. I have therefore written to the Holy Father, to ask him to grant me permission to resign my archiepiscopal see, in order that I may assume your habit, follow your rule, be with you in life, and if needs be also in death.'

The Pope, though he fully appreciated and highly approved the sentiments Mgr. Lavigerie expressed, and the motives by which he was actuated in resigning the archbishopric of Algiers, did not see fit to accept his resignation. The immense amount of good which he had been instrumental in effecting since his nomination to that important see, naturally rendered the Supreme Pontiff desirous, in the interests of the diocese, to retain as long as possible the services of this able prelate; he accordingly requested him to rescind his resolution, and continue to exercise the functions of his twofold charge, since he might be certain that in doing so he was fulfilling the will of God. The decision of Rome must not be disputed, and Mgr. Lavigerie remained at his post.

But as the Holy Father had consented to the permanent appointment of a bishop-coadjutor, with the right of succession to the see, who would relieve him of the greater portion of his episcopal functions, Mgr. Lavigerie lost no time in selecting a man suitable for the work. His choice fell on Mgr. Dusserre, formerly his vicar-general, then Bishop of Damascus. This prelate had in his early days distinguished himself in the service of the Church, for he had shed his blood on the battle-field whilst fighting bravely in the ranks of the Papal Zouaves. This choice met with the approval of the French Government, and received the sanction of the Holy See. In a letter wherein he announced to his flock the change about to be made, he speaks as follows :—

'. . . You are doubtless already acquainted with the reasons which necessitated the appointment of a coadjutor, as I have explained them in full to the members of the clergy who are my valued fellow-workers in this diocese. I should not again revert to them, were it not for the fear lest some might imagine that this new arrangement for the administration of ecclesiastical matters argued a diminution of the fatherly affection I bear my flock, or any laxity on my part in observing the rules laid down by Holy Church for the guidance of the bishops and pastors of souls. I feel it incumbent on me to answer these objections, should they suggest themselves to the minds of any, as they readily may even to my best and kindest friends, and I cannot do better than refer to the annals of the early Church of Africa, and appeal to the example of its greatest doctor, the Bishop of Hippo, who, when bending beneath the weight of years and accumulated labours of his pastoral office, acted some fifteen centuries ago as I have acted now. From the faithful and zealous priests who surrounded him, he chose one to share with him the duties of the episcopate while he lived, and succeed him after his death. History repeats itself; the records in which these proceedings are handed down to posterity might serve as the history of the present as well as of the past, for they are animated by the same vigorous life which causes the hearts of Africa's sons to throb in this our day.

'The prelate who is to be associated with me in my work is no stranger to you. Coming when a child to Algeria, he grew up in your midst, and having basked in the warmth of your African sun he could not return to a colder clime. He has consecrated his life to the service of the Church, and no eulogium from my lips is needed; it is enough that you know him, and the assurance that his presence is acceptable to you makes me content, for I wish nothing but what you wish yourselves. I can only repeat on his behalf the prayer which St. Augustine offered up for his fellow-labourer : *Qui misit eum ad me, servet eum, servet incolumem.* (May He who sent him to me, keep him, and keep him safe.)

'To my valued coadjutor, therefore, the management of all the business of the diocese will be committed. The general superintendence alone will remain in my hands. I shall be there to advise and direct, when counsel and guidance are needed. Thus will your wants be well provided for, and I shall, like the great doctor of the African Church, be able, should it please God to prolong my life, to spend the remainder of my days, not in repose, but in the labours of the Apostolate. The work to which St. Augustine devoted his last years was the Commentary on the Scriptures whereby he has rendered his genius immortal, and enriched the

Church to all ages. The work to which I desire to dedicate my days is one for which nothing is required but firm faith, which shrinks not from suffering, and this God does not deny to those who ask it of Him in prayer, but bestows it in proportion to the need of the suppliant.

'My spiritual sons have already gone forth to plant the standard of the Cross in distant regions. They are to be found at Tunis, amid the ruins of Carthage, on the spot where St. Louis of France breathed his last. They have established themselves at the Leptis of the ancients, and thence they have advanced by the old route into the desert, that desert which the resources and discoveries of civilisation render no longer impassable, and the sands of which are dyed with the blood of their young and generous hearts. They are in Palestine, at Jerusalem, where they are constituted the guardians of a sanctuary dear to the Christian world on account of its historical associations and traditional interests. And lastly, what is most important of all, they have penetrated into the interior of Africa, and reached the barbarous lands surrounding the great lakes discovered by Livingstone and Stanley; there they form the nucleus of a great army, an army of peace, whose mission is to deliver the unhappy negro race from the thraldom under which it groans. It is my task to direct the tactics of these warriors, and strengthen their hands in the distant lands where they are encamped, to provide them with their daily bread, the necessaries of life. For this I must toil in the sweat of my brow; do not, therefore, grudge me my leisure, a leisure which brings no lessening of labour; to you I can address the selfsame words that were spoken to the faithful of Hippo: *Nemo ergo invideat otio meo, quia otium meum magnum habet negotium.'* (Let no one grudge me my rest from labour, for with me rest from labour means plenty of fresh labour.)

The sanctuary in Jerusalem, alluded to by Mgr. Lavigerie, is a basilica of great antiquity, built over the spot to which Eastern tradition points as being the birthplace of the Blessed Virgin Mary, which was a sort of cave excavated in the rock, according to the Hebrew manner of constructing dwellings at that time. Since the taking of Jerusalem by Saladin, previous to which it had been a Benedictine convent, this sanctuary was for nearly seven centuries used as a Moslem mosque ; until in 1856 it passed into the hands of the French, and twenty-two years later the Holy See entrusted the guardianship of it to the Algerian missioners. Mgr. Lavigerie went in person to take possession of it and establish a community there; he also founded an apostolic school and seminary, for the education of young Greeks of the Melchite Communion, and other Oriental Christians.

But this work, although of considerable importance for the missions in the East, assumes, in common with the others which he mentions, a very secondary place in comparison with the missionary efforts in Central Africa, the most colossal and glorious enterprise of all that the illustrious Cardinal Lavigerie has inaugurated, on account of its vast extent, hazardous nature, and cosmopolitan interest. It has attracted the attention, excited the sympathy, and claimed the co-operation of the whole of Christendom. We shall now proceed to speak of its first commencement ; of the first duly organised expedition that was equipped for the crusade to Equatorial Africa. It was sent to a country whose barbarous inhabitants, more like animals than men, without proper clothing, without civilisation, without religion (except the grossest forms of superstition and most debasing fetish-worship), live in contented idleness, the weaker tribes in fear of the stronger, and both in mortal dread of the ruthless slave-hunter, who holds the whole continent under a reign of terror.

A brief account of the way in which this mission came to be entrusted to the Society of Algerian Missioners, founded by Cardinal Lavigerie, and of the perils and trials they encountered on their journey into the interior, may not be without interest to the reader.

CHAPTER VI

FOUNDATION OF THE CATHOLIC MISSIONS OF CENTRAL AFRICA

THE missions of Equatorial Africa, the object of which is at the same time the deliverance of the unhappy negro from the spiritual slavery of heathenism and devil-worship, and his rescue from the oppression and brutality of the Moslem slave-hunter, owe their rise, under the providence of God, to the movement which several years ago first directed the attention of the whole civilised world to the continent of Africa.

'One only needs,' Mgr. Lavigerie writes in 1880, ' to cast one's eye on the map of Africa, in order to see how the whole of the long line of sea-coast of this vast continent has been taken possession of by the nations of the Old and New World. From the provinces conquered by France in the north to the great English colony at the Cape, all along the western coast, we find settlements of almost every nation, who have acquired for themselves a portion of territory of greater or less extent; while the treaties concluded with the Sultan of Zanzibar have secured free trade to Europeans from Natal to the mouth of the Red Sea.

' And while the Christian nations with their armies and flotillas have blockaded the coast of Africa, the missioners, the pacific soldiers of the Cross, have also landed their victorious forces and established their spiritual dominion. On the shores of the Mediterranean, in Tunis, Tripoli, Egypt, the Gallas, we find the sons of St. Francis at work; in Abyssinia, those of St. Vincent of Paul; while in Zanguebar, Senegambia, Senegal, the Fathers of the Congregation of the Holy Ghost and of the Sacred Heart of Mary, through the charity and heroic devotion they exercise, make the name of Christian beloved. The African missioners of Lyons labour on the fever-stricken shores of Guinea, at the Cape, in Dahomey; the missioners of Verona, with the devoted Mgr. Comboni, in the recently conquered provinces to the south of Egypt. The Jesuit Fathers are in the island of Madagascar and the country bordering the Zambesi; the Oblates of Mary at Natal, besides all the secular priests in the European colonies; the English and Irish at the Cape, the Portuguese in Benguela, the Spanish in Morocco, the French in Algeria. There is not a single spot all along the shores washed by the Mediterranean, the Atlantic, and the Indian Ocean, where the footsteps are not found of the messengers of Divine mercy, whose errand is to put an end to the degradation of the sons of Ham. Who can doubt that we shall soon be called upon to witness one of those great upheavals whereby Providence is wont to change the destiny of nations?

'But although all along the countries bordering the ocean we behold numerous bodies of apostolic missioners engaged in spreading the light of the Gospel, it is otherwise with the interior of the Dark Continent. This has hitherto appeared impossible of access. From time to time individual travellers have endeavoured to penetrate the secret of this mysterious land, but almost all have lost their lives in the attempt. The veil which shrouds these unknown regions has, it is true, during the last twenty years, been partially raised by more fortunate, or more enterprising explorers, such as Cameron, Speke, Schweinfurth, Livingstone, Stanley. The bravery exhibited by these intrepid travellers, their adventures and their discoveries, excited enthusiastic interest, and the sympathy generally awakened soon assumed a definite and practical form.

'Up to that time all the efforts to penetrate into the heart of Africa were isolated and individual ones. Whether sent out by some scientific society, acting in the interests of commerce, or impelled by love of adventure, each traveller went out singly and shaped his course as he thought best. In 1876 the King of the Belgians conceived the idea of an International Association for combined and sustained effort, and in the opening conference at Brussels he sketched out a programme of action.

'"It appears to me," he said, "an undertaking worthy of this age of progress, to open to civilising influences the only portion of our globe that yet remains closed to them, to dispel the darkness in which countless tribes are still enveloped. For the success of such a scheme as this, it is necessary to secure the co-operation of the masses, the support of numbers—to appeal to the sympathy of the public, and the benevolence of the public. The great object of this association will be to abolish slavery, the ' open sore of the world,' to put an end to the abominable traffic in human merchandise which is the disgrace of the age in which we live. . . ."'

The African Society of Brussels was quickly organised, and a plan of action, worthy of its royal author, was set on foot. All Europe took part in it; neither money nor volunteers were wanting. Funds flowed in for what was termed the *crusade against barbarism*; distinguished scientists, brave soldiers, experienced travellers, offered their services in the cause of humanity. Stations—centres, that is, of scientific observation and civilising influence—were to be established both on the coast and in the interior, whence exploring parties and expeditions against the slave-hunter could be sent out and furnished with supplies, and a line of communication formed from Zanzibar to Tanganyika.

'These details,' continues Mgr. Lavigerie, 'may appear foreign to my subject, but in reality they form part of it. The field of exploration traced out for the International Society is identical with that subsequently assigned to the missioners of Equatorial Africa; the lands, that is, lying between the basin of the Zambesi on the south, and Egypt and the provinces of the Soudan on the north. The enterprise undertaken by the Conference of Brussels was undeniably a great and important one, far greater than those of which the object is merely to open out a way of communication across a trackless continent. It will be the means of bringing new light and new life to whole tribes and races of mankind. This task, however, the Association could only half accomplish, or rather it could only prepare the way for its accomplishment. In opening out a route across the equatorial regions for the explorer and the trader, an opening was made for the messenger of the Gospel, and thus, unconsciously to itself, the International Association achieved a glorious work. All connection with any religious body and all religious aims had been distinctly disavowed; and how could it be otherwise? It counted among its members those of every religious denomination; the majority were Protestants, a large proportion were professed freethinkers. However, far from opposing the work of the Apostolate, it extended its protection to the missionary, but without recognising the claims of religion to hold a place in its counsels, in which the interests of science, commerce, and manufacture alone were considered.'

Thus it was that in 1877 the attention of Christendom was attracted to the condition of Central Africa. Mgr. Lavigerie continues :—

'The Pontificate of Pius IX. was then drawing to a close. The aged Pontiff had entered upon the last year of his long and eventful reign, and while he stood almost on the brink of the grave, his gaze resting wearily and sorrowfully on a world wherein the rising tide of unbelief and irreligion threatened to sweep away all but the very fabric of the faith, his thoughts were directed to a new object of solicitude. Cardinal Franchi, the Prefect of the Propaganda, pointed out to him for the first time the proceedings of the Brussels Conference, and the promise of the future for the tribes of the interior of Africa. Pius IX. took in the situation at a glance, and appreciated its importance. The fate of a vast continent was at stake, a continent little inferior in size to the whole of Europe, and peopled by some hundred million souls. This estimate might, it is true, have seemed somewhat exaggerated, but the reports of recent travellers had furnished information of a novel nature. The interior of Equatorial Africa was no longer represented as a sterile desert, the tomb of every living thing, but as a densely populated region, rich in natural resources and in scenery of no ordinary beauty. The climate is said to be in many localities salubrious and mild, owing to the high tablelands in the vicinity of the great lakes, and the lofty mountains, some of them capped with eternal snow. . . . .

' The shadow of approaching death had not dulled the generous ardour of the venerable Pontiff, or diminished his apostolic zeal. He saw that no time should be lost in following out the discoveries of African explorers, and accordingly gave orders to the Propaganda to confer with the superiors of the principal African missionary societies as to the best means of realising his wishes. All were agreed as to the urgency of the case, and the necessity of founding new missions in the places where the International Association established its bases of operations. But a practical difficulty presented itself : where was a band of devoted men to be found, ready to risk their lives, and provided with sufficient resources for so vast and perilous a mission? The congregations already labouring in different parts of Africa barely sufficed for the exigencies of the work commenced, and could provide neither the men nor the funds required for a new undertaking.'

Mgr. Lavigerie was one of those who had been consulted on this occasion, and it was to the society instituted by him for the special purpose of evangelising the Arab and negro races that the Holy Father's thoughts recurred at this juncture. He had not forgotten how, five years previously, the Archbishop had conducted two of his missioners, the firstfruits of the newly formed congregation, to the Vatican, where, admitted to a private audience, they had in the name of all their brethren expressed their loyal attachment to the Holy See, and asked the blessing of the Supreme Pontiff before encountering the hardships and dangers of an attempt to work their way to the centre of Africa. Remembering this circumstance, Pius IX. assigned to the Algerian missioners the first share in the glorious undertaking he proposed to initiate.

'It was with a thrill of gratitude and enthusiasm' (we resume Mgr. Lavigerie's narrative) 'that our missioners received this intelligence. Three of their number had already shed their blood in the Sahara, on the way to Timbuktu, whither they had hoped to carry the light of faith. The remembrance of this, far from discouraging their comrades, inspired them with holy envy, and stirred them up to fresh emulation.

'All history has its heroic epochs, and religious societies are not exempt from the law that governs human associations. "Our missioners are still in the age of fervour." Such was the remark made to me by an experienced ecclesiastic, who was preaching a retreat at our mother-house. He was astonished at the severity of the rule, and the fidelity with which it was followed. To sleep on a board or on the bare ground, to be poorly clad, fed with the most frugal fare, exposed to the vicissitudes of the weather, and at the same time to observe every regulation with the utmost exactitude, keeping strict silence, persevering in prayer during the eight days of retreat—all this, he said, needs nothing less than the fervour of the early ages.

'Before starting on their perilous expedition the priests of the Society of African Missions desired to send a deputation to lay at the feet of the Pope an address expressing the willingness wherewith they made the sacrifice of their lives in order, conformably to his wishes, to enter on this new field of labour, which promised so abundant a harvest.'

Accordingly, in January 1878 the Archbishop deputed two of his missioners to be the bearers of this address, and solicit the benediction of the Holy Father on their institute and their mission. But before they reached Rome, the venerable Pontiff had been called to enter on his eternal rest. It remained for his successor, Leo XIII., immediately after his election, to attach his signature to the decree 'prepared by the Propaganda, and thus complete and sanction the plan marked out by Pius IX. for the creation of four extensive vicariates in the region of the equatorial lakes, namely Nyanza, Tanganyika, and the northern and southern Upper Congo. The charge of these was entrusted to Mgr. Lavigerie.

On March 25 in the same year, the first band of missioners, consisting of ten fathers, destined five for Nyanza, and five for Tanganyika, set out to take possession of their new inheritance. The starting-point of their enterprise was to be Zanzibar. Zanzibar is the focus of all African exploration; no matter whither the traveller is going in the interior, it is there his journey must begin.

Upon their arrival in Zanzibar, where they were cordially received and kindly entertained by the fathers who serve the mission of Zanguebar, the travellers at once set about the tedious work of organising the caravan for their long and perilous journey. It is well known that in a country like Africa, which is destitute of roads and abounds in forests and marshy jungles, one of the greatest difficulties of travel arises from the necessity of conveying everything by means of porters. Nor is it merely the personal baggage of the travellers, with the necessaries for their journey and future establishment, which have thus to be transported, but also an endless assortment of calicoes, beads, knives, and other articles, intended for the purpose of victualling the caravan, propitiating the native chieftains, and paying the tribute usually exacted by the petty monarchs of the country for the right of passage through their territories. Goods of every description are the current coin of the country, and a day's wage or the price of a basket of maize is estimated by yards of calico or strings of beads. Hence the negro porters, whom it is necessary to engage for a journey of many months, are counted by hundreds, entailing on the travellers both an enormous expense and a harassing responsibility. But this is not all. In addition to the *pagazis* or carriers, a corresponding number of *askaris* or guards must be engaged and armed, whose duty it is to enforce discipline and protect the caravan. Fortunately, the fathers, on crossing over to Bagamoyo on the mainland, were able to secure the services of a number of Unyamuezi negroes, who, having just arrived from the interior with an outgoing caravan, were not indisposed for another engagement which would bring them back to their homes and families.

On June 19, 1878, the little band of missioners started from Bagamoyo, turning their backs probably for ever on the glorious ocean, studded with the white sails of African dhows, and on the distant isle of Zanzibar, the last outpost of civilisation. The noble and generous sentiments wherewith their hearts were animated are best expressed in the following extract from a letter, written by one of them on the eve of departure from Zanzibar :—

'We are now going to complete our purchases, and make up into bales the outfit we brought from Algiers. Then, committing ourselves to the fatherly hand of Providence, and strengthened by grace, we go forth to proclaim the knowledge of God to the benighted peoples who have so long lain in the shadow of death, sunk in the grossest idolatry and barbarism. A new life is commencing for us ; we are breaking new ground, as the Apostles did when Christianity was in its infancy. Weak and unworthy as we are, we are yet the first who since the foundation of the Church have come to publish the name of God in this savage and almost unknown land. Out of its darksome depths we seem to see one, or perhaps two, hundred million souls, perishing in ignorance and degradation, stretch out their arms to us for help.

'Ours is a sublime mission, but at the same time a terrible one. It is ever present to our thoughts, almost always on our lips. To God we offer beforehand, for the success of the great work He has entrusted to us, all our trials, privations, and sufferings, and even the sacrifice of our lives, should He think fit to require it of us.'

In front of the caravan marched the guides, and a portion of the *askaris*, followed by some of the missioners mounted on asses, which they had purchased for the journey. Then come the *pagazis*, their bales of goods balanced on their heads, accompanied by the remainder of the fathers, while the procession is closed by another band of *askaris*, who have been told off for the duty of bringing up the stragglers and protecting the rear. Altogether they number five hundred souls, and, travelling for the most part in single file, form a train of considerable length. At one time their path lay through dense thickets or marshy jungles; at another through virgin forests peopled with myriads of beautiful birds and chattering monkeys; while frequently they traversed rich fields of maize or sugar-cane, and prairies of waving grass which towered far above their heads. Everywhere the vegetation was most luxuriant, and the narrowness of the path, sometimes closed in with reeds or underwood, joined to the intense heat of the sun, rendered the journey most trying and laborious. Malarian fever, too, is a certainty to every African traveller, and it is in these plains and marshes bordering on the sea coast that fevers are most prevalent. It was not long before our missioners became familiar with this insidious foe; but in the early stages of these attacks a few doses of quinine and a short period of repose sufficed to ward off the danger and renew their failing strength.

Although they were anxious to hasten their march across the lowlands and reach the more healthy table-land of the interior, they found it impossible, on account of the indolence of the porters and the difficulties of the route, to proceed except by very short stages. Owing to the intense heat of the midday sun, they usually began their march at a very early hour, and travelled till about noon. On arriving at the place of encampment, they pitched their tents, counted over their bales of goods, and secured them when possible under cover, setting over them a guard of *askaris*. They then proceeded to take their dinner, after which their time was fully occupied in bargaining with the natives for provisions, receiving the native chieftains, arranging differences among their followers, and issuing orders for the morning's march.

On July 26 the caravan arrived at Mpwa-pwa, in the more mountainous country of Usagara. After leaving the plain the route had become more difficult and laborious, leading often over crags and rocks, through narrow defiles, across rapid and dangerous streams, where the only means of passage was the slippery trunk of a tree, which it was often necessary to cross on hands and knees. The poor donkeys were pushed over the steep banks and dragged across with ropes, at the imminent risk of becoming the prey of the numerous crocodiles which infested the waters. In these regions the ass is the only quadruped which can be made available for the purposes of transport, and even it cannot always resist the attacks of the tzetzé, a venomous fly that infests a large portion of the African continent, and from the bite of which oxen and horses soon perish.

At length the missioners reached the inhospitable country of Ugogo, a land peopled by a savage and rapacious race, who frequently plunder and murder the passing traveller, and allow none to set foot within their territory without exacting at every stage an enormous and ruinous tribute. No sooner had the missioners arrived at their first place of encampment within the borders of this ill-famed region, than they were surrounded by swarms of negroes, almost naked and streaming with rancid oil, who pressed upon them from all sides, mocking and jeering at them, swarming in their tents, and hovering about in order to take the first opportunity of pillage. These unwelcome visitors being at length disposed of, it became necessary to treat with the principal chieftain or petty sultan of the district on the important subject of the *hongo* or tribute. The discussion and settlement of this vexed question usually consumed many precious hours, sometimes even days; for the rapacious tyrant refused permission to depart until his demands had been complied with, and to satisfy these demands was no easy task—sometimes, indeed, quite impossible. Guns, barrels of powder, hundreds of yards of white or coloured stuffs, coils of brass wire, necklaces and beads, were demanded with threats that made the timid *pagazis* tremble with horror and meditate a speedy desertion. No sooner was one demand complied with than another followed. In fine, it became necessary to yield to every extortion unless by long arguments the traveller could induce the tyrant to abate something of his pretensions. At each stage of the journey the harassing negotiations were renewed, while in the passage through the forests the poor *pagazi* who loitered behind ran every chance of being stripped of his burden and probably murdered by the robbers who lurked in the adjoining thickets. It would be difficult to describe the hardships, annoyances, and privations that the good fathers had to endure in their passage through this country. Repeated attacks of debilitating fever too had now begun to tell fearfully on their health, and they beheld with alarm that one of their little band was gradually sinking under the fatigue of the journey and the effect of the climate.

Father Joachim Pascal, the leader of the missioners destined for the settlement at Tanganyika, was the first to lay down his life for the salvation of the negro. The humility, piety, and heroic charity of this good priest, united as they were to a solid judgment and great prudence in the direction of others, had marked him out for the responsible office of Superior of the future mission. About a month before his death he wrote thus to Mgr. Lavigerie:—

'It cannot be denied that we have had trials, and that we still have them every day; but how could it be otherwise, and what else ought we to expect? It is in the service of God that we have undertaken this work. All our number have suffered more or less from the climate, and at the present moment four or five are a good deal out of health. But these things are far from discouraging us, Monseigneur, and you may be assured that we go on our way none the less cheerfully and gladly because of them. Those who are well nurse the sick to the best of their ability; and if they too in their turn fall ill, as generally happens, their comrades who are convalescent show them the same kind attention and care which they received from them. Thus we have every reason to consider ourselves fortunate, and to thank God for the slight troubles that in His providence He sends us.'

In the intervals between the attacks of fever, Father Pascal repeatedly offered to God the sacrifice of his life, and exhorted his brethren to practise submission to His holy will. About the middle of August, on the day of St. Joachim, his patron saint, he felt his end was near. As he lay on his mat in the tent, prostrated by extreme weakness, the missioners watching at his side thought each moment would be the last. He thought so too, and bade them all farewell, giving them his last messages to his superiors and to his parents; praying God to console the latter for his loss, and the grief it must cause them that he should die in this distant land. He lingered until the following day, and then, having received the last sacraments, he peacefully gave up his soul to God.

No sooner had he expired than it became necessary to think of the disposal of his remains; for the fathers well knew that, if the fact of his death within their territory became known to the natives, it would be the signal for a fresh outburst of superstitious fury and for still more extortionate demands of money. Accordingly, in the dead of night, a party of *askaris* was told off, with one of the fathers at their head, to convey the body into the adjoining district of Unyamuezi, the limits of which they had nearly reached. After journeying a few miles they selected a spot in the virgin forest, and there dug a grave for the last resting-place of the proto-martyr of the little band. After the funeral rites had been performed, they rejoined the caravan, which by that time had resumed its march. The missioners did not, however, escape the exactions of the natives—probably the secret was betrayed by one of their followers. They had not travelled far before they were overtaken by three chieftains, who accused them of concealing the death of a white man. In vain did the fathers challenge them to find the body; they were obliged to submit to a considerable fine before they were permitted to go on their way in peace.

At length the missioners, having passed through the territory of Unyamuezi, reached Tabora, where the two bands had to part company, in order to proceed, the one northwards to the Nyanza Lake, the other in a westerly direction to its destination on Lake Tanganyika, about 250 miles distant from Nyanza. The former were the first to depart. In the case of the other portion of the little band considerable delay was unavoidable, since in the first place it was necessary to recruit their shattered health by a short period of rest, and in the second place they had great difficulty in obtaining porters, since the Arab traders, who are the real rulers of that country, placed all manner of obstacles in their way. Being on the verge of war with the chieftain of the country through which the missioners must pass, they were unwilling that any of the natives whose services would be required for the coming contest should be taken from the neighbourhood, and therefore represented to the fathers in glowing colours the dangers of the journey. But they, well aware that if war broke out before their departure it would be impossible to proceed until peace was again established, hurried on their preparations, and, having succeeded in hiring a band of *pagazis*, they started immediately from Tabora, travelling almost due west, so as to strike the lake near Ujiji, the principal town on its shores.

Their way lay across fields of grass and maize, through dense primeval forests and over rugged mountains. Occasionally they came across melancholy evidences of the cruel scourge of the African continent, the slave trade. In the midst of rich but now deserted plains might be seen the blackened ruins of whole villages, the inhabitants of which had been massacred or carried off into slavery. In many districts once densely populated, not a single human being was to be seen, so wholesale is the destruction effected by the ruthless marauder. After seven weeks of painful and laborious journeying, the missioners reached the long-desired shores of Tanganyika.

Having taken the precaution to acquaint the Arab governor of Ujiji with their approach, they found on arriving at the lake boats in readiness to convey them to the settlement. At the place of disembarkation they were met and welcomed in the kindest manner by Captain Hore, a retired naval officer in charge of the station of the Church Missionary Society, who offered them the accommodation of his own house, and any other service which it was in his power to render them. While thanking him for his generous offer, the missioners considered it better to instal themselves at once in a house assigned to them by the governor. It was the same which had been occupied by the great explorer Stanley, in his last journey.

The reader may imagine that the town of Ujiji,[1] so

[1] The region about Ujiji is now the headquarters of the slave trade.

often spoken of in the journals of African travellers, and which in consequence of its advantageous position has become one of the most important markets of the interior, is a place of considerable size and population, laid out with some regard to order and furnished with roads.   He would be surprised, on descending the graceful hollow in which it lies, to behold peeping out of the densest foliage, and without any visible means of communication, the round tops of a few native huts resembling beehives.   There are, it is true, narrow winding paths conducting from house to house, but in the rainy months these are closed up with tall grass and underwood, through which it is difficult and often dangerous to force a passage.   Here and there is an Arab dwelling, a quadrangular building constructed of bricks, with a verandah in front and a spacious courtyard enclosed with walls and sheds, which afford accommodation for men and goods.   These are the residences of the Arab traders, who, though a mere handful in number, possess enormous influence, and have at their disposal hundreds of negro slaves.   The power of the native Sultan is merely nominal.

The first anxiety of the missioners was to establish friendly relations with the local magnates.   The Arab merchants received them favourably, owing to the letters of recommendation which they brought from the Sultan of Zanzibar.   Being French too, the new-comers were not regarded with the jealousy that was felt towards the English, whose observation of the traffic freely carried on in slaves was dreaded, British interference having already been actively exerted on the coast around Zanzibar.[1]   The French fathers did not

[1] Captain Hore states that when first the English missionaries established themselves at Tanganyika, their mere presence placed a consider-

excite the same suspicion, though in reality they did not yield to the English in abhorrence of a system which is a disgrace to humanity, not only on account of its cruelty and injustice, but because it is the means whereby a rich country, requiring only labour to render it one of the greatest producers in the world, is being rapidly drained of its population, ' bleeding out,' as has been said, ' its life-blood at every pore,' while its fertile plains are being reduced to solitary wastes. Though matters looked promising when the missioners first took up their quarters in Ujiji, they soon perceived it was not a suitable place to serve as a centre of operations. The influence exercised by the Mussulmans over the native population would, they foresaw, greatly impede their liberty of action. With the view, therefore, of selecting a position more favourable for their permanent settlement, they determined to explore the shores of the lake, directing their course northwards, towards the kingdom of Urundi, which they had heard described as a peaceful, populous, and fertile region. Having found a spot in an elevated and healthy district, the chieftain of which readily placed land at their disposal and assured them of his protection, they transported thither their effects, set about the erection of a hut, and received under their roof a few negro children whom they had redeemed from slavery. Their letters to their venerated Founder are expressive of gratitude and hopefulness.

' The country,' one of them writes, ' is broken and undulating, traversed from north to south by a chain

able check upon the slave trade in that district; but when it was found that their mission was an entirely peaceful one, it soon went on again much as before. The missionaries, knowing their inability to prevent the trade, were obliged to remain neutral, but their opposition to it was known to the Arabs.

of mountains. It is well cultivated and thickly populated. The natives are simple, but so timid as to run away in abject terror on our approach. Although not entirely free from swamps, Urundi seems much more healthy than Ujiji, and, what is more, there is not a single Arab here.

'We are getting on gradually; our house, or rather our hut, is finished. It does not do much credit to our talent for building, for it is nothing more than a shed, walled in and thatched with straw. One side is left open to admit air and light; in the night time it is closed by mats, which are rolled up by day. The natives come long distances to see it; they stand lost in admiration, contemplating for hours this marvel of architectural skill. We have goats, sheep, and shall soon have cows : I have been sowing large fields with rice and wheat—a bold venture, for I am quite a novice at this kind of work. At Ujiji there are only two Arabs who grow wheat, and the price asked for it is so exorbitant as to prohibit the purchase of it for any other purpose but to be used as seed and for the manufacture of altar breads.

'But the task on which we expend our energy most gladly is the training of some children whom we have redeemed from slavery. This method of commencing our mission bodes well, and we hope great things of these boys, who are extremely docile, and really appear to have no serious faults. The only fear is that they will run away : two have already done so, for no apparent reason. We have now three younger boys, whom we mean to teach to read, and four older ones, who will, we think, in a few years' time, form the nucleus of a future Christian village in Equatorial Africa. There is no lack of land; one might take

possession of any number of acres without one's claim
to ownership being contested.'

Meanwhile the fathers who were destined for the
mission of Nyanza, and who had been the first to leave
Tabora, pursued their journey northwards under the
leadership of Father Livinhac, the Superior of the
expedition. Daily had they more and more cause to
thank God for the protection He extended over them,
for their way led them among savage and barbarous
tribes, and through dense forests inhabited by a lawless
race, by whom they were frequently attacked, and at
whose hands they narrowly escaped massacre. It was
not until a year and almost three months had elapsed
since the departure from Zanzibar that the end of
their long and toilsome pilgrimage was finally reached.
They were received with cordial hospitality by Mtesa,
the powerful monarch then reigning in Uganda. A
revolution has taken place in that kingdom since his
death, and the struggle between Islamism and Christian civilisation now appears to be raging there with
almost unexampled violence. The kind reception
accorded to the missioners was probably due to the
forethought of Mgr. Lavigerie, who had furnished them
with gifts well calculated to dazzle and delight a savage
prince. Uncivilised man loves nothing so well as a bit
of finery, whatever its shape and size, whether it be old
or new. Now Mgr. Lavigerie had procured, for the
benefit of King Mtesa and his Court, a box of the discarded habiliments of official personages from a well-
known dealer in second-hand clothes in Paris, to whose
shop, thanks to the frequent changes of Ministry,
uniforms of all kinds often found their way. This
happy thought had been suggested by the remem-

brance of an anecdote related by a missioner of North
America, who had presented to the chief of a newly
converted tribe one of the scarlet coats, profusely
trimmed with gold lace, worn on Sundays by the
beadles of Paris churches. On occasion of the procession of Corpus Christi, which took place soon after,
the worthy missioner was highly diverted to behold the
chief stalking proudly at the head of his admiring
subjects, his sole article of apparel being the faded
garment of the *suisse* of St. Sulpice.

These relics of past grandeur were no less valuable
on the plains of Equatorial Africa than amid the Rocky
Mountains of the far north.   King Mtesa would not be
outdone in generosity.

'In all that concerns our material wants,' writes
Father Livinhac, ' we have every reason to be thankful.
Mtesa has been most liberal towards us ; he has given
us an acre at least of good ground, planted with bananas,
and thirty oxen.   He also provides workmen and
materials for the construction of a house large enough
to accommodate us all.   This dwelling will be made
of wooden stakes, the interstices being filled with reeds
and grass, after the custom of the country ; indeed, in
nothing but in shape will it be distinguishable from the
native huts.'

King Mtesa did not confine himself to the bestowal
of material benefits, but granted full liberty to the
missioners, and facilities for the prosecution of their
apostolic mission.   Here, as at Tanganyika, an orphanage was established for the negro children who were
rescued from slavery, and a class of adults was soon
formed, who flocked to the humble mission-house eager
for instruction, as of old the pagans of Rome went to
hear the teaching of St. Paul.   Several of these catechu-

mens expressed a wish for baptism, and on being sufficiently instructed were admitted into the Church by Father Livinhac at the following Easter.

These encouraging reports of the success of the missions decided the indefatigable Archbishop to organise and send out a second detachment of apostles. It consisted of twelve missioners, accompanied by six Pontifical Zouaves, who volunteered their services to direct and guide the caravan on its way from Zanzibar to the Great Lakes, four being Belgians and two Scotchmen. The idea of this escort of laymen had been suggested by one of the fathers of the first expedition, who had vividly described the anxieties and difficulties involved in the management of the numerous porters who were required to carry the baggage, as well as the *askaris* or guards, whose presence was necessary in order to ward off the attacks of the rapacious Ruga-Rugas. The command of the expedition, too, often obliged the priests to perform a part little in keeping with their sacerdotal dignity ; it was thought, therefore, that some of those who had formerly devoted themselves to the service of the Church in the ranks of the papal army might not be unwilling to risk their lives a second time for the good cause, by forming a military escort to share with them, and if possible protect them from, the perils of the route.

Before their departure an impressive farewell service was held in the Church of Our Lady of Africa, during which the Archbishop blessed and gave to each volunteer the sword he was to wield in the interests of the Gospel and for the cause of suffering humanity ; the colours also, which were to be carried before this company of soldiers of the Cross, were solemnly blessed. At the conclusion of the ceremony Mgr. Lavigerie

ascended the pulpit and delivered one of those stirring
discourses with which he has of late electrified his
hearers in almost every capital of Europe.

After some preliminary remarks on the solemnity of
the occasion and the sacrifice the young men present
before him were about to make in separating themselves
from all they held dear on earth, and going forth—
probably never to return—in order to carry the message
of life into the kingdom of death, he speaks thus of the
condition of the African continent :—

'From every part of this huge continent, from the
boundaries of the provinces France has annexed in the
north, to the English possessions at the Cape, one long
wail of anguish has gone up for centuries; a cry
wherein all the worst and keenest suffering our humanity
is capable of feeling, meets and mingles; the cry of
mothers from whose arms the ruthless marauder snatches
their little ones, to deliver them into lifelong servitude,
and who like Rachel weep for their children and refuse
to be comforted ; the cry of peaceful, happy villagers,
surprised by night in their sleep, who behold their dwellings reduced to ashes, all who resist put to death, and
the remainder dragged away and driven to the market
where human beings are sold like cattle; the cry of
interminable troops of miserable captives, men, women,
and children, sinking from hunger, thirst, and despair ;
slowly expiring in the desert, where they are left behind,
already more dead than alive, for the sake of economis-
ing the scanty nourishment doled out to them, or struck
down by a cruel blow as an example to strike terror
into others as wretched as themselves; the cry of
thousands of defenceless human beings, abandoned as a
prey to the passions of their pitiless captors : all this,
and much more, carried on daily through greed of gain,

desire of revenge, or lust of conquest. Such is the fate that overtakes, year by year, more than a million of our fellow-creatures ; and those who have witnessed the horrors of this iniquitous traffic assure me that one might heap words together without finding terms to adequately describe what African slavery really is.

'I have myself seen some of the unhappy victims of this impious trade. I have heard from their own lips the recital of their wrongs. I have heard children narrate, with a simplicity which gave unconscious force to their words, the story of their father's murder, their mother's death, the torture of the weary tramp over sun-scorched plains. I have seen some, long afterwards, beholding again in their dreams these revolting scenes, start from their sleep uttering fearful shrieks. Such is African slavery as it exists at the present moment, as it exists in our immediate vicinity, so near to us that those who will may see and hear it for themselves. The seaports are now closed against it ; it has spread far into the interior, and in an aggravated form.

'It is very well, my brethren, to discuss theoretically the amount of injustice involved in buying and selling black men ; but look at the slave trade in practice, see the brutal cruelty it fosters in the masters, the depth of degradation and suffering to which it reduces the slaves, and you will agree with me that one cry alone can ascend from human lips at the sight—a cry of horror and reprobation.

'Can you wonder, then, that I, a bishop, to whom the Holy See has entrusted the task of evangelising a portion of the wide tracts of country where slavery holds undisputed sway, should, standing in the house of God, lift up my voice in denunciation of this accursed trade, and in the name of humanity, in the name of faith, vow to wage against it a relentless and unceasing warfare? My only regret is that my voice is not powerful enough to make itself heard far beyond these sacred precincts; that I cannot utter what I know and what I feel in accents which will rouse everyone who deserves the name of a man and a Christian to join in putting an end to crimes which call to Heaven for vengeance.

' In vain have all the powers of the civilised world united for the abolition of this shameful traffic, which is draining the life-blood of Africa. Their efforts are powerless. Whether the reason why the measures adopted proved ineffectual is due to their having had reference to the vendors, not the buyers, of slaves, or whether it be that the root of the evil lies too deep for the hand of man to reach, certain it is that slavery flourishes as much as ever. The reports of the most recent explorers are full of its atrocities. Nor is it any longer the work of the stranger alone; the blacks themselves, having learnt contempt of their kind, become the authors of their own ruin, for the soul of man ever sinks lower when destitute of that true enlightenment whence strength is derived to resist the corrupt tendencies of fallen nature.

' What remains, then, for us to do, is to make these tribes, sunk, alas! in the deepest degradation, understand how great is their impiety; to teach them that all men are brethren; that in creating man, God gave him freedom, freedom of soul and body, a freedom which, when the whole world fell under the slavery of sin, Jesus Christ restored to him, not thinking it too dearly purchased at the price of His own blood.

' How beautiful to the eyes of Christians are the feet of those who are the messengers of these good tidings!

of those who offer themselves as victims to ransom the unhappy negro race ! . . .'

At the conclusion of the address, Mgr. Lavigerie descended the pulpit steps, and, arrayed in his pontifical vestments, knelt down before each one in succession of the missioners who were about to leave him, perhaps for ever, and humbly kissed their feet. After him came the cathedral clergy, several of whom, now bending under the weight of advanced years, had been the first to enter upon missionary work in Algeria ; they too stooped to kiss the feet of the youthful apostles who were starting on the rugged road.[1]

In speaking of the missioners before him as offering themselves in ransom for their African brethren, Mgr. Lavigerie's words were truly prophetic.

' Less than a year after,' he writes to the Propagation of the Faith, ' eight of them had already laid down their lives as the price of their heroic devotion. Four priests and three Zouaves were carried off by African fever, and a lay brother was killed during an attack made by robbers on the caravan. Eight times the grave has opened to receive the remains of my children, cut off by untimely death. On these I think with joy and with sorrow : sorrow at the loss of these young lives, at the loss to the mission of so much zeal, purity, faith ; joy at the remembrance that the Master they served never fails to reward generous service, and has doubtless already given them a place in His immediate presence among the martyrs and prophets. At the outset our

---

[1] This is a custom observed among Catholics when missionaries go forth to preach to the heathen. It is intended as a practical recognition of the words of Holy Scripture referred to by Mgr. Lavigerie : ' How beautiful are the feet of them that preach the gospel of peace, of them that bring glad tidings of good things ' (Rom. x. 15).

weakness was spared; the first band of missioners met with unhoped-for success, they arrived safely at their journey's end, and all obstacles were removed from their path. This time we are allowed to perceive the dangers of our mission and our want of foresight, lest we should presume on our first success, and forget that we owe all to the good providence of God.'

This fresh band of missioners arrived at their destination with sadly diminished numbers. Those who reached Tabora were worn out with fatigue, attacks of fever, and the privations of the journey. They had suffered greatly from want of provisions, which were extremely scarce in some parts and very costly. Had it not been for the kindness of some Protestant missionaries, they would almost have perished with hunger. As before, they divided into two parties, the one bound for Tanganyika, the other for Nyanza. The arrival of the latter enabled Father Livinhac, the Superior of the mission, to extend operations on the shore of the Nyanza, and to establish a permanent mission and orphanage at Tabora, in the kingdom of Unyanyembe. The central position of Tabora, where the road from Zanguebar branches out to the various districts of the interior, renders it a place of importance, both as affording a means of communication with the coast, and as giving the missioners established there the opportunity of redeeming the unhappy children belonging to the numerous slave gangs passing through on their way to the coast. The orphanage of Tabora has since grown into an institution of considerable magnitude, where the youth of many negro races, rescued from slavery and supported by the alms of Christians in Europe, enjoy the blessing of a Christian education.

On the reinforcement reaching the shores of Tanganyika, the missioners settled there at once resolved upon responding to an appeal from Massanzé, a district at some distance from the parent establishment at Urundi, soliciting that some fathers should be sent to them. This new field of labour would give access to the region of the Upper Congo, and the missioners lost no time in setting out on so important an expedition. They were received by the Chief and his subjects with every token of respect and welcome, for their presence was considered as affording security against the dreaded attacks of an adjacent tribe who were cannibals, and of whose ferocity vestiges were apparent in the ruined hamlets on the boundary of their realm; and also against the raids of the terrible slave-hunters who scoured the country and stayed their barks on the shores of the lake.

A few months later a sad calamity befell the mission of Tanganyika. Following out the plan of evangelisation which they had proposed to themselves as most likely to be productive of permanent results, the missioners in that region had devoted themselves principally to the purchase and instruction of young negro slaves, in the hope that when imbued with Christian doctrine, and habituated to the restraints of civilised life, they might become the means of winning their fellow-countrymen. The neighbouring tribe of Wabikari, however, did all in their power to thwart these charitable designs. They began either to entice the children to leave their protectors, or to carry them off by force, to be sold, when opportunity offered, to the slave-dealers. The remonstrances of the fathers were unheeded, nor were they allowed even to repurchase the children that had been stolen from them.

At length matters were brought to a crisis. A young boy who had been redeemed from slavery, and had been stolen from the charge of the missioners, was ascertained to be held in keeping by the Wabikari. All pacific means of procuring his restoration having failed, the missioners manifested some intention of sending a strong body of natives to demand his surrender. No sooner did the Wabikari obtain intelligence of this design, than, headed by their Chief, they swooped down upon the settlement and surrounded the mission-house. Two of the resident priests, with one of their lay helpers, issued from the hut to learn the cause of the disturbance ; they were assailed by a shower of poisoned arrows, and fell to the ground mortally wounded. When the other missioners, who had remained within the hut in charge of the children, went to the aid of their brethren, the savage marauders were already gone, for on seeing their victims fall, they fled from the spot as if terrified at the deed they had perpetrated. Father Deniaud, the Superior, was the only one still conscious ; he was carried into the house, where he expired in a few minutes, renewing with his dying breath the offering of his life for the salvation of the negro.

Such were some of the trials and triumphs which marked the early stages of the missionary work commenced in Equatorial Africa by Mgr. Lavigerie. The tidings of the sufferings and martyrdom of their brethren only served to inflame the zeal of the White Fathers in Algeria ; already in the close of 1881 a new detachment had gone out consisting of fifteen missioners.

'I am obliged,' their venerated Superior wrote, ' to do a thing that is seldom necessary, and least of all in this age of universal apathy and indifference ; I am obliged to moderate, nay, more, to condemn, their thirst for sacrifice, to reprove their rash ardour, their courageous devotion, and even treat it as foolishness, that sublime foolishness of the Cross which is found in all true apostles throughout the world, before which we all bow down in spirit, though obliged by prudence to restrain it.'

We shall have occasion later on to speak of trials more severe, and triumphs more glorious, which were reserved for the African missions. Meanwhile, we will quote some passages from the conclusion of Mgr. Lavigerie's letter to the Society for the Propagation of the Faith :—

'Amongst the obstacles with which our missioners have to contend in Equatorial Africa there are some which are common to all missions, especially those of Africa. Mohammedanism is one of these.

'At present there are but few of the adherents of this creed of Islam in these remote regions, not more than two or three hundred. They are Arab merchants, slave-dealers for the most part. Mohammedanism, overthrown and dying out in Europe, is, however, making rapid and alarming progress among the native population of Africa. It is imposed upon them by force. It created provinces and kingdoms, and is said to have subdued during the last hundred years no less than 50,000,000 souls to its iron yoke. Equatorial Africa will assuredly share the fate of the surrounding countries if its heathen population are left to themselves. Now the tribes conquered by the Crescent are lost to the Cross for centuries to come. The Moslem creed is the masterpiece of Satan, for whilst satisfying to a certain extent the religious needs of the human heart by the fragments of truth it retains, it legitimatises the indulgence of the baser cravings of our lower nature. . . . Its fatal shadow was already creeping over

Central Africa when our missioners arrived there, and we have since learnt that the Arab slave-dealers are endeavouring to nullify the influence of the Christians with King Mtesa, promising that if he will embrace their creed, they will guarantee his regal sway, of which he fears to be deprived by the Egyptian Government, and allow him to retain his numerous wives. . . . There is every reason to fear that should the Arabs find a pretext to demand the expulsion of our fathers, they will not let it pass.

'Protestantism is a great power, for it has immense resources at its command, and its missionaries are scattered all over the African continent. Our fathers have come into contact with them everywhere; they met with them at the Equatorial Lakes, but let it not be supposed that they found antagonists in them. On the contrary (with one exception), they experienced nothing but friendliness from them. I have already spoken of the courtesy and cordial kindness with which Captain Hore received Father Deniaud and his colleagues at Tanganyika, pressing his services upon them, and offering them hospitality; I can now add that his subsequent conduct has been of the same nature. Father Livinhac writes from Uganda in a similar strain.

' " Mention," he says, "has been made in our letters of opposition from the part of the Protestants, but I should be extremely sorry if anything were published to throw discredit on the behaviour of the Protestant ministers in general because of the hostility shown to us by a single individual. In every instance, save one, we have found them most obliging and ready to aid us, and have experienced nothing but kindness at their hands."

' A like testimony is given in respect to the two ministers at Ujiji. "They continue as kind as ever," our missioner writes; " the only thing I could wish is that these two excellent men were Catholics."

'Polygamy is another and a formidable obstacle to missionary effort. Of this I can but say that the Christian faith, which triumphed over the corruption of pagan Greece and Rome, ought not to despair of raising the negro from his moral degradation. . . .

'Over and above these difficulties, there are others peculiar to Equatorial Africa; they appear to me four in number: the climate, the indifference of the negroes to religion, slavery, and our want of funds. But experience has proved that with the help of God, and the charity of our fellow-Christians, not one of them need be regarded as insurmountable.

'The climate is specially fatal to the European in the tract of country which extends between the coast and the Great Lakes. The land lies low, and is often a swamp on account of the floods wherewith it is deluged in the rainy season. . . . Not one of our missioners escaped its attacks.

'"We had recourse to our medicine chest at the very outset of our journey," Father Deniaud writes. "The African fever brought on by the miasmas arising from the wet ground is like poison. It commences with violent headache, followed by shivering fits and general lassitude. Then delirium comes on, especially when the patient is lying down; almost every night morbid visions confuse the brain. These attacks may be cured by the timely use of proper remedies, succeeded by repeated doses of quinine. But they leave the system greatly weakened, the head feels heavy, ard sometimes even the faculty of thought seems gone." . . . Not only sickness but death is often the swift consequence of an attack of tropical fever. The least imprudence may have fatal results; over-fatigue, exposure to the sun, a chill at night, the evil effects of which, elsewhere, would be but trifling, are mortal under the equator. The blacks alone, accustomed from their youth up to these pestilential vapours, inhale them with impunity. In the region of the Lakes it is otherwise; there the climate is salubrious and temperate, and the health of the missioner living there is in comparative security. . . .

'The religious indifference of the negro in these lands,' Mgr. Lavigerie continues, 'is the second obstacle to the success of our missions. It is a greater one in some localities than the superstition or even the bloodthirsty fanaticism prevailing in other parts of Africa. This brutish indifference is so great that many travellers have declared the black man to be ignorant of the existence of God and the necessity of any form of worship. This statement—militating as it does against the doctrine of a natural law implanted in the heart of even the most barbarous people, whence theologians draw the strongest argument for the existence of God—made a great impression on me, and led me to question our missioners on the subject. They affirmed most positively that all the negroes believe in powerful spirits, whom they fear and worship, propitiating them with prayer and sacrifices. They may practise gross idolatry, but they are not destitute of all belief in the supernatural. Thus one of the fathers writes :—

' " On one occasion, when we were coasting along the lake, a terrible storm arose, which threatened to engulf their rude and fragile bark. The negro rowers were much alarmed, especially as they were passing Cape Cabogo, a place of evil fame which no one can pass with impunity without appeasing the spirit of the neighbouring rock with presents. Accordingly, upon approaching the cliff, one of the sailors advanced to the prow, bearing in his hands some strings of beads and a piece of calico. He then addressed the spirit, praying him to withhold his wrath and not impede their voyage. Having finished his prayer, he cast into the water the offerings destined for the spirit, and, resuming his seat, began to chant a song with his comrades, while they rowed vigorously away from the perilous rock, convinced that the presiding *muzimu* was appeased, and would allow them to reach their destination without difficulty."

'But if the African negro believes, as he certainly does, in a supernatural world, his ignorance and apathy are none the less real, and these are in fact the great obstacles to his conversion. Hunting, fishing, and puerile amusements occupy his attention, to the exclusion of any idea of what is spiritual and eternal. To instil into his mind higher thoughts and lead him to the practice of virtue is therefore a laborious task, but not a hopeless one, as our missioners experience in regard to the children whom they redeem from slavery. In the case of adults this is a matter of greater difficulty, but even with them grace can work wonders. And who needs the help of God more than this unhappy race, groaning under the weight of its many woes, and of that which is the parent of them all, the curse of slavery?

'Without having been in Africa, and having been brought into contact with those who are or have been slaves, it is impossible to form a just idea of the crimes, the cruelties, the horrors of every kind which slavery and the slave trade bring in their train. I am not speaking of the past, but of what goes on at present,

of what I have seen myself, or heard from the lips of
some of the sorrowful victims of the atrocities daily
practised. The transport of slaves by sea is stopped,
it is true, but it still goes on inland, and has in many
parts assumed proportions of greater magnitude, and
a character yet more revolting.

'In the North and East of Africa it is either the
Mussulmans themselves, or the negro chiefs whom they
associate with them in their commercial transactions,
who supply the trade. And it may be said, in passing,
that no blow could be struck more fatal to Mohammedanism than the abolition of slavery, since Moslem
society is so constituted that it cannot exist without it.
The black men are regarded as beings of an inferior
order, something between man and beast, to whom no
mercy need be shown. The Mussulmans have in their
pay bands of marauders and assassins, who invade the
territories inhabited by heathen tribes in order to
capture and carry off their victims.

'The Berber States, and, I am ashamed to say,
Algeria itself, Egypt, Zanzibar, the Soudan, are the
principal places whence these expeditions set out.
Sometimes they confine themselves to hunting down
isolated individuals, women or children who have
strayed to a distance from their dwelling-places. But
generally the expedition is a regularly organised raid.
The villages of the interior are suddenly surrounded
at night by these merciless adventurers. Seldom do
the negroes, who are unprovided with firearms, offer
any resistance; if they do so, they are instantly massacred by their assailants, who are armed to the teeth.
Some fugitives escape in the darkness; the rest are
seized, chained together, and hurried off, men, women,
and children, in the direction of some market in the

interior. Captives are brought from countries at a distance of sixty, eighty, or even a hundred days' march. This is the first step on their *via dolorosa*.

'A series of unspeakable miseries then commences for them. The slaves are on foot. The men who appear the strongest, and whose escape is to be feared, have their hands tied (and sometimes their feet) in such fashion that walking becomes a torture to them; and on their necks are placed yokes, which attach several of them together. They march all day; at night, when they stop to rest, a few handfuls of raw " sorgho " are distributed among the captives. This is all their food. Next morning they must start again.

' But after the first day or two, the fatigue, the sufferings, and the privations have weakened a great many. The women and the aged are the first to halt. Then, in order to strike terror into this miserable mass of human beings, their conductors, armed with a wooden bar to economise powder, approach those who appear to be the most exhausted, and deal them a terrible blow on the nape of the neck. The unfortunate victims utter a cry, and fall to the ground in the convulsions of death!

' The terrified troop immediately resumes its march. Terror has imbued even the weakest with new strength. Each time some one breaks down the same horrible scene is repeated.

' At night, on arriving at their halting place, after the first days of such a life, a not less frightful scene awaits them. The traffickers in human flesh have acquired by experience a knowledge of how much their victims can endure. A glance shows them those who will soon sink from weariness; then, to economise the scanty food which they distribute, they pass behind

these wretched beings, and kill them with a single blow.
Their corpses remain where they fell, when they are
not suspended on the branches of the neighbouring
trees; and it is close to them that their companions
are obliged to eat and to sleep.

'But what sleep that is may be easily imagined.
Among the young negroes snatched by us from this
hell and restored to liberty, there are some who, long
afterwards, wake up every night, shrieking fearfully.
They behold again, in their dreams, the abominable
and bloody scenes which they have witnessed.

'In this manner the weary tramp continues—sometimes for months, when the caravan comes from a
distance. Their number diminishes daily. If, goaded
by their cruel sufferings, some attempt to rebel or to
escape, their fierce masters cut them down with their
swords, and leave them as they lay, along the road,
attached to one another by their yokes. It has been
truly said that, if a traveller lost the way leading from
Equatorial Africa to the towns where slaves are sold,
he could easily find it again by the skeletons of the
negroes with which it is strewed.

'It is calculated that each year no less than 400,000
negroes are sacrificed to this Moloch.

'When at length the market is reached the ranks
of the unhappy captives are indeed sadly reduced;
rarely do more than a third or fourth part of the
original number survive the journey.

'In the town where the slave-market is held, a
scene of a different, but not less revolting, nature may
be witnessed. The captured negroes are exhibited for
sale like cattle; their feet, hands, and teeth are looked
at, and all their limbs examined, to see what work can
be got out of them; the price to be given for them is

discussed in their presence, just as if it were a question of purchasing some brute beast; and, the sum agreed upon being paid, they belong body and soul to the man who has bought them. No consideration is made for the ties of blood, for father, mother, and children are ruthlessly separated; conscience is not respected, for the slaves are required to adopt forthwith the creed of the Mussulman whose property they have become; even the natural feelings of modesty and shame are disregarded, for they are obliged to submit to the most disgraceful demands. In a word, the life of the slave is at the disposal of his owner. In Central Africa no one is called to account for the death of his slaves.

'I have entered at some length on these details, because I know of nothing better calculated to awaken the sympathy of Christian Europe for the unhappy negro, better calculated to give an idea of the obstacles wherewith the zeal of our missioners has to contend. What can be expected of a race thus decimated, crushed, tortured, and who themselves add day by day to the tale of their woes? What, above all, can be expected of those who carry on and profit by this vile traffic? Our missioners will reply to this question. They tell us they could have no more bitter foes. The slave-dealers and the slave-hunters are aware that the spread of the Gospel will put an end to their gains, and they spare no pains to hinder its progress. This the latest reports from Nyanza prove; for there, as has been said, endeavours are being made to poison the mind of King Mtesa against us, and induce him to put the fathers to death. But we must trust to the support of the civilised world, which will find a means of suppressing the slave trade in the markets of the interior, as it has been suppressed in those of the coast.

'Meanwhile our missioners will act with prudence and charity, and carefully abstain from arousing angry passions by impotent protestation; striving to alleviate by kindly deeds and the hope which comes of faith, the cruel wrongs they daily witness.

'When taken to the dwellings of their owners to be employed as servants, the slaves are, it is true, fairly well treated as a rule, for otherwise they might die before their time. But when they are old, or if they become disabled from work, they are often driven away with blows, until they crawl to the cemetery to die there.

'Such are the frightful atrocities of African slavery. Ask the missionaries of Zanzibar, who have heard and seen as I have, and they will say the same. As for Central Africa, we have the corroborative testimony of all explorers; I will mention Livingstone only, the most celebrated of them all, who says that in speaking of the slave trade he keeps far short of the truth, lest he be suspected of exaggeration, although on that point there is no room for exaggeration. It would be utterly impossible to overrate the wretchedness it produces. . . .

'Finally, the last, and in one sense the greatest obstacle to the success of our missions, is the enormous outlay required and our inability to meet it. Every one can understand the immense expenses of such journeys and such a mission, where, too, such misery has to be relieved: in every letter our missioners complain of the lack of funds, and to supply them we must appeal to the liberality of Christians in Europe.'

CHAPTER VII

DEVELOPMENT OF THE MISSIONS OF CENTRAL AFRICA

In spite of the formidable obstacles against which, as we have seen, the Catholic missioners in Equatorial Africa had to struggle, the labours of the White Fathers of Algeria had met with splendid and almost unhoped-for results. The missions were extended and formed into four districts, viz., the two Apostolic Vicariates of Nyanza and Tanganyika, and the two Provicariates of Unyanyembe and the Upper Congo. Over the Vicariates Mgr. Lavigerie placed two bishops chosen from among his first subjects; the charge of Tanganyika was given to Mgr. Charbonnier, in the place of Father Deniaud, the former head of the mission, who, as related above, fell a victim to the poisoned arrows of a savage tribe; whilst Father Livinhac, who had been one of the first who reached the shores of the Nyanza, was raised to the episcopate, and received jurisdiction over the district lying around the lake.

It was in 1884 that Father Livinhac was summoned to Algeria to receive episcopal consecration at the hands of Cardinal Lavigerie. At first he declined the dignity, entreating that it might be conferred on one more worthy, and that he might be permitted to remain in obscurity amongst his beloved catechumens in Uganda. He was, however, constrained to yield; and the ceremony of consecration took place at Carthage, in the

Chapel of St. Cyprian, of which we shall presently speak ; on the spot which was formerly the scene of the combats and triumphs of the early martyrs.

Immediately after, Mgr. Livinhac hastened back to his distant post, accompanied by a fresh band of labourers, anxious to join in the toils and perils of the Apostolate; to aid in gathering in the rich harvest of souls which lay ready for the sickle in the region of the Equatorial Lakes, before Islamism could cast its blight over the corn in the ear, and Moslem influence counteract the influence of the Christian missioner.

On arriving at his post, Mgr. Livinhac found that a cruel persecution had broken out in the mission. The letter which he addressed to the Society for the Propagation of the Faith contains an account of the persecution, and shows the spirit in which this severe trial was borne by the natives. Under the mysterious transforming power of Divine grace, and the elevating and regenerating influence of Christianity, the debased and down-trodden negro, the object of contempt and aversion to the white man, whose life is held of no value, and who is hunted, captured, and sold like a brute beast, becomes capable of sublime devotion and heroic courage. In fact, the faith and steadfastness exhibited by the African converts under torture and in face of death, bear comparison with the acts of the martyrs in the early ages of Christianity, and could only be accounted for by their savage persecutors as the result of charms and magic.

'Before my departure for Algeria,' writes Mgr. Livinhac, ' the message of salvation had, by God's help, begun to produce abundant fruit amongst these unhappy tribes, who are sunk in superstition and vice. Several missionary stations had been established, and were extending their influence ; hundreds of catechumens and neophytes attended our instructions. But King Mtesa, stirred up by the Moslem slave-dealers, showed signs of an intention to stop the progress of the faith amongst the natives, by recourse to violence. The missioners therefore thought themselves obliged in prudence to withdraw for a time from a position which they could not hold without danger to their lives, and quitted Uganda. It was at this juncture that I was called upon to undertake the cares of the episcopate and the administration of these widespread territories.

'Meanwhile Mtesa died, and his son Mwanga, whom I had known personally, and who had always been a good friend to us, insisted upon our missioners returning to their former quarters close to his capital. But in a very short time the same influences which had excited suspicion and hostility towards us in Mtesa's mind brought about a complete change in his son's feelings in regard to us. On my return from Carthage, where I had been consecrated bishop by his Eminence Cardinal Lavigerie, I learnt, to my inexpressible grief, that sad calamities had befallen our mission settlement at Uganda.

'When the missioners, at the request of Mwanga, had again taken up their residence near him, they had met with a warm welcome. He declared openly that he owed his elevation to the throne to the prayers of the Christians, and to show his gratitude to their God would boldly break off with the old superstitions of his forefathers. He habitually recited the Lord's Prayer, and desired that instruction should be imparted to his subjects by some of the native Christians. These latter soon had occasion to give a striking proof of their loyalty, by apprising Mwanga of a plot formed by the chief men of the realm, who were displeased at his departure from the heathen customs of the country.

They intended to assassinate him, and place his younger brother on the throne. On being charged with this conspiracy, the prime minister, who had been the ringleader in it, pleaded guilty and was pardoned. From that day forth he vowed undying hatred to the Christians, and resolved upon their destruction. Gradually he succeeded in poisoning the mind of the King against them ; and indeed it was no very difficult task to induce him to repudiate a religion which forbade polygamy, and condemned cruelty and injustice, which constitute the regal prerogative in those regions.

'Open hostility was, however, not declared; but while matters were in this state, tidings reached the King's ears of the conquests of Germany in Equatorial Africa. To the mind of the negro all white men are confederated together. Might not we perhaps be crafty spies, come to prepare the way for the invader ? Just then news arrived that a white man with a strong escort was approaching by way of the Boussaga, and this caused general alarm. The traveller in question was the Anglican Bishop Hannington. Mwanga saw but one way to avert the supposed danger, and gave orders to his troops to kill the white man and all his company.

'Joseph Mkasa, a native Christian, and one of the King's councillors, did his utmost to prove that the dreaded stranger was no enemy, and that if Mwanga did not wish him to enter his territory, he need only forbid him to cross the frontier, without imbruing his hands in his blood. One of the fathers added his entreaties, and finally the King promised to countermand his order ; but whether the messenger was sent too late, or was not sent at all, it is impossible to say; at any rate, the poor bishop and all his men were massacred, and the interference of the Christians on his behalf served as a pretext for persuading the King that all " those who prayed " were his mortal foes. The prime minister, Katikiro, took occasion to demand the death of Joseph Mkasa (by whom his conspiracy had been revealed), and the King, although reluctant to lose the services of so faithful and valued a servant, consented to the proposal.

'Fearing lest Mwanga should revoke his decision, the minister ordered that Joseph should be beheaded immediately. When led to the place of execution he remained perfectly calm, and addressing his executioner said: "Tell Mwanga that he has condemned me unjustly, but I forgive him with all my heart. Tell him, too, that I advise him to repent, for unless he does so, he will have to answer for me before the tribunal of God." His head was then struck off, and his body committed to the flames.

'Joseph's last message was delivered to the King. At first he pretended to laugh at it, but it evidently made a great impression on him. In his brutish anger he thought to prevent Joseph from appearing against him at the judgment seat by killing another man, and causing the ashes of the two to be well shaken up together. "Now," he exclaimed in triumph, "nobody can distinguish between them, so how can he plead against me before God?"'

Several other native converts were put to death at the same time, for no other crime but that of professing the religion of Christ. The King also announced his intention of exterminating all the Christians in his dominions, and murdering or driving away the missioners. The good fathers therefore lived in daily expectation of having to lay down their own lives,

and to see the rising Church swept away in torrents
of blood. But Mwanga contented himself for a time
with uttering threats, and imprisoning a few neophytes,
though his feelings remained unchanged. "I shall
make an end of these Christians," he said to his cour-
tiers ; "they obtain from God all they wish. Formerly they regarded me as a friend, and prayed for
me, and God preserved me from harm ; now they will
implore Him to overthrow me, so I must rid myself of
them all."'

A spark only was wanting to kindle the conflagration. Clara Nalmasi, one of King Mtesa's daughters,
had been converted to the faith a short time previously.
She held the office of guardian of one of the tombs of
the former kings, and had, with injudicious zeal,
destroyed some of the amulets which were hanging
there, and banished the sorcerers in whom the spirits of
the dead were supposed to reside. These proceedings
gave great offence, but matters came to a crisis when
she broke into fragments and threw away a heathen
charm, of an indecent and revolting nature, which
belonged to her. One of these charms is possessed by
every member of the royal family, and is regarded as
sacred, since after the death of its owner his soul is
said to inhabit it. Too often it becomes the object
of superstitious worship, human sacrifices being offered
to it. In order to prevent anything of the sort in
her own case, Clara destroyed the charm, displaying
thereby, perhaps, more courage than prudence. This
act brought a storm of persecution on the native converts ; all manner of public calamities were predicted
as likely to follow upon such a profanation, calamities
that could only be averted by a general massacre of the
Christians.

A few days after, Mwanga, when out walking, came upon one of his pages, a Christian youth, who was teaching something to one of his comrades. 'What are you doing there?' inquired the King. 'I am teaching the catechism,' replied the boy. The monarch, transported with anger, drew his sword and ran him through the body.

This gave the signal for a universal outbreak of hostility. That same evening the King sent for his minister, and declared that he would put to death every one of 'the people who pray' (the name given to Christians by the savages). The gates of the city were instantly closed, and orders given that no one should pass out. One of the Christians, however, managed to escape, and carry the tidings to the missioners. Father Lourdel resolved to set out at break of day, in order to intercede with Mwanga for his beloved children. It was raining heavily, and the roads were fast becoming a morass, when he left the mission house at Rubaga, for his weary tramp of three hours. The following is the account he gives of his adventures :—

'I soon met bands of men hurrying along, armed with guns and spears ; they were being despatched to the principal missionary stations, to plunder them and arrest the chief inhabitants. "Alas!" I said to myself, "I am too late to allay the tempest. What will be my own fate? I can only commend myself to God, ready, if it be His will, to make the sacrifice of my life." I went on my way with a heavy heart, and on reaching the royal residence found all tranquil. It was the lull before the storm. Every one I met stared at me, astonished at my audacity in venturing into the King's presence at such a moment. Striving to conceal my agitation, I walked boldly up into the hut which serves as an antechamber for royal audiences, greeted the minister who was seated there, just as usual, and passed through to the inner apartments, no one attempting, to my great surprise, to hinder my progress. I was still more surprised to see all the Christians attached to the court going about just as if nothing extraordinary had happened. Was it possible that I was the victim of a trick, or had I been dreaming? Alas! all was but too true. I was to have the melancholy satisfaction of seeing my spiritual children bound and led away before my eyes, and of bidding them farewell by look if not by word, before they entered on their last conflict. Already the officers were collecting the Christians together in the courtyard on which the royal apartments opened. The faces of many of our converts beamed with joy, some looked rather frightened, whilst others answered boldly, when their heathen friends told them they ought to have run away, " Run away!—why should I ? "

'The first called out was Charles Luanga, the head of the King's pages, many of whom were Christians. He and his comrades were greeted with yells of derision in which the King's stentorian voice was plainly audible. Mwanga addressed bitter reproaches to them ; then he said : " Let all who pray stand apart." Charles Luanga instantly stepped out, hand in hand with Kizito, a catechumen, a mere boy, but whose courage and firmness were far beyond his years. All the Christians in the company followed their example. At a sign from the King, they were seized, bound with ropes, and roughly dragged out of the courtyard.

'The young men of 18 to 25 years of age were bound together ; the children formed a second troop. They were tied so tightly and so close to one another that they could only walk with the greatest difficulty, taking tiny steps and continually knocking up against each other. I noticed that little Kizito laughed at this as merrily as if he were at play with his companions. He is the son of one of the greatest lords in the kingdom, several of his brothers are Christians, and very fervent ones too. Kizito had long been entreating me to baptise him, on the plea that the King would soon put him to death, and I had promised, seeing him in such good dispositions, to do so in a month's time. But God had decreed that this chosen soul should be regenerated in the baptism of blood.

'As they passed before me, these brave confessors looked their last farewell, and I prayed for them, that their courage might not fail under the tortures they were to undergo. I was not allowed to speak a word of encouragement to them, and had to content myself with reading on their countenances the resignation, the holy joy, the manly courage of their hearts; and in all my sorrow I thanked God that He had chosen these negro children to bear the first witness to the faith in Uganda.

'After the officials of the court, a young soldier, named James Bouzabaliao, was brought before the King. He had attracted notice by his zeal in imparting religious instruction to the children in the town; Mwanga, who knew him, had threatened him with death if he did not desist, but nothing could induce him to discontinue his apostolic labours. The King even accused him of having tried to make a convert of him; a crime of so dark a hue merited speedy punishment.

'As soon as he was summoned to the King's presence, he came running up to the royal hut, knowing well what was in store for him.

' " You are the one," the King said to him, " who is the chief of the Christians here ? "

' " I am a Christian, it is true," replied James ; " but the title of chief, which you give me, does not belong to me."

' " This young fellow," continued the King, " gives himself out for a great man ; to look at him, one would take him for a lord."

' " I humbly thank your majesty," answered James, laughing, " for the high rank you give me."

' " This is the man," resumed the King, " who actually wanted me to adopt his religion. Take him away, executioners, and cut off his head at once. I mean to begin with him."

' " Farewell, then ! " the young Christian said, without betraying the least emotion ; " I am going up to Paradise, and I will pray God for you."

' These words provoked a shout of mocking laughter from the heathen bystanders, to whose ears they conveyed no meaning.

' " These Christians must have lost their senses," they said, " to talk in this way."

' James passed close to where I stood, a rope round his neck, led by the executioner who was going to behead him. I raised my hand to give him the last absolution. In response he lifted his hands, which were tightly bound, towards heaven, pointing upwards to show me whither he was going, and where he hoped we should meet again. As he looked at me he smiled, as if to say : " Father, why are you so sorrowful ? This is but a trifling thing in comparison with the eternal joys to which you have taught us to look forward."

' I waited several hours, in the expectation of being allowed to have an interview with the King. It was not granted me. At last, fearing lest Mwanga, in a fit of fury, might send his men to loot our house and massacre the orphans, I turned my steps homewards. Hoping to gain some information respecting his intentions, I walked part of the way with the minister, who was leaving the court at the same time. He behaved with exaggerated politeness, but I learnt nothing from him. On taking leave, he discharged a parting shot, saying with an odious sneer: " The men of God know everything, but they did not foresee what was going to happen to-day." I made no answer, and went on my way, with sad misgivings as to the future of our infant Christian community, for which there seemed no hope but in the succour of Divine Providence.

' The sun is burning in these regions, and I was parched with thirst. But so great was the consternation inspired by the King's action, that on this occasion no one dared to give me anything to drink for fear of compromising himself. Not until I reached the hut of one of our converts could I obtain any refreshment.

' On the road I met an old man, a good honest heathen, but very friendly to us, three of whose sons were converts. His usual cheerfulness was gone ; when he accosted me I saw his eyes were full of tears. " My three sons were dragged away in chains," he said ; " why are they treated so cruelly? What harm have they done ? They have not robbed any one, or insulted the King. They are accused of praying ; is that a crime ? " I was quite touched by the way the good old man took my hands and expressed his sorrow for the misfortune that had befallen us ; and I felt it all the more because I had encountered many a hostile glance, and heard many a threatening word as I went along, from the parents of the persecuted Christians, who saw in me the cause of their affliction. One woman when she caught sight of me exclaimed : "Oh, would that I were a man! I would soon run a spear through this wretched white man who taught our children, and has brought them to this misery!" Poor creatures! If they did but know how much we love them, how earnestly we desire their welfare! If they did but know all it has cost us to leave our country and our friends, and live in exile amongst them! But the disciple is not greater than his Master, and we must be content to be the objects of hatred and mistrust on the part of those for whom we are ready to lay down our life.

'During the night a considerable number of neophytes came to us for consolation and encouragement. They gave us details of how the Christian stations had been plundered, and also said that the King had spared several of the catechumens attached to the court, as he could not dispense with their services.'

Later on Father Lourdel made another, and this time a successful attempt, to obtain an interview with Mwanga.

'I represented to the King,' he writes, 'with tears in my eyes, the harm he was doing to himself by putting to death his most valuable servants ; but all I said appeared to make no impression, he only laughed at it. "I will not any longer allow my servants to pray," he said ; "I am *kabaka* (king)—every one cannot say that ; I am master here, and no one shall resist my authority."

'I would not be silenced, but went on to intercede for our beloved converts, endeavouring to convince the despot that the accusations brought against them were false. He laughed loudly, and said : "They shall not all die, I will spare a few." That was the utmost concession I could gain.'

Father Lourdel had hardly quitted the royal presence when the most influential of the native converts, Andrew Kagoua, was arrested. This man had always manifested the greatest attachment and loyalty to the King, and was a universal favourite, being intelligent, courageous, and pleasing, ready to do any one a good turn. The King himself called him his friend, and wanted to make him general-in-chief of his army; he always kept him near his person, as he knew he could be relied on in case of an insurrection breaking out. But Andrew had been a zealous proselytiser. It was well known that he had converted his wife, and had collected about him as many as a hundred and fifty catechumens, who loved him as a father. The terrible crime of having converted two of the prime minister's children was laid at his door; this was an unpardonable offence, and Katikiro only awaited a suitable moment for vengeance. When the King decreed the massacre of the Christians, he hastened to denounce Andrew; but the King could not at first be persuaded to sacrifice one whom he considered as his best friend. The minister, however, was so persistent, and painted Andrew in colours so black, that Mwanga gave way. Andrew was accordingly arrested, and arraigned before the tribunal of Katikiro, who, pretending not to recognise him, asked who he was.

' "How is it that you do not know me?" replied Andrew calmly. "You have seen me a great many times, and, if you remember, I came with my men to thank you on my promotion to the rank of *Mgoa*."

' " Was it you," continued the minister, " who taught my children your religion?"

' " Yes, I did teach it them," Andrew answered.

' Then the minister went on :

' " Before he died, Joseph Mkasa " (the first victim of the persecution, and a great friend of Andrew) " gave you a gun to shoot the King."

' " If I had had such a murderous intention I did not want that gun to execute it.   Had I not a number of guns that Mwanga had given me, just as good ones as the one I had from Mkasa?   Look at all the guns you had from Mtesa—were they given you to take away his son's life ? "

' " Take him away and put him to death," said Katikiro.   " Put him to death at once," he added, addressing the executioner, " for I will neither eat nor drink until you bring me his hand cut off as a sign that he is dead."

' Now the executioners were accustomed to keep condemned culprits several days, and torture them cruelly, promising milder treatment if they would give them slaves, cattle, &c.   Only when no more bribes were to be extorted from them or their friends was the *coup-de-grâce* given.   Thus when a criminal was handed over to the executioner, it was considered a piece of good luck, for which he thanked the King effusively, especially if the prisoner was a wealthy one.   But the man into whose charge Andrew was delivered stood in awe of the minister, and dared not defer the execution of his sentence, as he would fain have done ; for Andrew was rich, and his friends were numerous.

' Andrew on his part, dreading lest the executioner, who seemed sorry for him, should postpone the happy moment when he should receive his crown, urged him to carry out his orders at once.   " If your master tells you he is hungry, and bids you kill a fatted kid, you make haste, in order to set it before him as soon as possible. Be quick then, and put me to death, or else he will scold you. Take my hand to him, as he will not eat anything until he has seen it."

'Andrew was beheaded close to Katikiro's hut, and his hand taken to his enemy. We could not learn what became of his body.'

Such was the situation of affairs when Mgr. Livinhac arrived in Uganda on his return from Algeria.

'Hearing of our approach,' he writes, 'Mwanga and his councillors thought it prudent to prevent our holding communication with our brethren at Rubaga : five white men in one house would be almost as good as an army, and would be able to conquer the whole district ! So in their wisdom they determined to assign to us as our residence some wretched huts about two hours' march from our station, where we should be kept close prisoners. Happily, Father Lourdel, having been apprised of these designs, hastened to meet us, and acquaint us with the fate in reserve for us. I immediately pushed on to Rubaga with Father Denoit, whilst Father Lourdel remained behind to look after the baggage. A heavy downfall of rain sheltered us from observation ; but from time to time, as we pursued our way, some of the native converts came out of their places of concealment in order to give us an affectionate welcome. It was a great pleasure to me to give my blessing to these beloved members of my flock, who since their conversion had given proof of such filial attachment and firm adhesion to the faith they had learnt of us, and for which they might, on the morrow, be called upon to shed their blood.

'We reached Rubaga wet through and tired out ; rejoicing, however, at having defeated the schemes of the King and his councillors, who imagined us on the shores of Nyanza, while we were resting under the roof of our dear colleagues. The next day, Father Lourdel went again to the capital, to acquaint Mwanga with our arrival. He seemed astonished, but accepted the *fait accompli*.

'Some days later, I went with some of the fathers to pay my respects to him, and hand over to him, in the form of a present, the toll expected of us for our journey on the lake. I confess that it was no small effort to me to pay this visit and present this gift, but the neglect of either would have been the utter ruin of our mission.

'The King seemed somewhat embarrassed on seeing me, but he soon recovered his self-possession. Whilst abstaining from reproaches, which would only have irritated him and made matters worse, we pointed out to him that the line of conduct he had recently adopted would be the means of depriving him of his most valuable subjects, and banishing all foreigners from the kingdom. We added that, under present circumstances, we could not all remain there, and I therefore asked for boats to carry us further south. This request staggered him; he declared he could not allow me to go so quickly, but he carefully refrained from holding out hopes that the persecution would soon be at an end. We persisted, urging all manner of arguments, appealing to his feelings, and even resorting to menaces; all were of no avail. Finally, he consented to my departure, and ordered one of his officers who was present to get the boats ready.

'I knew how slowly everything was done, and felt sure that I should have time to visit the mission station and confirm all the converts who could make their way thither. While the persecution lasted it would have been very unsafe to go round to the villages; in fact, the neophytes themselves could not venture out in the day-time, and only came to us, as in the early days of the Church, under cover of the darkness. During the month that I remained at Rubaga, not a single night passed without a visit from several of our converts. Sometimes I was called up four or five times during the night to receive them, and I was able to administer confirmation to ninety-seven individuals. I cannot say how deep was the impression made on me on beholding the marvellous effects of grace in the hearts of these Africans, who but yesterday were enslaved by the debasing errors of paganism. They expected every moment to be handed over to the executioner; but, far from being intimidated by this prospect, they confronted torture and death with a calmness and intrepidity which is the result of divine grace and steadfast faith alone. "The executioner," they said, "can destroy our bodies, but he cannot destroy our souls; we shall have to suffer, it is true, but these brief sufferings will be followed by eternal happiness." We were often asked if concealment were not a sort of apostasy, and whether it would not be better to court death, by openly declaring that they were Christians.

'The good dispositions evinced by these generous souls afforded us great consolation, and the time spent in instructing and exhorting them flew by rapidly. But nature asserted her rights, and often, overcome by fatigue, I tried to dismiss my visitors for the purpose of obtaining a few hours' sleep. "Do not send us away," they would entreat; "to-morrow I shall be brought before the judge and probably sentenced to death. I shall never see you again!" "It was only by means of a large bribe," another would say, "that I got the gaoler to take off my fetters and let me come to bid farewell to my friends; this is the last opportunity I shall ever have of speaking to you."

'Who could harden his heart against such appeals? Our conversations were prolonged late into the night; far from being sorrowful, all present were cheerful, almost gay, and, looking at the bright countenances around us, we almost forgot the heavy storm that had broken over our infant Church. Those whose life was in greatest danger, and who could remain with us until after midnight, received Holy Communion; and, fortified by the Bread of Heaven, they went forth bravely to their last conflict.'

Mgr. Livinhac adds some details respecting the death of Charles Luanga, the chief of the King's pages, of whom mention has already been made.

'He had been separated from his comrades, probably in the hope that, if their leader was gone, they would be more easily prevailed upon to renounce their faith. One of the executioners, to prove his zeal, begged that Charles might be given to him, and he would torture him as he deserved.

'He was burnt to death by a slow fire, beginning with his feet. Whilst kindling the fire, his tormentor said to him: "Now then, let your God come and take you out of the flames." The martyr replied calmly: "Poor man, you do not know what you are saying. I only feel as if you were pouring water over me; but do you beware, or the God at whom you mock will one day cast you into a fiery furnace!" He then kept silence, and bore his lingering torture without ever allowing a murmur to escape his lips.

'Three of the youngest pages excited the compassion of the head executioner, who in the course of a long life had never had to practise such cruelties on children of such tender years. " Only tell the King that you will not pray any more," he said to them, " and he will pardon you ! "—" We will never leave off praying as long as we live ! " was the indignant reply of the boys.

' They were accordingly bound, and led out with the others, to the number of thirty-four, on to a hill which rises opposite to the mission house. A quantity of dried reeds had been taken there, and of these the executioners made huge faggots, in each of which one of the victims was bound up. They were then laid on the ground, side by side, the feet of all being turned the same way.

' Among these boys was one of the chief executioner's own sons. The unhappy father used every endeavour to induce him to utter a word which could be construed into a denial of his faith ; but his efforts were fruitless. He hoped that the sight of the torture in store for him might change the boy's mind, but he hoped in vain ; the child allowed himself to be bound in the bundle of reeds without a word or a struggle. At the last moment his father made a final attempt : " My boy," he entreated, " only let me hide you at home ; nobody comes that way, you will never be found out ! "—" No, father," replied the boy, " you shall not hide me. You are the King's slave : he has commanded you to kill me. If you disobey him, you will get into trouble ; I will not be the cause of it. I know well enough why I am put to death ; it is because of my religion. Let me die, father ! "

' To make his death easier, the executioner ordered one of his men to unbind the boy, and give him a hard blow on the back of his neck. Death was instantaneous ; and the body was replaced in the bundle of reeds to be burned with the rest.

'Then the reeds were ignited at the end where the feet of the victims were, in order that their sufferings might be more protracted, and that some might, perhaps, when the flames reached them, be prevailed on to deny their faith. A vain hope ! The martyrs' voices were heard, it is true, but only when joining in the prayers which we had taught them to recite !

'Half an hour later the funeral pile had burnt down, and nothing remained but rows of charred corpses, covered with ashes. Three of the youngest pages had been spared by the executioner ; the terrible fate of their comrades had not daunted their courage, on the contrary, they waited with impatience for their turn to come.

'The executioner, seeing children so young despising death, could hardly believe his senses. He determined to cut their bonds, and take them back to the prison. Grieved to the heart to see the hoped-for crown fade from before their eyes, "Why," they exclaimed, "do you not put us too to death ? We are Christians like those whom you have burnt; we will never forsake our religion—*never, never !* " The executioner was deaf to their entreaties. Some days later he told the King what he had done, saying that he hoped now that the evil influence of their comrades was removed they would *repent.* The King blamed him, but their lives were spared. These generous boys were the only survivors of the glorious band of martyrs.

'Another of our converts, named Mathias Muromba, had for a long time been the object of special aversion to the enemies of God. Ever since his baptism, four years previously, he had been most strict in the practice of his religion, for he was one of those who, having once known the right way, never depart from it. He lived quietly with his Christian wife and children, exercising the functions of magistrate in one of the largest districts of the realm. As soon as the persecution broke out, he was arrested and brought before the judge, who looked scornfully at him, and asked, " Can that be Muromba ? Can he at his age have taken up with religion ? "

' " Yes, I am he," Mathias replied. The judge continued : " Why do you pray ? "

' " Because I wish to pray," was the answer.

' " You have sent away all your wives," the minister said with a sneer; " pray who cooks your food for you ? "

' " Is it because I am thin," Mathias asked, " or on account of my religion, that I have been brought before you ? "

' The minister vouchsafed no reply. " Take him away and put him to death," he said to the executioners.

' " That is just what I wish for," Mathias replied.

' " Executioner," resumed Katikiro, " you are to cut off his hands and feet, and tear strips of flesh off his back, and broil them in his sight. And," he added, " no doubt God will deliver him."

' Mathias, stung by the affront offered to God, spoke out boldly : " Yes, God will deliver me ; but you will not see how, for He will take unto Himself my immortal soul, and leave only my perishable body in your hands."

' The barbarous orders of the King were exactly carried out. To avoid attracting a crowd, the valiant

Christian was taken to a hill at some distance. Bound with ropes, he walked with a brisk step and joyous countenance to the place of torture. Another Christian, baptized on the same day as himself, was led out with him to be beheaded.

'With the help of his men, the executioner chopped off Mathias' hands and feet, which were broiled before his eyes. Then, laying him on the ground face downwards, they tore pieces of flesh from his bones, and burnt them too in the fire. This excruciating torture did not elicit a single complaint from the heroic sufferer.

'The executioners possessed the art of stopping the flow of blood, so as to prevent their victim from bleeding to death; thus they prolonged his agony. They did this so effectually that three days afterwards some slaves who came to cut reeds close by, heard a faint voice calling to them. They went to the spot whence the sound proceeded, and found the dying man, who entreated them to bring him some water. But the slaves were so horrified at the sight of his mutilated form that they ran away, leaving him to consummate his sacrifice and his sufferings after the example of his Divine Master, without the slightest alleviation for his burning thirst, or any human succour.

'The constancy and contempt of death exhibited by the native converts, and their calm resignation under torture, seemed incomprehensible to the King and his heathen subjects. The only manner in which they could account for it was by attributing it to the power of witchcraft, supposing that we cast over those who came to us for instruction a spell which rendered them indifferent to the pleasures of life, and made death attractive. Acting on this notion, one of the chiefs whose daughter was a Christian had recourse to a strange expedient to force her to apostatise. Finding that caresses and threats were alike ineffectual, he took a cutlass, and cut deep gashes about her head and body, saying, " Those openings will surely let out the ideas with which you have been indoctrinated, and the charm by which you are bound."

' A great deal of blood escaped by these outlets, but the faith remained, and the spell that attached the poor girl to it was still unsevered.'

On hearing of these sad occurrences, Cardinal Lavigerie considered it binding upon him, as Apostolic Delegate, to interfere officially to arrest this sacrifice of life. He therefore appealed in the name of humanity and of religion to the European Powers who had representatives in Zanzibar, requesting them to unite in bringing pressure to bear upon the Sultan Said Bargash. He alone had sufficient influence with the Arab traders to induce them to put a stop to atrocities which rendered it dangerous for any white men to remain in the districts between the Great Lakes and the coast. National rivalry, however, prevented united action, and no effectual steps were taken. It was not until tidings of the English expedition for the support of Emin Pasha reached Uganda that Mwanga was seized with salutary alarm. Fearing lest Stanley should come southwards, and enter his territory, the King stopped the ruthless slaughter, and Mgr. Livinhac, writing in July 1887, reported a more happy condition of affairs. Conciliated by the gift of a new rifle, Mwanga had actually paid a visit to the mission house; and this had had a good effect in encouraging the native converts, as well as the heathen, who were deterred by dread of the tyrant from receiving instruction. The number of catechumens

increased rapidly, although the war which was being
waged in the neighbouring territory prevented the
natives from coming from a distance for instruction.

Since that period a rebellion has broken out in
Uganda ; Mwanga has been deposed and forced to take
flight. The tyrant had made himself thoroughly unpopular with a considerable portion of his subjects, and
even with the Mussulmans ; for, although at one time
he favoured their creed, latterly he had begun to show
active dislike to the followers of the Prophet as well as
to those who professed the Christian religion. At
length the people grew tired of his severe rule and acts
of robbery. It used to be his custom to take journeys
in all directions through his dominions for the purpose
of robbing his subjects, and these periodical raids
caused him to be almost universally hated and feared ;
the more so as the King did not scruple to seize and
carry off any of the women whom he deemed worthy to
be placed in his harem. Several of the Mohammedan
chiefs united with the discontented among his subjects
in dethroning him. The capital was surrounded.
Mwanga made little show of fight ; he quickly retired,
and fled towards the lake followed by about two hundred attendants.

A new prince was placed upon the throne, who
was most lavish in his promises. He proclaimed
liberty of trade to the Arabs ; no heavy duties were to
be levied on goods imported or exported. He gave
permission for the Moslem creed to be taught, and announced that a mosque should be built. To the Christian missioners also he promised liberty to teach without hindrance. He even showed himself so friendly to
the native Christians that he appointed some of them
to the highest posts in his court.

But the Arabs stationed themselves round the new King, poisoning his mind against the Christians. They persuaded him that an attempt would be made to depose him in favour of a princess whom the Christians had determined to set on the throne, as they wished to be governed by a woman, as was the case in England. The King believed this calumny; regarding the Arabs as his friends, he naturally considered the Christians as his enemies, and on the very first pretext that presented itself declared war upon them. The mission houses were sacked and many native Christians massacred; the missioners had a hairbreadth escape, but they saved their lives. Protestants and Catholics alike were involved in this sudden calamity; every white man was banished from Uganda. The Europeans and some native converts were taken down to the lake and put on board the Church Missionary Society's boat *Eleanor*. Their perilous and eventful voyage across the lake is described by the Rev. E. C. Gordon, an English Church missionary :—

'The captain carried us on board, and gave us a parting message. It was this:—Let no white man come to Uganda for the space of two years. We do not want to see a white teacher back again until we have converted the whole land to the Mohammedan faith. Such was the farewell given us.

'All the food we had on the *Eleanor* was provided by our friends the French priests. They alone had been allowed to keep such cloth and shells as were required to provision us with food for the voyage. We had a little rice on board, also a small quantity of wheat. We were hoping to be able to buy food at the first port we should reach. As it was, it came to this —we helped each other through. The boat was ours,

and the money to procure food was the French priests'.
The one party was rendered almost helpless without
the other. The priests had left behind a large native
canoe, for they were forbidden to take it. We, too,
should have been almost helpless without their shells.

'We had put ashore to cook some food, and, this
over, had got on board the boat, and were about to
hoist sail, when a couple of hippopotami showed their
heads. The great creatures were both very near, and
one of them nearer than our captain was aware of.
However, when we thought we were steering a clear
course between the two monsters, we found out our
mistake. On a sudden the boat seemed to strike
against something with considerable violence. The
truth was that the hippopotamus had struck the boat
with such force as to make two holes in the port
side, sufficiently large to give entrance to a great
quantity of water. The boat was much crowded with
passengers, and contained almost no cargo. She soon
began to fill with the rush of water entering her.
Almost before we knew it we found ourselves in the
water. By a merciful Providence the land was near,
so many of us immediately struck out for the shore.
All the sailors could swim, and we found ourselves
making way. Of the six Europeans, four of us could
swim—Père Lourdel, the Bishop, Walker, and myself.
But we found ourselves at a considerable disadvantage,
seeing that we were weighted with our boots and all
our clothes. In spite of these drawbacks, we safely
reached the island.

'Our eyes turned back to the spot where the boat
had sunk. To our surprise and joy we saw her still
afloat, lying right over on her side, and we saw the two
remaining Frenchmen with, we hoped, all their boys

and girls, clinging to the wrecked vessel. The sailors had meanwhile some of them been scouring the island, Père Lourdel and Walker aiding lustily with their lungs. The mainland was not far off. These united efforts of the searching and the shouting awoke the only inmate of the small island, a Musese, who possessed one small canoe. Soon after we had the joy of seeing the man coming along at a rapid pace in the direction of the still floating boat. He was very much excited, nor could we understand his language. With the aid of this true friend in our desperate need, the poor frightened boys and girls were gradually, by threes and fours, with the two Frenchmen, brought safely to the now friendly island.

'The captain and all the sailors deserved great credit for their behaviour on this occasion. The captain and some of the best swimmers were seen to return to the wreck to endeavour to bring off some of the sufferers, though without success. Others made a large fire on the shore for the benefit of all. Then when all were removed from the wreck, at about nine o'clock at night, it was found that we had suffered great loss. Some of Père Lourdel's children were missing. It was found that five of the elder lads had been drowned. The night passed very slowly, though the wife of the owner of the island acted as our hostess. She handed over her houses for our use and benefit, and showed us every kindness and hospitality,

'The next day it was determined to right our own boat, which was still visible lying on its side. But for this work more help was needed, so our good host beat his drum to invite the assistance of the Buganda from the mainland. Maybe we felt rather shy of these Buganda, with their shameful treatment of us still fresh in the memory. They came, however, to our aid, and behaved very well, being probably ignorant of the treatment we had received from the authorities. Meanwhile some of the sailors had dived down to get the things out of the boat, and lighten the vessel. These goods were brought ashore and dried in the sun. Many things were lost in the wreck and never recovered. All the cloth allowed to Père Lourdel was lodged at the bottom of the lake, but we managed to save plenty of cowries. The few books we had put in our pockets disappeared at this time. Many things were saved from the waters, but many things were left in the water and destroyed.

'The rest of the day was occupied in recovering our boat and beaching her for repairs. She was still our only hope, and we must manage to make her again fit to weather the changes and chances of the great lake. Mr. Walker and the captain set to work to repair and mend our crippled craft. In spite of the fact that there were no suitable tools, they succeeded in their difficult task with much rapidity, and the boat was launched the next day shortly after noon.

'After making our kind host and hostess a suitable and well-deserved present, we hastened to depart. For many days forward the voyage was made in slow stages. For, first, it was necessary to purchase all the food we could during the early part of the voyage while passing among natives whose current coinage was cowries; and, secondly, favourable winds failed us. In this way many long days passed by; then when more favourable winds were granted us, we made more rapid progress, which brought us quickly towards the end of our voyage, the south of the lake.

'On November 3 we landed the French priests and

their boys at Ukumbi. Here our friends kindly entertained us for one night. Towards the close of the next
day, Sunday, November 4, we arrived in sight of the
Church Missionary station, to our eyes a most refresh-
ing and gladsome sight.'

The struggle between Islam and Christian civilisation
seems to have been the cause of the unfavourable turn
which has been taken by events in Uganda. Opinions
vary as to whether the slave-trade has anything to do
with the present disastrous state of affairs, but the
testimony of the Arabs themselves points to it as at least
an important factor in what has taken place. Exulting
in their triumph, they write in insulting tones, saying,
' Uganda has now become a Mohammedan kingdom,
and in revenge for England's anti-slave trade policy
missionary effort in Central Africa is to be exter-
minated.' [1]

[1] Vide *Illustrated Cath. Missions*, Feb. 1889, p. 149.

CHAPTER VIII

TUNIS—ELEVATION TO THE CARDINALATE—CARTHAGE— CONCLUSION

It is foreign to the purpose of the present work to enter upon the history of the occupation of Tunis. The question is a purely political and military one, in which Mgr. Lavigerie had not to take any direct part. France and Italy had long been seeking to obtain an exclusive influence over the Government of Tunis : the former for the sake of her extensive Algerian colony, of which Tunis forms one of the boundaries ; the latter because of the close vicinity of Sicily, and of the great number of Italians already settled in Tunis, as well as out of regard to her own commercial interests.

Up to the year 1880 the two Powers had contented themselves with watching each other's proceedings, and endeavouring so skilfully to manœuvre at the Court of the Bey as to gain those advantages which would secure for them the coveted preponderance. But in 1880 the representative of Italy at Tunis, having succeeded in assuring himself of the support of the favourite of the Bey, unexpectedly assumed an attitude which French agents considered eminently disrespectful to France. He boasted that, far from being disowned by his own Government, his proceedings were supported by it ; and after an interview with King Humbert, he redoubled his irritating behaviour in regard to France, openly asserting that he was authorised to pursue this course of action, and imprudently allowing himself to be urged on by the Italian colony in Tunis. The representative of France having laid a full account of the situation before his Government, the latter was induced to resort to arms. Taking advantage of the depredations perpetrated by the tribes of Kroumeria, France determined to repress them by force, entered the province, and took military possession of it. The Bey saw, when it was too late, the error of which his Minister had been guilty in throwing himself into the arms of Italy, and accepted by means of a formal treaty the French Protectorate.

The missions in the Regency of Tunis had in 1841 been entrusted by the Holy See to the Italian Capuchin Fathers. Their Superior, who was Bishop of the place, and a man greatly advanced in years, resigned his post shortly before the occupation of the province by the French. In virtue of the new Protectorate, the latter demanded that a French bishop should be appointed to the vacant see; whereas the Italians, who formed an equally important element in the colony, naturally wished for one of their own nationality. In order not to foment the rivalry already existing in consequence of the political relations between the two nations, the Holy Father postponed his decision, and nominated the Archbishop of Algiers to administer the ecclesiastical affairs of the province *ad interim*.

One of the principal reasons for appointing him to this post was that he already exercised a certain amount of ecclesiastical jurisdiction in Tunis, on account of his Algerian missioners having the charge of the Church of St. Louis on the hill of Byrsa, in the centre of the ancient city of Carthage. How it came about that they were established there will now be told in Mgr. Lavigerie's own words.

'This corner of African soil is for ever sacred and
venerable in the eyes of Frenchmen and Italians, as
being the spot where King Louis breathed his last, in
1270, whilst besieging Tunis, before proceeding to join
the Crusaders in Palestine. It might have been feared
that at so great a distance of time, considering that
during the intervening centuries the Mussulmans have
held sway over these regions, every trace of such
memories would have disappeared. Facts, however,
prove that such has not been the case. I refer not
merely to the Christians who have from time to time
visited the coasts of Tunis. It was only natural that
they should desire to behold the scene of so holy a
death. I am alluding to the Mussulmans, who have never
ceased to entertain feelings of respect for the memory
of St. Louis ; and their homage touched me, in a certain
sense, even more than that paid by Christians.

'It is now upwards of twelve years ago that I
visited Carthage for the first time and made a pilgrimage
to the hill of Byrsa. As is usual in that part of the
country, I was followed by crowds of ragged children,
who had come together from the surrounding villages,
attracted by the sight of a foreigner and a priest.

They begged an alms "*for the love of God!*" But
as I remained deaf to their entreaties—for I was thinking
solely of the object of my visit, and of the glorious past
of my country—after a moment's pause they burst out
again, exclaiming simultaneously, "*For the love of St.
Louis!*" I am not ashamed to confess that I was moved
to tears on hearing these ignorant Arab children, from
whom one would certainly not have expected any
knowledge of our national history, thus pleading for
alms, with the delicate tact of Orientals, in the name of
one of our own kings.

'It was in the course of this, my first visit to the tomb of St. Louis, that I began to understand the duties incumbent on France. If strangers and barbarians thus honour the name of one of our kings, and hold it in such high esteem, it is surely not fitting that we should allow ourselves to be, to say the very least, left behind by them.

'On the taking of Algiers in 1830, Charles X., who then filled the throne of France, obtained from the Bey of Tunis the cession of the plot of ground where tradition states that St. Louis breathed his last. Ten years later, a chapel and dwelling-house were erected there by Louis Philippe, in memory of his illustrious ancestor. This memorial of the past was, it must be confessed, utterly unworthy of the sacred and glorious associations connected with it, as well as of the enormous sum expended on its construction. The chapel itself, a poor specimen of architectural art, barely held fifty persons ; the adjacent buildings reminded one of those of an African farm. Frenchmen visiting the spot blushed for their country, which knew not better how to honour a hero and a saint. Worst of all, after a time the church was closed owing to the culpable indifference of the authorities, mass being only said there once a year. The whole place wore a melancholy aspect of dilapidation and neglect.

'Upon first entering the Church of St. Louis my feelings were those of sorrow and shame. Even the very statue above the altar contributed to the depressing effect of the whole ; for, by an unaccountable mistake, the statue of Charles V. (le Sage) had been sent from France to Tunis instead of the statue of St. Louis, and the massive proportions of the marble figure were a sorry representation of the angelic features and attenuated form of the saintly Crusader.

'As I knelt before this statue, which was never destined to occupy the place where it now stood, I could not help blushing for my country and for the Church; and before quitting the chapel I made a solemn promise before God that I would do all that lay within my power to make such changes as would render it no longer a disgrace and a grief to every Frenchman and every Christian.

'But before attempting the restoration of this memorial of the past it was necessary to gain possession of it. I am not speaking of the occupation of Tunis— that only took place six years later. The territory on which the chapel stood, in the centre of Carthage, belonged, as I have already said, to France; but I had, as bishop, no authority over it. The ecclesiastical jurisdiction rested entirely in the hands of a foreign prelate; and merely to obtain permission to send our priests there, it would be necessary to go to war, though in a very gentle and pacific manner. I had to lay siege to the heart of the saintly Pontiff, Pius IX., the memory of whose kindness and beneficence is fresh in the hearts of us all.

'On leaving Carthage I went straight to Rome, and, kneeling at the feet of the Holy Father, humbly represented to him the neglected condition in which this sanctuary of Christian France had been left, adding that it seemed only suitable and natural to entrust the care of it to French hands, and finally proposing that my Algerian missioners should undertake the charge. Doubtless mine was the eloquence which comes straight from the heart; for scarcely had I finished speaking when the Holy Father said to me with a benignant smile : " I grant what you wish. It is fitting that the sanctuary of a king of France should be under the care of Frenchmen, as is the case even in Rome." '

Thus it was that at the period when Mgr. Suter, the Capuchin bishop to whom we have alluded, sent in his resignation, Mgr. Lavigerie had already, by means of his missioners, obtained a definite footing in the very centre of Tunis, and was in a position to render substantial services of a religious nature to that colony. The Holy See and the French Government therefore concurred in appointing him Apostolic Administrator of the diocese; and when the proposal was laid before him, he felt that he could not do otherwise than obey. Although already overburdened with work, he did not refuse the additional labour, saying with the Apostle, ' I will most gladly spend and be spent myself for your souls.'

It was with feelings such as these that Mgr. Lavigerie quitted his archiepiscopal city in order to repair to Tunis, where the situation was in every respect a difficult one. With truth it has been said that he rendered signal services to France, even the Italian newspapers, the *Riforma* in particular, having affirmed that his presence in Tunis was worth more to his country than that of an army. But it would be a mistake to imagine that his presence assumed in the slightest degree a political character. In Tunis as everywhere else, he was simply a missionary bishop.

On assuming the jurisdiction of Tunis, the first act of the Archbishop of Algiers was to erect new churches, the existing accommodation being utterly inadequate for the 20,000 Catholics of the town. An episcopal residence was also wanting, as his predecessor had dwelt in the Capuchin monastery. Mgr. Lavigerie undertook to construct one. The next thing was to

create a secular clergy; and in order to raise funds for
building seminaries, he appealed to the bishops of
France to make a collection in their respective dioceses.
This appeal did not meet with a response equal to his
hopes; yet he did not on this account falter in his task.

Although he was extremely popular among the
people, he had considerable opposition to contend
against. The Italian Capuchins naturally objected to
being under a French prelate; and though his policy
was invariably one of pacification and conciliation, it
was impossible to avoid exciting national feeling. The
aged bishop Mgr. Suter, however, who, at the advanced
age of eighty-six, was now about to quit the shores of
Africa and retire to Ferrara in order to end his days
in peace, exhibited the true spirit of Christian charity.
Before leaving he paid Mgr. Lavigerie a visit to make
a formal act of submission to his authority, and to
present him with a stole which he had himself received
forty years ago from the hands of Queen Marie-
Amélie.

'It is the emblem of the pastoral office,' he said;
'allow me to hand it over to you. It will be acceptable
to you, coming as it does from France; and I am
happy, in offering it to you, to have an opportunity of
showing that we, who are brethren in the episcopate,
are of one heart and one soul. Looking at outward
circumstances, it might be imagined that this was not
the case. But if you are seen wearing the stole here
which I too wore, every one will see what is the true
state of things.'

Mgr. Lavigerie, on his side, behaved most generously
towards the aged prelate. The Holy See had made an
express stipulation, on the nomination of Mgr. Lavigerie,
that the French Government should grant a retiring

pension to Mgr. Suter, as well as an ample subsidy to
his successor in the see. Neither the one nor the
other had been done ; and Mgr. Lavigerie, anxious that
Mgr. Suter should not suffer through the remissness
of France in fulfilling her obligations, allowed him an
annuity of 6,000 francs, to be paid out of his private
purse.

As soon as possible, the newly-appointed Administrator Apostolic began his pastoral visitation of Tunis.
He commenced by visiting those parishes which lie
along the coast. Everywhere he met with an enthusiastic reception ; and though it would be useless to
attempt giving an account of one scene of welcome
after another, we may narrate the circumstances which
attended his stay at Sfax, as they serve to show the
respect in which he was held by the Mussulmans, and
the idea they had formed of his power and influence.

A short time previously the town had revolted
against the Bey, who, after recapturing the place, had
condemned its inhabitants to pay a heavy fine in
punishment of their insubordination. The heads of all
the principal families were arrested and thrown into
prison as hostages ; and as the unhappy natives of Sfax
were totally unable to furnish in the allotted time the
indemnity required of them, they feared that the
hostages would be condemned to death, and they themselves driven forth from their homes, which would become the property of the Bey.

The day but one before the term of payment
expired, the Archbishop of Algiers arrived at Sfax.
Hearing of his advent, the inhabitants, almost all of
whom were Mussulmans, begged him to grant them an
interview, in order that they might induce him to
intercede with the Bey on their behalf. To this pro-

posal he readily agreed, and received them in the church, the only place spacious enough to contain so numerous an assembly. The building was speedily crowded. Standing on the altar-step, robed in his pontifical vestments, Mgr. Lavigerie reminded the subjects of the Bey how wrongly they had acted in rebelling against their Sovereign, and asked them whether they repented of their conduct.

'We repent! we repent!' they cried. 'We acknowledge that we have done wrong and behaved like madmen. The Bey is our master; France is strong, and we are weak.'

'But,' resumed Mgr. Lavigerie, 'at this very moment the leader of the previous revolt makes it his boast that a fresh rebellion is preparing for the spring, and he disseminates this assertion all over the world.'

'He lies! He is a liar!' shouted the audience; 'we do not mean to revolt again. He has made victims of us.'

'Then promise me,' added the Bishop, 'swear to me solemnly, that you will never again rebel against the Bey, who is your lawful Sovereign, nor against France, his ally and protector.'

'We swear it! we take a solemn oath! God be our witness!' cried the Arabs.

The Archbishop then promised to intercede for them; and having succeeded in calming their excitement, he listened while they explained what it was they wanted.

'We will do everything thou wishest!' they exclaimed. 'May God bless thee! May He increase thy happiness! Truly thou art our father and deliverer!'

He then dismissed them with the assurance that he would pray Heaven to bless them and their city. In accordance with his promise, he made representations to the Bey, through which their request for an extension of the term of payment was granted to the full.

Mgr. Lavigerie addressed pastoral letters to the clergy and laity of the province soliciting their aid and co-operation in the different good works he desired to found and carry on, and expressing his pleasure at the opening of various colleges and schools. After declaring that it was in no way to himself that thanks were due for these benefits, but to the generous contributors who had come forward from all quarters, frequently in the most unexpected manner, he concluded with the following anecdote, which we give in his own words :—

'Some months ago a lieutenant in the French army presented himself at the door of the Archbishop's palace in Tunis, and asked if he could see my secretary in order to consult him in regard to a plan he had formed.

' " The campaign is ended," he explained, " and I am on the eve of returning to France. But before sailing I am desirous of contributing to the *œuvre* which, among all those at present being carried out in the province of Tunis, is the most thoroughly French and the most entirely Christian. On this subject I wish for the opinion of his Eminence."

' I was at once informed of the occurrence, and I simply replied that a school was the good work which at the present moment most entirely corresponded to the conditions prescribed.

' The officer called again as he had promised to do. He fell in with my proposal, and immediately remitted to my secretary the sum of 10,000 francs, which has served to erect a school in the Maltese quarter of the city.'

The buildings which the prelate caused to be erected

on all sides furnished employment to a large number
of workmen, and augmented his influence with the
townspeople. But the hostile attacks on the part of
Italy, after having been temporarily suspended, soon
broke out afresh. One day the consular agent of that
country, happening to meet the Archbishop ·at the
railway-station, could not refrain from exhibiting his
jealous dislike by exclaiming in the hearing of the
bystanders, 'Oh, Monseigneur, how much good you
are doing! And how much harm all that good does
to us!'

Yet Mgr. Lavigerie held steadily on his way, seeking
to conquer his adversaries by kindness. At the very
time when the annoyances they caused him were at
their height, he issued an appeal to the faithful in
Algeria and Tunis on behalf of the inhabitants of
Northern Italy, who were suffering from the effect of
a series of inundations. In answer to this appeal a
large sum was contributed, which Mgr. Lavigerie
remitted to the manager of the *Osservatore Romano*
with the following letter :—

'Tunis : Sept. 10, 1882.

'You opened in the columns of your excellent
journal a subscription in aid of the sufferers by the late
inundations in Upper Italy. Allow me to forward to
you the sum of 6,159 fr., which I request you to add
to the offerings already received by you and to hand on
to its destination. It has been collected in the parishes
belonging to the diocese of Algiers and in those of the
province of Tunis.

'The sum is a small one compared with the greatness of the calamity; but colonists are not rich over
here, and I am sending you what can truly be termed
" the widow's mite." More deeply than by anything else

I have been touched by the manner in which all nationalities have, without any distinction, responded to my appeal; even the Mussulmans of Tunis, headed by their newly-chosen Bey, having come forward as contributors. For myself, it has been a twofold satisfaction to evoke this manifestation of sympathy towards the afflicted sons of your beloved Italy. Whilst thus fulfilling the primary duty of my pastoral office, which is the practice of charity, I have been able once again to preach, both by word and example, the duty of unity, peace, and the forgiveness of injuries, without which it is impossible for us to take part in the great work which the whole Christian world is evidently called by the providence of God to accomplish in the North of Africa. "Be not overcome with evil," says the Apostle St. Paul, "but overcome evil with good."'

The Italian Government could not leave this charitable act unnoticed, and its vice-consul at Tunis—the very same individual who had complained to Mgr. Lavigerie of the harm his good works were doing to Italy—wrote him the following letter:

'Monseigneur,—On hearing the news of the terrible disaster which has fallen upon the provinces of Upper Italy, with characteristic charity you asked the help of Africa for the relief of such widespread misery.

'Only the other day you gathered together in your cathedral the *élite* of Tunis society, and made a touching appeal, referring to the common bond which unites nations in times of calamity, addressing yourself not only to ourselves but to those also who, to borrow your own words, have not the happiness of being natives of that fair Italy with which you so truly sympathise.

'Allow me, Monseigneur, in my turn to thank in your person all contributors, of whatever nationality, and more especially those who belong to your generous country. I do so in the name of all those whose sufferings have been relieved, and also of all who know how to appreciate high-mindedness and generous feeling.

'Accept, Monseigneur, the assurance of my profound respect and gratitude.

'RAYBAUDI MASSIGLIA.'

The prelate pursued a similar line of conduct in his relations with the Anglo-Maltese colony, which at that time composed, together with the Italian colony, almost the entire European population of the province of Tunis. On the occasion of the last attempt made on the life of our own most gracious sovereign, Queen Victoria, Mgr. Lavigerie showed the same friendly spirit to England. He caused a service of thanksgiving for her escape to be held in the pro-cathedral of Tunis, and himself delivered an appropriate discourse, from which we give a brief extract addressed to the English who were present :—

'Your first feeling, dear brethren, on learning the failure of the sacrilegious attempt made upon the life of your Sovereign, was one of thankfulness to God. You remembered that He, according to the words of Scripture, disposes of life and death at His own pleasure, and you blessed the Fatherly Hand which turned aside the blow that threatened to strike you all in the person of your Queen.

'I have been an admiring spectator of your pious feeling, while I saw how faith and patriotism were united in the expression of your grief.

'No sentiments of loyalty could possibly be more just, if one looks at the character of the royal lady who has called them forth in your hearts. A model of every virtue which can adorn a throne, a model of devotion to the good of her people, and of respect for its liberty, laws, and constitution, a model wife and mother, a model of humble Christian resignation beneath the blow which shattered her life and left in her heart a wound which can never cease to bleed, she is the object of devoted gratitude on the part of her subjects, because of the blessings which have marked her reign— one of the longest to be found in the annals of your monarchy. She has likewise won the respect of every nation because of the wisdom of her rule, which knows how to respect the rights of all.'

England, like Italy, recognised in an official manner, by the mouth of her representative at Tunis, the pacific and friendly dispositions of the Archbishop. We will for a moment anticipate the period when he was raised to the Cardinalate, in order to quote the following speech, made by the English Consul whilst proposing the health of the Cardinal-elect, at a banquet where all the authorities of the country were assembled :—

'To my lot has fallen the honour and pleasure of proposing the health of his Eminence. I am certain that every one present has been deeply moved and equally well-pleased on hearing that the Pope has shown his esteem for Mgr. Lavigerie by bestowing on him the highest dignity of the Church. His Eminence has assuredly given proof in this country that he possesses two noble qualities : the spirit of conciliation, and that of benevolence. We see rising up refuges for the poor, hospitals and schools ; and we owe all these benefits to his Eminence.

'As to his conciliatory spirit, I need merely allude to the service held in honour of Queen Victoria—a service at which I was myself present, and by means of which he gained the hearts of all Englishmen, both here and at home. Whilst proposing his health, I cannot but at the same time give utterance to the wish that God may grant him to live many years, and carry on in our midst the work he has so nobly begun—that work of charity, humanity, and conciliation by which he has made us all his friends.'

While Mgr. Lavigerie, as Apostolic Administrator of the province, was busily engaged in setting on foot many useful institutions, and reviving and fostering Christian life in Tunis, a new and unforeseen danger arose, which threatened the existence of the religious congregations under his jurisdiction. The decrees of March 29 for the expulsion of the religious communities—especially the teaching Orders—had been put in force in France, and it was announced that before long they would be executed in Algeria also, against all Orders which had not obtained the formal authorisation of the civil power. The Abbot of La Trappe at Staouëli, fearing to find himself, with his hundred and fifty religious, compelled at brief notice to vacate their monastery, applied to the Archbishop to know whether they could obtain a house in the province of Tunis, where, at any rate for a time, they could take refuge if driven out of Algeria. Mgr. Lavigerie could not but feel indignant at the proceedings of the French Government towards the religious in his diocese, seeing how much he was doing at the time to advance the interests

of his country in Tunis, and he raised his voice in bold
expostulation.   The Consul-General, admitting the justice of his arguments, obtained an order from France
to the effect that the decrees in question should for a
time remain in abeyance.   This did not content the
energetic prelate.   He addressed a memorial to M.
Freycinet, then President of the Council, pointing out
not only how unjust, but how highly impolitic, was the
contemplated measure.

'Three reasons,' he wrote, 'may be urged against
the execution of the decrees of March 29 in Algeria.

'1. Legally, these decrees are not applicable to
Algeria, because they do not refer to that country,
whose case, owing to the presence within her territory
of numerous Moslem associations, is entirely different
from that of France.   Consequently, in a matter like
this a special decree is necessary, such as that which
has been issued for the other colonies.

'2. Politically, it is impossible, from want of due
authorisation, to dissolve in Algeria the Catholic religious communities composed of French subjects,
without dissolving at the same time the Moslem religious associations, which are far more numerous and
powerful.   These latter have their vows, their colleges,
and even their monasteries.   Now reasons connected
with higher policy forbid alike either the dissolution
or the authorisation of Moslem associations in Algeria.
Hence it follows that Catholic religious associations
must be permitted to remain.

'3. As an international question, France cannot
banish the religious congregations from Algeria without
relinquishing the political influence accruing to her
from the official protectorate she exercises over the
same congregations in the Moslem provinces of the

Mediterranean. Algeria is still, in fact, to a great extent, a Moslem country, nine-tenths of its inhabitants being Mohammedans. What would be said of us if we were seen to claim in Tunis or Tripoli the protectorate over those very congregations we were banishing from Algeria? Italy is only waiting for an error like this on our part in order to deal the final blow to our secular influence. The French Ambassador at the Papal Court is in a position to furnish useful information to his Government on this head.'

These representations had the hoped-for result; Mgr. Lavigerie received a formal promise, both verbal and written, from the Government that the religious communities in Algeria should not be interfered with.

In March 1882 Mgr. Lavigerie received from the hands of the Roman Pontiff an honour he had well deserved. From the very commencement of his Pontificate Leo XIII., who entertained the highest possible opinion of the Archbishop of Algiers, had wished to confer on him the dignity of the Cardinalate, on account of the virtues that adorned him, the zeal and perseverance with which he had laboured, both in France and Algeria, to revive religion and propagate the faith; the prudence and tact with which he had acted under circumstances of great difficulty; the eminent services he had rendered in Africa to his country, and to the Church of God, by the formation of a congregation specially destined to carry the light of the Gospel into the heart of the Dark Continent. Previous to his appointment to the see of Nancy, he had filled the office of Auditor of the Rota—a post which generally forms a stepping-stone to the Cardinalate: and for several years the seniority amongst

French bishops had been his. The Holy Father had accordingly sounded the French Government through the French Ambassador in order to ascertain whether the proposal to confer the purple on the Archbishop of Algiers would be favourably received. Marshal Mc-Mahon, with whom, as will be remembered, when he was Governor-General of Algeria, Mgr. Lavigerie had some differences, was then President of the Republic, and the suggestion was negatived. In the following year, however, a new President having taken office, and another vacancy occurring in the Sacred College, the dignity of the Cardinalate was bestowed on Mgr. Lavigerie, at the request of the French Government, and to the satisfaction of all the bishops and clergy both in France and Northern Africa.

The future Prince of the Church was at Carthage, busy with the organisation of his various charitable works, when the news reached him. In the reply wherein he expressed his gratitude for the honour his Holiness did him by this choice, he intimated his wish to receive the Papal envoy who was commissioned to remit to him the scarlet *calotte*, and invest him with the title and dignity of Cardinal, at St. Louis of Carthage, which, though situated in Tunis, is on French territory. This wish was complied with. But the fact that the ceremony of presentation took place on French soil in no wise obviated the necessity of the new Cardinal's journey to France, since custom requires that when a French subject is raised to the purple he should receive the red biretta from the head of the State, to whom it is handed by a sublegate of the Holy See. Cardinal Lavigerie accordingly repaired to Paris, where he met with a kind reception, and was presented with the insignia of his office. In replying to the speech in which the Cardinal expressed his thanks, and claimed the favour of France on behalf of his beloved missioners, the President spoke as follows :—

'My Lord Cardinal,—The touching picture your Eminence has just drawn of the priests who, attached to foreign missions, abandon home and country, in order, at the risk, and often at the cost, of their life, to carry on their sacred ministry, and who make the name of France honoured and beloved all over the world, convincingly proves the Holy Father to have been inspired by the spirit of wisdom and justice when he raised to the highest rank of the episcopate the illustrious prelate who represents in his own person those heroic missioners, and represents them most worthily. It was therefore with much pleasure that I recommended you to the choice of the Sovereign Pontiff, and I am most happy to present you to-day with the insignia of a dignity which is the due reward of the virtues which adorn you and of the signal services you render to your country.'

But all formalities were not yet ended, for from Paris the Cardinal had to proceed to Rome, where, in the commencement of July, he received the Cardinal's hat from the hands of the Holy Father, with the ceremonial customary on such occasions. Immediately after he set out once more for Africa, and on his homeward way landed at Malta, for the purpose of baptizing twelve young negroes whom he had sent thither to study medicine, in view of associating them later on with the missioners who were carrying on the work of the Apostolate in Central Africa. These youths were some of the children ransomed from slavery in the Sahara or the regions of the equator, and for whom a home had been provided about a year previously in

Malta. There they were taught and trained, firmly grounded, above all, in the fear of God and the practice of virtue, so that when their studies were completed they might employ the knowledge they had acquired for the spiritual and temporal welfare of their suffering fellow-countrymen. Of these negro students only three had been baptized, the others having remained catechumens up to that time. But they all desired baptism, and had often written to their kind patron entreating earnestly that he would come and baptize them. At last their prayer was granted, and these first-fruits of the African missions were admitted into the fold of Christ.

The reception given to the Cardinal at Malta was most enthusiastic, and the greeting which awaited him on his arrival in Algiers, from both clergy and laity, was no less cordial. The military authorities and civil functionaries wished to receive him with ceremony; but alas! the anti-Christian principles of the Municipal Government had caused all religious processions to be prohibited, and the Cardinal accordingly refused all honours in which the Church could take no part.

'His Eminence Cardinal Lavigerie,' wrote the correspondent of the *Monde*, 'arrived in Algiers yesterday. He had declined every kind of official reception, since he wished, as he said in a letter addressed to his coadjutor, and read in all the churches, for no other homage than that of the faithful who desired his paternal blessing.

'Crowds filled the streets through which he passed on his way to the cathedral, where he was to make a solemn entry, and receive the congratulations of the bishops and clergy, regular and secular. The cathedral square especially was thronged with people, who, when

he alighted from his carriage, rent the air with their
acclamations and cries of *Vive le Cardinal!*'

Addresses and demonstrations of respect and affection were presented to the newly made Cardinal from
all quarters. It was impossible for him to be otherwise
than touched and gratified by these proofs of the gratitude and love of his flock; yet he regretted the loss of
time, which he would fain have spent on the prosecution
of his schemes of usefulness. When all the ceremonies
were over, he turned again with a feeling of relief to
the labours to which he had devoted himself.

Numerous indeed were the various good works
which Cardinal Lavigerie commenced and carried on
in the province of Tunis : churches, schools, hospitals,
refuges, were constructed ; different religious orders
and congregations, cloistered and active, were invited
to found houses, in order that the former by their life
of prayer and penance, the latter by engaging in
charitable works, might convert the sinner, reclaim the
fallen, teach the ignorant, and call down the mercies of
God upon the land from which His face had for a while
been hidden. But in the midst of these arduous apostolic labours, the desire long present to Cardinal
Lavigerie's mind, to restore to the see of Carthage—the
see of St. Cyprian, the scene of the glorious triumphs of
so many martyrs—the privileges and glory which it
enjoyed in the early ages of Christianity, was still
uppermost in his thoughts. The establishment of
French rule in Tunis seemed to present a favourable
opportunity for the accomplishment of this desire ; and
he accordingly presented to the Holy Father a petition
requesting the revival of the metropolitan see of Carthage, to mark the resurrection of the ancient African
Church. Pope Leo XIII. graciously acceded to this

proposal, and published an Allocuticn and a Bull in which the decision was announced. In this Bull he speaks of the regret with which the Church ever views the relapse of a people once enlightened with the light of faith into the darkness of superstition and error, as had been the case with the inhabitants of Northern Africa. The African Church, so great and glorious in the early ages of Christianity, had long since ceased to be an example to the nations. Carthage too, which had been amongst the first to receive the faith of Christ, had become a heap of ruins—Carthage, whose name recalled the memories of so many saints and martyrs, so many Bishops and Doctors—of Perpetua and Felicitas, of Augustine, Tertullian, and of Cyprian. Carthage had been the scene of much heroism and courage under the persecution of proconsuls, the violence of Vandals, the merciless onslaught of Moslems; she had, moreover, until her final destruction, held unrivalled sway over the Church of Northern Africa, for hers was the metropolitan see, and to her authority seven hundred and fifty churches were subject.

After thus glancing at the past Leo XIII. turns to the present, and speaks of the happy revival of religion in the country, in consequence of which he has been led to re-establish the ancient primatial see of Carthage, in the following words :—

'The Archbishop of Algiers, Mgr. Charles-Martial Lavigerie, Cardinal of the Holy Roman Church, having been appointed to the administration of the vicariate of Tunis, has applied himself, like a wise and energetic man, to propagate the faith in those countries, and establish the Church on a solid basis. He has, within a short space of time, founded a great number of useful works, and has undertaken many others destined to raise Carthage from her ruins. In the quarter of *Megara*, near the spot hallowed by the blood of St. Cyprian, and not far from the place where his remains are interred, in the very midst of the ruins of Carthage, he has erected an episcopal palace with a chapel, where the poor and distressed can daily find relief in their woes. In the episcopal residence, as well as at Tunis, and in all the most thickly populated parts of the vicariate, he has placed priests to exercise the sacred functions of the ministry; while the Capuchin Fathers continue zealously to carry on their work. In the part called *Byrsa* he has founded the Seminary of Carthage, where the young men, the future hope of the diocese, are being taught and trained by the care and the instructions of learned teachers in theology, philosophy, and classics. He has added several fresh parishes to those already existing, one of them being established in the chapel dedicated to St. Louis, on the spot where that most pious king passed from this brief life to the eternal felicity of heaven. Furthermore, he has opened a home for those who are suffering from poverty and old age, a hospital for the sick poor, schools for the education of both boys and girls. Attracted by these advantages and benefits, many have come to reside in these regions, in the hope of seeing the city revive.

'Finally, he has taken measures to secure in perpetuity the funds necessary for the support of the Archbishop, and the carrying out of the works that have already been commenced.

'We therefore, after having pondered over with diligent consideration and attention each and all of these things which have been mentioned, re-establish the archiepiscopal see of Carthage, with the consent of the Sacred College of the Propaganda, by the authority of these letters. May this act conduce to the prosperity of the Universal Church, and, above all, to the salvation and glory of the people of Africa.'

Shortly after a Brief was issued definitely fixing the limits of the archdiocese of Carthage, in which the whole regency of Tunis was comprised, and nominating Cardinal Lavigerie to the see. By this he became Metropolitan of Africa. The province of Algeria was to remain under his charge, being administered in his name by an auxiliary bishop.

In the midst of his apostolic labours Cardinal Lavigerie had found time to devote to the interesting study of the Christian antiquities of the country. The glories of the ancient African Church were ever present to his mind, and he loved to trace the footsteps of her illustrious saints, and bring to light the scattered monuments which still bore testimony to their sufferings and heroic deeds. On coming to Tunis he found a fresh and fruitful field for research amid the ruins of ancient Carthage, now almost entirely buried beneath the sand of the desert, and overgrown with grass, situated on the shores of the Mediterranean, about ten miles from the city of Tunis. It was Mgr. Lavigerie's laudable ambition to erect over the ruins of the past, within sight of the amphitheatre where St. Perpetua, St. Felicitas, and so many other glorious martyrs had won their crown, a Seminary dedicated to St. Louis, whose memory is so intimately connected with a later period of the history of the African Church. A number of interesting discoveries, zealously prosecuted during a period of several years by Father Delattre, a priest attached to the new Seminary of St. Louis, were commenced under the following circumstances.

One day a message was brought by an Arab to Father Delattre requesting him to visit a sick person dwelling in a little village at some distance. Whilst on his way thither, the priest was accosted by two shepherd boys, who offered him for sale some rusty coins found among the ruins. On his refusal to purchase them the boys withdrew, but still kept their eyes on the traveller, whose attention had meanwhile been attracted by the fragment of a marble slab bearing a mutilated inscription, lying at the edge of the path. This he at once perceived to be a portion of an ancient funereal tablet, probably of Christian origin. While he was examining it the boys came up again, and assured him that many similar stones were to be found in the neighbourhood, offering to procure him some specimens. Father Delattre accepted their proposal, and on his return, two hours later, found that in the interval they had gathered together eleven fragments, a cursory inspection of which convinced him that he was standing on the site of an ancient Christian cemetery. Having rewarded the young Arabs with a few sous, he encouraged them to pursue their researches, and bring to the Seminary all similar specimens which they might be able to discover. On the following morning one of the boys presented himself with twenty-six fragments of Christian inscriptions wrapped in the folds of his garments. The rumour that the Christian marabout was in search of ancient monumental inscriptions brought him many willing assistants, and the collection began to assume extensive dimensions. Even the young negro boys from the orphanage, when out for a holiday ramble, found no amusement more exciting than a hunt for fragments of tombstones. Thus was the foundation laid of a valuable collection which now comprises many hundred specimens of mortuary inscriptions, symbols, figures, carvings, lamps, mosaics, &c.

The cemetery thus accidentally discovered was evidently of large extent, and had been devoted exclusively to the purpose of Christian burial. Situated outside the ramparts of the ancient city, in accordance with the law forbidding intramural interment, it extended along them for a considerable distance in the direction of the sea. Unlike the Roman catacombs, it is above ground; and if we except some subterranean chambers, which were probably destined for a martyr's tomb, and covered in course of time by a basilica, it must have borne a strong resemblance to our modern cemeteries. It may appear strange that an open Christian burial-ground, which evidently dates back to the ages of persecution, should have been permitted to exist in the immediate vicinity of a populous pagan city. But in the works of early African writers mention is frequently made of these *areæ*, which were tolerated, and even protected, by public law. The facilities they afforded for the exercise of the proscribed religion were so well recognised, that a common cry of the angry mob in times of persecution was, ' *Areæ non sint!* ' Away with the Christian cemeteries!

The inscriptions upon the fragments found in the cemetery of Carthage were difficult to decipher on account of their state of extreme mutilation. This is to be accounted for by the fact that they have not only been exposed to the outrages of pagans and Mussulmans, but have for centuries been broken to pieces by the Arab ploughshare, the fields wherein they were found having been for ages devoted to the purposes of tillage. But these African remains, most of which appear to range from the second to the sixth century, are of great value, and those who are acquainted with the ancient Christian formulas are able to interpret the symbols and fill up the gaps with certainty. This renders these fragments reliable witnesses to many doctrines and practices of the early African Church. It will be understood that these archæological discoveries added greatly to the interest and importance attaching to the see of Carthage. The very soil on which stood the ruins of pagan edifices, as well as of Christian temples, was hallowed ground; it had been watered with the blood of martyrs; it was the resting-place of innumerable saints and confessors; it formed, as Cardinal Lavigerie expressed it, one vast reliquary—hidden, indeed, from the eyes of man, but precious in God's sight, and watched over by the angels.

The Church of St. Louis of France had, on account of the more recent historical associations connected with it, been selected and mentioned in the papal rescript as the metropolitan church of the diocese, at least provisionally, until a cathedral should be erected. But the narrow dimensions of the building rendering it unsuited for the performance of any ceremony at which more than a very limited number of persons would be present, permission was given to use the Church of St. Cyprian as a pro-cathedral. This chapel, too, was not without its touching memories of the past, for it was there that St. Monica passed the night in tears and prayer, while Augustine, without her knowledge, and against her will, set sail for the shores of Italy.

Previous to his elevation to the dignity of metropolitan, Cardinal Lavigerie had already commenced the construction of a cathedral church which was to be in every respect worthy of the primatial see of Africa.

In less than two years the building, although still far from completion, was ready to receive the bells. The ceremony of blessing them drew together an immense crowd, consisting of several thousand persons, many of whom had travelled long distances in order to be present. The spectacle was both singular and picturesque; every variety of dress to be found on the shores of the Mediterranean, every variety of colouring of which the human skin is capable, from the ebony blackness of the natives of Timbuktu to the rosy whiteness of the children of Albion, might be seen side by side, as the eager pilgrims wandered over the hills, inspecting the new buildings which had risen up as if by enchantment—the Carmelite convent, the school under the direction of the Marist missionaries, and above all the cathedral. At four o'clock the procession set out towards the spot where the bells had been temporarily placed until the tower intended for their reception should be completed. First came four confraternities of Italians and Maltese, in their picturesque costumes, and carrying their banners. The clergy walked next, with the forty-three African missioners, wearing their white dress. The Cardinal took his place beneath the daïs in his pontifical vestments. It had been his intention to address the assembled throng at the conclusion of the ceremony, but the crowd was so vast that it was not possible for him to make himself audible, and he could only call to the ringers, who were standing ready on their platform, ' Now, my children, let your bells ring out and proclaim the resurrection of Christian Carthage ! '

At the conclusion of this ceremony another took place of an entirely private nature, but one which possessed a touching interest peculiar to itself. It had been the wish of Cardinal Lavigerie to determine beforehand the place of his burial, and he had caused to be constructed beneath the sanctuary of the new cathedral, at the very foot of the episcopal throne, a vault wherein he desired to be interred. A flight of seventeen steps leads down to this vault, the dimensions of which are the very narrowest. His Eminence resolved himself to bless, in the evening of the day of which we have just spoken, the spot destined to serve as his last resting-place. He accordingly proceeded thither, preceded by the students of the Seminary and the scholastics, to whom he addressed the following words :—

' I should have hesitated to sadden you by means of this ceremony, dear children, were it not that I believe it may suggest to your mind some salutary reflections. God has vouchsafed to me the grace of never passing a single day of my life without thinking upon death ; and the precarious state of my health has served to render this thought still more familiar to me. As the years slip away and bring me nearer to my final hour, the thought dwells more habitually in my mind, and takes the foremost place there. I have always felt, and I still feel, that such a frame of mind is useful in two ways, which the Holy Spirit Himself teaches us. The first is, to learn from the thought of death to be more careful in regulating one's life—" *Remember thy last end, and thou shalt never sin.*" [1] The second is, to stir oneself up each day to work, in proportion as time is passing away—" *I must work the works of Him that sent me whilst it is day ; the night cometh when no man can work.*" [2] This is the reason why I have come down to-night to this grave, when I am on the eve of leaving you for a short

[1] Eccl. vii. 40.   [2] St. John ix. 4.

time, in order that I may learn how to spend my remaining days on earth more profitably and how to labour
unto the end.'

He concluded as follows :—

' The day will come—and it cannot be very far
distant—when I shall descend into this grave, not for a
few brief moments, but to remain permanently there.
Then shall I have need of your prayers, for then will
the time have come when I must render to the Supreme
Judge an account of my stewardship. I have wished
that my tomb should be in the midst of you, because
you at least will remember your father and implore for
him the mercy of God. This is what I humbly beg of
you in return for the love I have borne you, for the
fatigue and suffering I have endured on your behalf:
*" Have pity on me, have pity on me, at least you my
friends."* ' [1]

The missioners could not restrain their tears as they
listened to these words ; but it was without any outward
sign of emotion that the Cardinal recited the formula
for blessing the vault, into which he immediately afterwards descended, remaining there for some time in silent
prayer. The procession then re-formed and returned
to the Seminary in the same order in which it had come,
the *Miserere* being chanted as before. A deep impression
was made by the sight of the example thus given by
the venerable prelate to his sons in the priesthood,
and by the manner in which he taught them to
sanctify their souls by the thought of death and of
eternity.

He likewise desired to compose his own epitaph,
and dictated it, in fact, while suffering from severe
illness.

---

[1] Job xix. 21.

It runs thus : [1]

HIC

IN SPEM INFINITÆ MISERICORDIÆ REQUIESCIT

KAROLUS-MARTIALIS ALLEMAND-LAVIGERIE

OLIM

S. R. E. PRESBYTER-CARDINALIS

ARCHIEPISCOPUS CARTHAGINIENSIS ET ALGERIENSIS

AFRICÆ PRIMAS

NUNC CINIS.

ORATE PRO EO.

The brilliant success of these numerous undertakings excited, however, the malice and envy of some of the townspeople, especially of the Italian Jews, of whom there were as many as forty thousand in Tunis. The elevation of Mgr. Lavigerie to the Cardinalate was represented as a direct affront to Italy, and as a measure intended to damage her interests in Africa. This hostile feeling, of which the air had long been full, broke out at length into a storm of open and decided hostility, the occasion which called it forth being one of the most unlikely that could possibly be imagined—a measure, namely, of a purely sanitary nature, and one which every unprejudiced person must have at once perceived to be absolutely free from all religious import or national colouring.

As far back as 1882 the Cardinal, at that time Administrator Apostolic, had felt the imperative necessity of providing a new Catholic cemetery for the city of

[1] Here rests
In the hope of infinite mercy
Charles-Martial Allemand-Lavigerie;
Formerly
Cardinal-Priest of the Holy Roman Church,
Archbishop of Carthage and Algiers,
And Primate of Africa;
Now dust and ashes.
Pray for him.

Tunis. The existing cemetery had been in use for two hundred years; it was situated in the centre of the more modern part of the European quarter, and owing to its narrow dimensions had become a veritable hotbed of infection. The dead were literally heaped one upon another, under conditions too revolting to be dwelt upon; some of the corpses being prematurely exhumed in order to make room for fresh coffins. So crying, indeed, was the need for a remedy, that in the course of the first visit paid by Monseigneur Lavigerie to Tunis the French Consul begged him to provide an extramural cemetery of sufficient size which might serve as a place of interment for Europeans, in order that the old cemetery might be completely closed on hygienic grounds. The first thing was to procure the necessary funds. In the course of a year, thanks to the energy of the Cardinal, these were forthcoming. A suitable piece of ground at a sufficient distance from the city was purchased and walled in, a chapel being erected there dedicated to our Lady of Dolours. All being thus in readiness, his Eminence, who had spent upon this good work the sum of nearly 80,000 francs, proceeded to bless the cemetery, and gave orders that for the future no burials were to take place in the former graveyard, except in the case of persons who had private vaults there, and were permitted to retain the right of burying in them members of their own family.

Could any one have imagined that such an action as this would have called forth any feelings but those of gratitude in regard to the author of it? Strange as it may appear, the result was the very opposite of gratitude. The anti-French faction took advantage of the occasion to stir up a fierce manifestation of enmity and dislike among the lower orders, by representing to them that the regulations recently made constituted a violation of the rights of those families whose relatives had been interred in graves in the old cemetery. The tide ran so high that the tombstones were mutilated and defaced, especially as the ignorant populace believed in addition that the clergy had gained enormous sums by the whole transaction. It became necessary to procure a decree from the Bey absolutely forbidding any interment to take place in the original burying-ground, and placing the management of cemeteries for the future in the hands of the municipality. The commotion gradually subsided, and for a time there was peace.

Unfortunately the truce was not of long duration. In 1884 the church belonging to the Italian Capuchins was burnt down, in consequence of some carelessness on the part of those who had charge of the sacristy. The next day there appeared in the *Sentinella*, an Italian newspaper published at Tunis, an article concluding as follows:[1] 'Some persons say that in this event is shown *the finger of God*. But ninety-nine out of a hundred say that *the finger of the cathedral* has something to do with it.' An insinuation like this amounted to nothing less than a charge of incendiarism against the Archbishop and his clergy. As a matter of fact, Cardinal Lavigerie had risked his life during the conflagration in order to assist the Capuchin Fathers in rescuing the sacred vessels from the midst of the flames. It was not possible for him to allow such a calumny to remain unnoticed; he therefore answered it, in the first

---

[1] 'Alcuni dicono che in questo fatto si mostra *il dito di Dio*. Il novantanove per cento dice che in questo fatto c' entra *il dito della Cathedrale*.' (*Sentinella*, 14 Settembre, 1884.)

place, by heading with a liberal donation the list of subscriptions for the restoration of the church ; and, in the second, by bringing an action against the proprietors of the *Sentinella* in order to obtain a public vindication of his own conduct and that of his clergy. An ample apology was, however, speedily forthcoming, and the legal proceedings were therefore withdrawn.

Fresh accusations were soon brought forward against this exemplary prelate. The French atheists, enraged to see him advancing the cause of truth, said that he had amassed great riches for himself in Africa, and also that the public safety was imperilled by the fanaticism of his missioners. In regard to his supposed wealth, we may here relate an amusing anecdote, which shows the deep root these absurd ideas had taken in the popular imagination.

About fourteen years ago, a brother of his Eminence, M. Félix Lavigerie, who held a commission in the African army, being on a visit to Algiers, went one day into a tobacconist's shop in order to get some cigars. Whilst he was engaged in making his purchases, the Archbishop happened to drive past in an ordinary hired carriage, as was his invariable custom. The woman who was serving in the shop, totally ignorant as to who her chance customer was, said to him :—

'Would you like to see the richest man in Algeria? He is just going by.'

'Whom do you mean?' asked M. Lavigerie.

'The Archbishop of Algiers,' was the reply.

'Is he, then, really so very rich?'

'Yes, sir, he owns all the land which stretches from Algiers to Oran, on both sides of the railway.'

'That is certainly a great deal,' remarked the officer.

' But it is not all,' his informant went on ; ' he is also the proprietor of all the steamboats in the port.'

' I imagined them to belong to well-known companies—the Messageries Maritimes and others.'

' Yes, they do bear these names,' the woman replied, ' but in reality they belong to the Archbishop.'

' What can he do with all this money ? '

' He makes use of it in order to enrich his family.'

' I am glad,' rejoined the officer, ' to be able to assure you that such is not the case. I am the Archbishop's brother, and never, I solemnly affirm, has he made a present of money to any of his relatives ! '

This statement was, indeed, nothing but the simple truth. It was well known to all the clergy of Algiers, and to all who knew the Archbishop, that it would be difficult to find a prelate more strict in his observance of the laws of the Church in this respect, or one who more rigorously maintained them, not in the letter alone, but in the spirit also.

The subjoined epistle was addressed by the Cardinal to an individual, who, although personally unknown to him, had in a public conference held at Hyères boldly defended his *œuvres* against the attacks of a freethinker :—

' I find that in your presence I have been accused of being a millionaire, an arch-millionaire even. Certainly I should be anything but displeased if such were really the case, for did I in reality possess these riches I should most assuredly soon find a use for them. But I do not possess them, or rather I have ceased to possess them, since whenever large sums of money have been entrusted to me by the faith and charity of Catholics, they have been expended in building, in founding *œuvres*, and in providing daily bread, the latter in the most literal sense; for in the exercise of my apostolic ministry I come in contact with none but those who are poor.

'The truth is, that in spite of appearances I am myself a poor man—so poor, indeed, as to be compelled to beg in order to support our missions, and in great part my diocesan works also.

' What deceives the superficial observer is, that while the properties I purchased twenty years ago in Algeria, and those I have more recently acquired in Tunis, in order to found my various charitable institutions, can be seen by all with the greatest ease, it is far from being as generally known that I have made a formal legal renunciation of every one of them, and that the income derived from them bears no proportion whatever to the outlay it is expected to cover.'

His Eminence next enumerates the different institutions and charitable works founded by him in Algeria, Kabylia, Tunis, and elsewhere, among which we find mention of the college in Malta for young negroes who, having been ransomed from slavery, had been brought over at great expense from the interior of Africa in order that they might study medicine, and afterwards return to their native land, the complete conquest of which could be accomplished through their means alone.

'I am thoroughly persuaded,' the Cardinal continues, 'that a Minister of Finance who had to balance a budget under circumstances such as mine would believe himself utterly ruined. I should do the same if I were not able to place for my aid and encouragement the charity of Catholics side by side with my expenses.

' In order to silence these absurd reports, I declare

by means of the present letter that I will make over to
the editors of your journal all the land which has ever
been bestowed upon me by any Governor of Algeria.
If the story about me is a true one, you will be enriched
for years to come, and I shall sincerely congratulate
you. But if the reverse is the case, what do you deserve
said to you ?

'In fact, I formally empower you to declare to those
who in future talk to you about *my millions* that I
herewith bind myself in writing to hand over to them
by a deed of gift all lands which belong to me *personally*,
either in Africa or elsewhere.

'Should this plan not meet with their approval, I will
induce the society which has been regularly formed
in Africa for the carrying on of our missions and other
works of charity, and to which I have legally made
over everything, to make a present of all they hold
from me, to any one who will engage, subject to reliable
security, to pay annually in return a quarter only of
what is necessary for the work of the apostolate and
the maintenance of our charitable undertakings.'

But calumnies of this nature in regard to the ima-
ginary wealth and extensive possessions of the Cardinal
were not the only ones directed against him by the
enemies of Christian charity. It was further pretended
that his agents stirred up fanaticism, and that his proceedings were calculated to excite a spirit of revolt among
the native population of Northern Africa. On this point
also he felt it to be his duty to justify his conduct.
He accordingly wrote as follows to the director of the
Society for Promoting Education in the East :—

'You must be aware how prejudicial the attacks of
which I have lately been the object are to the influence
of France in this country. It is a lamentable thing that

the strife of parties is waged so fiercely in France; but that this petty warfare should be carried on in a foreign land, in full view of our enemies, is indeed a fatal sign of national decadence.

'What a different example England sets in this respect! I know that in the recent campaign in Egypt her conduct has not always been blameless; but all those who took part in it—generals, politicians, the very soldiers—are respected by the nation. No one lifts his voice to diminish their prestige or hamper their action.

'Ordinarily I leave accusations like those now brought against me unanswered; but this time I cannot pass them by in silence, because they affect our Catholic charities even more than they do myself personally.

'You will see in the papers the letter wherein I have replied to some odious insinuations in regard to the use to which the sums we have received have been put. Another charge has been brought against us: we are accused of fanaticism. It is actually said that my presence here, and that of the priests with me, imperils the public peace—that we put a pressure in regard to religion on the Mussulmans. It has even been alleged in the parliamentary reports that—

'"The Archbishop of Algiers has been sending missioners into some of the towns of Tunis, where there is not a single Catholic at the present time, and that he is carrying on a work of proselytism most displeasing to the people."

'Again it is said that three of the White Fathers were assassinated at the gates of Kairwan, just at the time the Committee of the Budget was sitting; and that it was most imprudent, highly dangerous in fact, to

send missioners into the heart of Tunis, and thus pro-
voke insurrection and crime.

'Not a single word of all this is true.   No missioner
has ever been sent by me into any town of Tunis
where there were no Catholics; not a single one of the
White Fathers has been murdered in Tunis, nor has one
of them set foot in Kairwan or the immediate vicinity.

'The Algerian missioners can boast some martyrs, it
is true; but it was at Lake Nyanza, at Tanganyika, or in
the Sahara that they met their death.   They may be
accused of fanaticism for penetrating at the risk of their
lives into the depths of the Dark Continent.   But how
many of all nationalities have gone before them—travellers, scientists, Protestant missionaries.   They too have
risked their lives on this heroic enterprise.   Why
should France be left behind, and why should she not
now count it her glory that there are more of her sons
on this barbarous soil than of any other Christian
nation whatever ?

'But we are speaking of Tunis now, and I can safely
assert that I should consider it both foolish and wrong
to excite the fanaticism of the Mussulmans by indiscreet
attempts at proselytism.   One need not be a priest, however, it is enough to call oneself a man, in order to
desire the regeneration of the degenerate races of
Northern Africa; to rescue them from the evils under
which they groan; to release the women, the children,
all who cannot help themselves, from the cruel and
selfish yoke of the oppressor; to deliver the men from
the blind fatalism, the indolence, the vices by which
they are enslaved.

'The true civiliser, the only effectual preacher at this
present time, is the action of events which change the
political aspect of the country. Unwittingly, unwillingly

even, our Commandants, our soldiers are the chief factors in this change. They represent force, and force to the Mussulman is the hand of God. We see proof of this in Algeria, where, without any other apparent action, a general disintegration is taking place in Moslem society, from which religion is not exempted.

If you were with me in Carthage you would often find my house full of Mussulmans come to solicit my assistance; some ask for work, others beg for alms. Close by, the priests of St. Louis tend and relieve the sick; and in a house at some little distance the sisters render the same kind service to the women and children. Never is a word said to them at which they could take alarm. We leave God to carry on, in His own good time, His work in their souls. Our part is to do His will and fulfil His commands by showing them that in our labours of love we are obeying a law of charity higher than their own. Our greatest happiness, after all our sacrifices, is to hear the Mussulmans exclaim: " Really, what good people these French are!"'

Somewhat later, another attack of illness, more severe than the former one, caused great alarm to the Cardinal's friends. Scarcely had he recovered before he repaired to France to solicit alms for the support of the African Seminaries, on account of the withdrawal of the Government grant. His appeal was warmly responded to, the sum subscribed surpassing all expectations. Catholic France, as we know well, is ready to forward every good work, and in her generous support of foreign missions more especially she distances by far all the rest of Europe. And the same eloquent voice that then evoked her ready sympathy has lately been heard amongst ourselves; it is still heard throughout Christendom, where it has made a deep impression, appealing for the liberation of the African from the savage cruelties of his Moslem conqueror.

On March 22, 1888, Cardinal Lavigerie celebrated his episcopal jubilee. This occasion called forth most enthusiastic expressions of esteem and affection. A grand and imposing ceremony took place in the cathedral, previous to which the following address was presented to his Eminence by Mgr. Dusserre, the Bishop-Coadjutor of Algiers :—

' May it please your Eminence,—In the name of the bishops of Northern Africa, of the secular and regular clergy, and of the religious communities belonging to the dioceses of Carthage, Algiers, Constantine, Hippo, and Oran, I have the honour and pleasure of laying at the feet of your Eminence our respectful homage, together with a souvenir of this memorable occasion.

' It has been my privilege to receive the proofs of the heartfelt affection your Eminence has inspired ; and as I beheld one community after another approach me in order to express, with equal dignity of language and delicacy of sentiment, their enthusiastic admiration, their filial love and loyal devotion, my heart swelled with proud emotion on thus contemplating the strength and depth of the feelings your Eminence has called forth in the hearts of us all.

' We desire to approach you as one united family, without even the division of separate dioceses. The Church of Africa—that Church to which you have given new life, and which has thus become your own—is here gathered together in the person of its representatives. We approach the throne of its common Father with one heart and one soul, in order to offer him a tribute of feeling as sincere as it is unanimous.

' Accept it, therefore, beloved and honoured Father,

from the hands of your grateful and affectionate children.'

His Eminence could not at first restrain his tears, but as soon as he had sufficiently mastered his emotion he replied in the following terms :—

'Monseigneur,—To the expression of such feelings, couched in terms such as those to which I have just listened, I could at first, as you have all seen, only answer with my tears.

'It is with deep gratitude that I accept the souvenir of my episcopal jubilee just offered me by my spiritual children. On such a day as this, nothing could more profoundly touch me than the sight of you all thus gathered around me, and forming as it were my crown of honour.

'You, Messeigneurs, are the elder sons of my great sacerdotal family, from whom, ever since I first came amongst you, I have received most cordial support and sympathy, and whom I have seen increasing day by day in virtue, in power, in wisdom, until you too were raised to the dignity of the episcopate. You most especially, Monseigneur, who have made yourself the spokesman of your brethren, I have closely associated with myself in the work of the diocese, since you will be called upon to undertake the government of it alone when God has taken me to Himself. You have just presented to me, in the name of your brethren, a new pastoral ring. I intended to beg you to accept, after my death, the one I have hitherto worn. Let me give it to you now ; take it, and in return let me ask of you this favour, that when my hand is cold in death, and yours is raised to bestow your blessing on my flock, you will sometimes remember that though parted from them by the grave I love them still and bless them with you.

'And you, my dear fellow-labourers, the priests of our four dioceses, and the members of our Society of Missioners—for your happiness I offer my prayers daily, and for the success of the ministry you carry on in the midst of so much hardship, toil, and even danger. But at the present moment I feel I can offer these same petitions to God with greater confidence, for I know that He has promised to reward with abundant blessings the sons who honour their father, and who support and cheer him with their filial devotion and thoughtful love.'

The souvenir alluded to consisted of a gold pectoral cross studded with diamonds and rubies, and a pastoral ring set with similar precious stones. Many other splendid gifts were offered to his Eminence, among which we may enumerate a chalice of solid gold; a second pectoral cross, also adorned with diamonds and rubies; a valuable mitre, to be worn when officiating pontifically; besides a number of vestments and sacred vessels intended for distribution among the poorer churches of his two dioceses.

The religious ceremony was succeeded by a banquet at which nearly three hundred members of the clergy sat down. In the evening there was a general illumination of the whole city, and the festival concluded amid universal rejoicings.

'Amid all the varied scenes and different demonstrations which gave interest to this auspicious day, none was more touching, and at the same time more genuine, than that which took place when the Cardinal left the cathedral, at the close of the service, and appeared on the top of the flight of stone steps which leads down from the principal entrance. Each step was covered by a dense mass of persons, a closely packed

crowd filling the square, the adjoining streets, the
windows of all the houses, and even their very roofs.
When his Eminence raised his hand to bless the people,
the enthusiasm of those present could not be restrained.
He was surrounded and almost suffocated by the number
of persons who pressed up to him endeavouring to kiss
his hands or his vestments, and to utter, each one indi-
vidually, their good wishes and congratulations. Italians,
Spaniards, Maltese, and French—every one spoke in his
own language, and offered him an ovation which lasted
more than a quarter of an hour, until he reached the
door of the episcopal palace.

The Cardinal was exhausted with the fatigue and
excitement of the morning, but his eyes beamed with
joy and pleasure. Who can describe his feelings on
such an occasion? Who can describe the emotion that
filled his paternal heart when, on the way back to St.
Eugène, on passing by the Church of our Lady of
Africa, he found assembled there the Arab Christians
from his two villages of St. Cyprian and St. Monica,
built some ten or twelve years previously. They too
had come to bear a part in the general rejoicing, to
join in the universal tribute of gratitude and affection.
Standing in groups by the roadside, the parents, surrounded by their children, held up the little ones to
receive the blessing of the Cardinal, to whom they owed
the training of their early years, and whom they had
not ceased to love and venerate as a father and
protector.

We may here quote from Cardinal Lavigerie's
pastoral letter a sentence which briefly sums up the
work he accomplished in Algiers :—

'At the period when my episcopate commenced,
the resources of the Church in Algiers scarcely sufficed

for its own needs. Its funds were scanty, its clergy few in number, and it was consequently unable to make the teaching and the influence of the Gospel felt in the barbarous countries which lie around it. But now it can already chant the joyous hymn of the victor: " Rejoice, thou barren that bearest not. Thou shalt pass to the right hand and to the left, and thy seed shall inherit the Gentiles and shall inhabit the desolate cities." [1] The tents of its ambassadors are spreading far and wide; they have penetrated to the very heart of the Dark Continent. By their means the sound of the Gospel has reached those unknown lakes where the great rivers, celebrated in ancient days, take their rise.'

The Bishop of Oran, one of Cardinal Lavigerie's suffragans, speaks, on the occasion of his Eminence's jubilee, as follows in regard to the result of his labours on behalf of Africa:—

' If there is, in the days wherein our lot is cast, one sight better calculated than another to make our hearts thrill within us, it is that of the manner in which the minds of men are being drawn to interest themselves in this Africa of ours. You are aware how closely the whole world is watching what goes on there, with what special attention the progress of the Faith and the extension of the work of civilisation is observed. All Christendom rejoices to see that in these days the mercy and goodness of God is made known in these vast regions of Central Africa, where His name has hitherto been unknown. Equatorial Africa is no longer, of all portions of the globe, the only one entirely destitute of the light of truth—given over, as it were, to the darkness of ignorance and paganism. The Gospel has

[1] Is. liv. 1-3.

been preached there, and the soil has already been watered with the blood of many heroic martyrs.

‘ Let us unite our voices to the anthem of praise which we hear rising from beyond the vast deserts which separate us from those of our fellow-Christians who have so lately been admitted into the fold of the Church ; with them let us thank the God of all mercy who has granted to us to behold such wonders of grace. Let us join with these newly made converts in blessing the name of Him who has rewarded our labours by bestowing upon us not only the costly crown of souls regenerated in the waters of baptism, but the still more precious diadem of glorious martyrs and confessors purified in the fire of persecution.

‘ All this is due, under Divine Providence, to the indefatigable efforts of our venerated Primate. He it is who, after having carefully trained and formed them for the warfare upon which they were to enter, sent forth bands of valiant missioners to explore this new world and carry to it the light of faith.

‘ Yet at the price of how many labours and fatigues, of how much suffering and sacrifice, has this great result been achieved ! God alone knows all the weary journeys which have been undertaken both by land and sea, all the fervent appeals which have been made, the stirring discourses which have been delivered, not only in France but in the neighbouring countries also, in order to obtain the funds needed for the establish-ment and maintenance of so many works of charity. What we have seen for ourselves of all this has filled us with ever-increasing admiration for the illustrious prelate whom it is our privilege to call by the name of Father. An episcopate of twenty-five years repre-sents an incalculable amount of contradictions and vexations, of trials and disappointments, borne as far as possible in silence, and courageously endured for the sake of Jesus Christ and for the good of souls.'

In conclusion, it may be well to quote the Brief addressed to Cardinal Lavigerie by his Holiness Pope Leo XIII. in acknowledgment of a valuable relic discovered amongst the ruins in the vicinity of Tunis, of which the Cardinal had begged his acceptance. We rejoice also at the same time to re-echo the laudatory words contained in this Brief ; words which, coming as they do from the lips of the Supreme Pontiff, have a value that they could not possess were they the utterances of any individual of less exalted station.—' *The name of Cardinal Lavigerie merits, on account of the eminent services he has rendered to Africa, a place in the ranks of those who have deserved the most of Catholicism and civilisation.*'

To Our dear Son,

Health and apostolic benediction.

' We both hold especially dear, and shall keep with the greatest care, the precious treasure (κειμήλιον) that you sent Us not long since. We refer to the silver reliquary dug up from the ruins of a Christian house on the confines of Tunis, and to which a particular value is given both by its anti-

' Dilecte Fili Noster,

' *Salutem et apostolicam benedictionem.*

' Et habemus apprime carum, et tuebimur perquam studiosè missum abs te non ita pridem κειμήλιον. Lypsanothecam intelligimus argenteam, e ruderibus ædis christianæ ad Tunetanos fines egestam ; cui pretium sane magnum planeque singulare sua facit tum vetus tum periucunda ad recor-

quity and by the pleasant memories it calls forth.

'For when we cast our eyes on that memorial the prosperous days of the Church of Africa recur spontaneously to our thoughts, and the times when the Gospel was carried further from Rome, and when Numidia above all and Mauritania were adorned with the most brilliant instances of virtue and learning. How terrible were the disasters and calamities which followed on that period! In truth it is a most difficult task to build together again ruins of long duration and wide extent.

'Yet, trusting in God and the strength of united effort, we must with perseverance and good courage make the attempt. For Ourselves, We indeed have aided, and will aid as much as in us lies. It is for you to direct the means, you, whose eminent services to Africa give you a place in the

dationem origo. Nam in istud mnemosynon cum coniiciuntur oculi, sponte in memoriam redeunt A-fricanæ Ecclesiæ felices anni, quo tempore, maturime hinc accepto evangelio, maximis virtutum doctrinæque ornamentis Numidia præsertim ac Mauretania florebant. Quam formidolosi eam ætatem excepere casus, quam variæ calamitates! Profecto caussa perdifficilis inveteratas latissimeque diffusas sarcire ruinas: nihilominus Deo fretos coniunctisque viribus eniti constanter et animose oportet. Nos quidem et dedimus, et dabimus, quantum poterit, operam. *Te scilicet ad omnia adiutore, quem singularia in Africam merita sic commendant, ut cum viris de catholico nomine urbanoque cultu summe meritis comparandus videare.* Interea laboribus curisque tuis perpetuam a Deo felicitatem precati, tibi, dilecte fili Noster, et universo

ranks of those who have deserved the most of Catholicism and civilisation.

'Meanwhile We beg God to grant enduring success to all your labours and plans, and We most cordially give to you, beloved Son, and to all your Clergy and your people, Our Apostolic benediction.

'Given at Rome, at St. Peter's, the 10th November, 1887, in the tenth year of Our pontificate.'

LEO XIII. POPE.

Clero populoque tuo apostolicam benedictionem peramanter impertimus.

'Datum Romæ apud S. Petrum die X Novembris Anno MDCCCLXXXVII, Pontificatus Nostri decimo.

'LEO PP. XIII.'

PART THE SECOND

THE AFRICAN SLAVE TRADE

CHAPTER I

SLAVERY IN AFRICA

THE anti-slavery crusade in Africa is one of those exceptional schemes of benevolence in which religion and politics do not interfere with the common action of all civilised nations. It is directed not so much against slavery as an institution as against the systematic slave-trade, the necessary accompaniment of slavery, which is carried on in Central Africa with a barbarous cruelty unparalleled in the most savage nations of ancient and modern times. Cardinal Lavigerie has expressly disclaimed any intention of interfering with domestic slavery where it is one of the recognised customs of the country. It would be mere folly to undertake a practically impossible task, and however serious are the evils that slavery of its own nature entails, yet on the one hand self-interest, and on the other general public opinion, not to mention the natural kindliness which exists in a majority of mankind, do much to mitigate the condition of slaves and to keep in check the brutality even of the most hard-hearted and unprincipled of slave-owners. With some marked exceptions the general treatment of slaves all over the world has not been very much below the treatment of ordinary domestic servants and labourers who are free. The bondage of one rational being to another is always one of degree. It cannot from the very nature of things be absolute and complete, and the distinction between servant and serf and bondsman and slave is shaded off by various degrees of subjection which often make it difficult to draw the line between those who are captives and those who are free.

Slavery has been in some stages of social development most beneficial to the interests of those who were enslaved. It was often the alternative for wholesale butchery, and, moreover, enforced settled habits of industry on those who before had been subject to the demoralising effects of a nomad life. The objections to slavery are drawn from a consideration of its moral influence on the master, rather than from that of any habitual cruelty practised on the slaves. Any hardships they endured were rather the results of their changes of condition than of their actual servitude. Slaves born in their master's house, for the most part, have had an easy time of it. Horace's *verna procax* was but a type of the class both in ancient and modern times. Even in 'Uncle Tom's Cabin,' though it was written with the object of painting slavery in the blackest colours, 'Topsy' was quite a favoured child of fortune. The real objection to domestic slavery is the moral licence it engenders, the facilities it gives to libertinism, the petty tyranny it encourages in the master, the spirit of servile, crouching, degrading subjection which it begets in the slave. It was because of the social and moral corruption which accompanied it, rather than because of any physical sufferings on the part of the slaves, that the Christian Church always set her face against it. It is as the moral educator of mankind that she has taught them to abolish slavery as an institution wherever she has been able to exert her due influence, The work has been and ought to be a gradual one, but from the moment when Christianity began its work slavery was doomed. It must needs fade away and disappear under the standard of the Cross. It could not withstand the Divine proclamation of universal freedom, that there is neither barbarian, Scythian, bond, nor free, but all are one in Christ Jesus.

In the present day slavery is all but abolished in Christian countries. But wherever Islamism prevails slavery always accompanies it. It is, for the most part, domestic, and slaves are rarely employed in field-labour. Mohammedans in general treat their slaves well. The Koran inculcates gentleness and kindness to them. The child of a slave by her master is *ipso facto* free in all Mohammedan countries, and polygamy gives every facility for the conversion of the female slave into the lawful wife. In the East there is no such hard and fast line between wife and mistress as is the case where monogamy prevails. One of the curious features that mark the religion of the prophet and perpetuate its blighting influence on mankind is the way in which it is bound up with slavery, but, at the same time, makes a compromise which mitigates the hardships of the slave's condition, without, however, lessening its demoralising effects on master and slave alike. Dr. Schweinfurth's testimony respecting slavery in Egypt illustrates this extremely well :—

'Whether Egyptian officials wear an Oriental dress or a European dress, their ideas about slavery and the slave-trade are stereotyped. It is the fashion in good society to have a house full of slaves, and their presence is considered indispensable. Now if a man were to keep two, or even three, properly-paid servants, and see that they did their duty with order and punctuality, he would be making some advance in civilisation; but, now, what is the impression upon entering the homes of the rich Egyptians? There, comfortably settled on the divan, sits the master of the house, silent and contemplative, a man of peace and quietness; nothing seems to disturb his composure; all the nobler passions are quite alien to his nature; hunting and fishing, riding and boating, are quite unknown to him, and he never puts himself to the trouble of taking a walk. If he is thirsty, he has only to raise his hand and say, " Ya, wolled " (Here, fellow !), and in an instant his slave hands him a glass of water; or if he wants to smoke or to go to sleep, it is, " Ya, wolled," just the same : everything is done for him, and he does not stir an inch to help himself. Now, supposing, some fine day, all these " wolleds " were to take themselves off, what would befall these fine gentlemen on their divans, and where would they turn for all the trifling comforts of their daily life? Their sluggish nature would be invaded by a feeling of disquietude that they had never felt before; they must either die or become new creatures. This description, which applies to every rank of life, is only a reflection of the lethargic apathy that prevails in every Oriental state; an inference necessarily follows that *of equal importance with the abolition of slavery is the dawn of a new life in the East.* If this regeneration is impossible, then slavery is a permanent necessity.

'The kind treatment of slaves, and the comfortable lot that they enjoy, in comparison to the hardships of their rude, rough homes, are pleas that often have been urged in extenuation of slavery in the East. It is certainly true that the contrast in slave labour is very great, and, whilst Europeans have looked upon their slaves as little better than useful domestic animals, the Oriental slave is a mere object of luxury. Only a small proportion of the slaves that are brought annually from the interior are employed in field labour in Egypt, though rather more frequently in the Eastern provinces. The European, although he deprived the negro of his ordinary rights, still compelled him to become a useful member of society; the Oriental allows him a portion of his rights, but trains him up to general incapacity; the occupations of filling pipes, handing water, boiling coffee, and holding a salver, are not employments worthy of a man.'[1]

We may therefore leave out of our consideration the domestic slavery of Islamism, as an ineradicable evil which it is quite useless to attack directly. It is a source of wholesale moral corruption and social and political degeneracy, inseparably bound up with the religion of the prophet. Whether the crescent is waning before the cross—whether the enervating and paralysing influences of Mohammedanism are such as to check its career of conquest and to force it in the end to yield to the superior vitality inherent in the religion of Christ—is a question that does not concern us. For our purposes, the slavery of Mohammedan countries is an established fact, the existence of which we may bitterly lament, but cannot hope by any amount of anti-slavery crusades to destroy.

Putting aside, then, the domestic slavery of Egypt, Turkey, and all other countries where the crescent still prevails, we find ourselves face to face with two tremendous evils, existing over a large portion of central Africa. Both of them cry aloud to heaven for vengeance. One of them is more directly opposed to the

[1] *Heart of Africa*, ii. 435, 436.

law of nature and must infallibly disappear as any sort
of civilisation, whether Mohammedan or Christian,
takes the place of the fetichism and devil-worship which
prevail among the native heathen tribes. The other is
less revolting, but more dangerous : more difficult to
encounter, more closely interwoven with the selfish
interests of a large, wealthy, and unprincipled class.
The one prevails chiefly among the tribes on the Niger,
and in Western Africa; the other all over Central
Africa. The former of these is the domestic slavery
among the pagans, with its accompaniment of human
sacrifices and other atrocities to be hereafter related ;
the other, the slave-trade, as practised on the native
tribes by the Mohammedan and Portuguese traders with
the assistance and co-operation of the natives themselves, and in many parts with the connivance and
consent of Egyptian officials. The crusade of Cardinal
Lavigerie is directed primarily against the slave-trade.
If only this could be effectually put down, domestic
slavery would, of necessity, gradually disappear.

Slavery requires a continual supply from without.
The children of domestic slaves are found by universal
experience not to be sufficiently numerous to fill up the
ranks. It is not easy at first to see why it should be
so, as the negro is remarkably prolific and of strong
physique. But men, like other animals, do not seem to
breed when they are in captivity as they do when they
are free, and it is not as a rule to the interest of their
masters that they should do so. Slaves who grow up
in the house occupy quite a different position from those
that are purchased. For them slavery is a light yoke,
one so light that a great many of them shake it off
altogether and are virtually if not actually free. There
is a sort of moral obligation on slave-owners to give their

liberty to faithful slaves, and their ranks are in this way considerably thinned. In all slave-holding countries in the present day the offspring of a white man and a slave is by the law born free, and thus the licence existing among the owners of slaves in their intercourse with female slaves increases the free population in comparison with the slaves. Moreover, a prosperous man gradually increases his family of slaves, and such a one will go into the market or to the trader, and look out for a healthy boy or girl lately imported from the slave-producing countries, rather than purchase one who is home-bred. He will thus get a cheaper and more serviceable article, one more completely in his power, and less likely to run away than if parents or a former owner were near at hand. Whatever the cause, an import trade is a necessity to the existence of slavery. Destroy the trade, and slavery itself will not last long.

But this is not the primary motive of the strong feeling that prevails respecting the African slave-trade, or of the vigorous onslaught that all good men are preparing to make upon it. The hope of the ultimate destruction of slavery is secondary to the desire to abolish the horrors that surround the traffic. It is the frightful atrocities committed in the process of capture— wholesale massacres, committed in the African villages; the inhuman barbarity with which the slaves are treated on the march; the murder, pillage, rapine, which are the accompaniments of every slave-trading expedition; the line of victims who mark the track of the slave-caravan, left to perish or pitilessly beaten to death because their fainting limbs refuse to carry them further; it is the gradual depopulation of large districts of central Africa, once the home of prosperous tribes, the scenes of desolation which mark this accursed traffic, the demoralisation of the tribes wherever these fiends in human shape, who make slave-trading their livelihood, turn their footsteps; it is the utter impossibility of ever carrying with any hope of success either healthy civilisation or Christianity to countries liable to these visits; it is these and many other accompanying evils that stir the blood and rouse the indignation of all those who have any benevolence in their hearts, and above all those who have learned the sublime lesson that Jesus Christ came to teach by word and by example. Wherever the slave-traders are able to do their work unchecked, missionaries, whether Catholic or Protestant, have no chance. Sir Samuel Baker's testimony on this subject is very remarkable. He says:—

' The Austrian Mission has failed, and the stations have been forsaken; their pious labour was hopeless, and the devoted priests died upon their barren field. What curse lies so heavily upon Africa and bows her down beneath all other nations? It is the infernal traffic in slaves—a trade so hideous, that the heart of every slave and owner becomes deformed, and shrinks like a withered limb incapable of action.

' Thus is Africa accursed: nor can she be raised to any scale approaching to civilisation until the slave-trade shall be totally suppressed. The first step necessary to the improvement of the savage tribes of the White Nile is the annihilation of the slave-trade. Until this be effected, no legitimate commerce can be established; neither is there an opening for missionary enterprise :—the country is sealed and closed against all improvement.' [1]

[1] Baker, *Albert Nyanza,* ii. 294.

The traders are the deadly enemies of those who come to preach the gospel of freedom. The great mass of them are moreover Mohammedans, and have therefore a double reason for their hatred to the Christian missionary. In some parts of Africa they unite a religious crusade with their commercial enterprise, and proselytise whole villages partly by force and partly by persuasion, and by representing to the chiefs the advantages they will gain and the ills they will avoid by adopting the religion of the prophet. In this way Islamism is making way far more rapidly in the interior of Africa than Christianity. Unless the slave-trade is suppressed, it bids fair to subdue the greater portion of central Africa as it has subdued the north of it. European and Christian nations may nominally parcel out Africa among themselves, or at least establish a nominal protectorate, but the fierce tide of proselytising Islamism will, with all the help of the slave-trade, sweep on resistlessly, and gradually encroach even on those portions which England or France or Germany considers as her own.

These are facts which do not depend on the unsupported representations of Cardinal Lavigerie or his missionaries. There is the concurrent testimony of all those who have had the best opportunity of collecting evidence on the spot, and have witnessed with their own eyes the awful, the heartrending scenes that they describe. We have, moreover, the pitiful tale of some of those who have themselves endured the inhuman atrocities of the slave-traders, and have experienced the awful miseries and seen the revolting scenes which are the accompaniment of the march of slave caravans to the coast. The evidence here is so plentiful that we

scarcely know where to begin—most of our readers
have probably made themselves acquainted with the
testimony of Stanley, Livingstone, Baker, and Schweinfurth.

We must, however, quote the following description
which Sir S. Baker gives of a slave-raid of White Nile
traders :—

'On arriving at the desired locality the (piratical)
party disembark and proceed into the interior, until
they arrive at the village of some negro chief, with
whom they establish an intimacy. Charmed with his
new friends, the power of whose weapons he acknow-
ledges, the negro chief does not neglect the opportunity
of seeking their alliance to attack a hostile neighbour.
Marching throughout the night, guided by their negro
hosts, they bivouac within an hour's march of the un-
suspecting village doomed to an attack about half an
hour before break of day. The time arrives, and, quietly
surrounding the village while its occupants are still
sleeping, they fire the grass huts in all directions, and
pour volleys of musketry through the flaming thatch.
Panic-stricken, the unfortunate victims rush from their
burning dwellings, and the men are shot down like
pheasants in a battue, while the women and children,
bewildered in the danger and confusion, are kidnapped
and secured.   They are then fastened together, the
former secured in an instrument called a *shéba*, made
of a forked pole, the neck of the prisoner fitting into
the fork, secured by a cross piece lashed behind,
while the wrists, brought together in front of the body,
are tied to the pole. The children are then fastened by
their necks with a rope attached to the women, and
thus form a living chain, in which order they are

marched to the head-quarters in company with the captured herds.' [1]

Commander Cameron, writing from a different part of Africa, bears similar testimony. Travellers are unanimous as to the barbarous treatment of the unhappy captives on their long and weary march to the coast. They are driven sometimes for the distance of 1,000 miles, to be packed on board the Arab sailing boats called *dhows* and conveyed to the slave markets of Western Asia.

'Slaves were usually gagged by having a piece of wood,.like a snaffle, tied into their mouths. Heavy slave-forks were placed round their necks, and their hands were fastened behind their backs. They were then attached by a cord to the vendor's waist.' [2]

Elsewhere he says : 'Coimbra arrived in the afternoon with a gang of *fifty-two women* tied together in lots of seventeen or eighteen. Some had children in arms, others were far advanced in pregnancy, and all were laden with huge bundles of grass cloth and other plunder. These poor weary and footsore creatures were covered with weals and scars showing how unmercifully cruel had been the treatment received at the hands of the savage who had called himself their owner. . . The misery and loss of life entailed by the capture of these women is far greater than can be imagined except by those who have witnessed some such heart-rending scenes. Indeed the cruelties perpetrated in the heart of Africa by men calling themselves Christians can scarcely be credited by those living in a civilised land.

[1] Baker, *Albert Nyanza*, i. 19.   [2] Cameron, *Across Africa*, i. 341.

'To obtain these fifty-two women, at least ten villages had been destroyed, each having a population of from one to two hundred, or about 1,500 in all. Some may, perchance, have escaped to neighbouring villages; but the greater portion were undoubtedly burnt when their villages were surprised, shot whilst attempting to save their wives and families, or doomed to die of starvation in the jungles unless some wild beast put a more speedy end to their miseries.'[1]

Speaking of another caravan he says: 'I had noticed the bad condition of this gang several times on the road, the poor wretches being travel-worn and half-starved, and having large sores caused by their loads and the blows and cuts they received; the ropes that confined them were also, in some instances, eating into their flesh. And I saw one woman still carrying the infant that had died in her arms of starvation.'[2]

Another of Cameron's experiences is no less distressing.

'. . . The whole of the caravan passed on in front, the mournful procession lasting for more than two hours. Women and children, foot-sore and over-burthened, were urged on unremittingly by their barbarous masters; and even when they reached their camp it was no haven of rest for the poor creatures.

'They were compelled to fetch water, cook, build huts, and collect firewood for those who owned them, and were comparatively favoured if they had contrived some sort of shelter for themselves before night set in.

'The loss of labour entailed by working gangs of slaves tied together is monstrous, for if one pot of water is wanted twenty people are obliged to fetch it from the

[1] Cameron, *Across Africa*, ii. 136-8.   [2] Ibid. ii. 164.

stream; and for one bundle of grass to thatch a hut the whole string must be employed. On the road too, if one of a gang requires to halt, the whole must follow motions, and when one falls five or six are dragged down.'[1]

At another stage of his journey, where the road was so difficult as sometimes to render progress almost impossible even for able-bodied men, he describes the traces of the slave caravan :—

'Numerous skeletons testified to the numbers whose lives had been sacrificed on this trying march, whilst slave clogs and forks still attached to some bleached bones, or lying by their sides, gave only too convincing proof that the demon of the slave-trade still exercised his influence in this part of Africa [Benguela.] Clogs and forks were also hanging on trees, some being so slightly affected by the weather, that it was evident they had not been there longer than a month or two. Doubtless they had been removed from some flagging wretches in the belief that weakness of body had extinguished all idea of escape, and in the hope that the strength which was insufficient to bear the weight of the clog might still prove sufficient to drag the unfortunate human chattel to the coast.'[2]

Of Liowa, the chief village of Western Ugara, where the fertile soil would have yielded a rich return to industrious cultivators, he gives the following account :

'Passing through the ruins of so many deserted villages, once the homes of happy and contented people, was indescribably saddening. Where now were those who built them and cultivated the surrounding fields ? Where ? Driven off as slaves, massacred by villains

---

[1] *Across Africa,* ii. 147–8.   [2] Ibid. ii. 256.

engaged in a war in which these poor wretches had no
interest, or dead of starvation and disease in the
jungle.

'Africa is bleeding out her life-blood at every pore.
A rich country, requiring labour only to render it one
of the greatest producers in the world, is having its
population—already far too scanty for its needs—daily
depleted by the slave-trade and internecine war.

'Should the present state of affairs be allowed to continue, the country will gradually relapse into jungles
and wilds, and will become more and more impenetrable
to the merchant and trader.' [1]

The Fakis or priests are often the agents of wholesale dealers, and never, Dr. Schweinfurth says, did I
see slaves so mercilessly treated as by these fanatics,
who, in spite of everything, are held by the people in
the greatest veneration.

'In one of their convoys were some poor miserable
Mittoo-slaves almost too emaciated to bear the heavy
yoke (the sheyba) that was fastened to their necks.
One morning, hearing an unusual outcry, I paused to
inquire what was the matter. A scene such as my pen
can only indignantly depict, met my gaze. A dying
man had been dragged from the hut, and was being
belaboured by the cruellest of lashes to prove whether
life was extinct. The long white stripes on the withered
skin testified to the agonies the poor wretch was enduring, and the vociferations I heard were the shouts
of his persecutors, who were yelling out their oaths
and imprecations. "The cursed dog! he is not dead
yet. The heathen rascal will not die!" Then, as though
resolved to accumulate cruelty on cruelty, the Faki's

[1] Cameron, *Across Africa*, i. 209.

slave-boys not only began to break out into revolting jeers, but actually played at football with the gasping victim; the horrible contortions of the sufferer's countenance were sufficient to melt the hardest hearts.'[1]

'. . . The environs of the Sheriba of Shereefee were only scantily cultivated. . . . Exposing itself far and wide there was the naked rock, the barrenness of which was only interrupted at intervals by a covering of human bones! Carried off in groups, the captured slaves here succumbed to the overwrought exertions of their march. At times they literally died of starvation, as there was no corn to be had in the barren land. The overland dealers in slaves here make their purchases at the most advantageous prices. In these Eastern Sheribas, as the result of perpetual raids, there is always a superabundance of the living black merchandise on hand, but rarely is there an adequate supply of food for their maintenance. . . . It is no unwonted thing for the gangs to melt away a dozen at a time. Bones of men and charred palisades of huts are too true an evidence of the halting-places of Mohammedanism, and day by day there was awaiting me the miserable sight of a number of helpless children, perfect little pictures of distress and wretchedness, either orphans or deserted by their mothers, who dragged on a pitiable existence, half-starved, burnt by falling into the fire in their sleep, and covered with loathsome sores.'[2]

The unhappy captives often contrive to effect their escape in gangs, as many as twenty at a time, and the whole caravan halts for a day or two whilst search is made for them. If the fugitives are overtaken and

[1] Dr. Schweinfurth, *The Heart of Africa*, ii. 414.   [2] Ibid. i. 346.

brought back, a terrible flogging is the usual punishment, but sometimes death is inflicted.   Sir Samuel Baker relates that on one occasion—

'From the trader's camp a girl about sixteen and her mother, who were slaves, were missing; they had escaped.   The hue and cry was at once raised.   Ibrahimaiva, who had himself been a slave, was the most indefatigable slave-hunter.   He and a party started on the track of the fugitives.   They did not return until the following day, but where was the runaway who could escape from such a bloodhound?   The young girl and her mother were led into camp tied together by the neck, and immediately condemned to be hanged.' [1]

The loss of slaves on the march from the interior to the coast is enormous.   From one cause or another, desertion, disablement, or death, never more than one-third, sometimes only one-tenth, of the original number reach their destination.   When the caravans pass through missionary stations, the missioners frequently ransom a few of the very young or feeble, of whom the traders are glad to rid themselves.

From a letter of Mgr. Bridoux, the Vicar Apostolic of Tangányika, to Mgr. Lavigerie, we take the following lines :—

'Yesterday we met two caravans of slaves, and baptized two little children who were nothing but skin and bone.   I baptized one, a little boy, to whom I gave the name of Charles, in the river Mpwapwa, into which he had just been dipped for the purpose of washing him.   The other was a little girl; I baptized her in the Arab camp.   Words fail me to describe the painful impression made on us all by our meeting with

[1] *The Albert Nyanza,* ii. 254.

these caravans. One consisted of about one hundred
slaves, the other numbered perhaps three hundred;
forty of the band were literal skeletons, and they can
never reach the coast. Some of the men had the fork
(*shéba*) on their neck, and a certain number of the
women were chained together. They seemed hardly
able to drag themselves along, yet several had a little
child on their back. Though I was prepared to witness
similar horrors, I confess that those I have just described surpassed my expectations, and while I write
these lines my heart still bleeds at the recollection of
them. One of the caravans has encamped in our
vicinity, and I am going to return to the halting-place
in a short time, taking our doctors with me in order to
see what can be done for the sick.'[1]

Another of the Algerian Missioners writes from
Kibanga, near Lake Tanganyika, in December 1887:—
  'Once more we can breathe freely. Thank heaven!
. . . At seven o'clock this morning the oppressors, the
slaughterers of our peaceful people took their departure
in the midst of drenching rain, followed by the execra-
tions of all the native population. They numbered
nearly three hundred in all, and were a troop like
those that come from the coast with drums and flags,
porters, women and children, &c. In the rear the
slave-caravan marched, a melancholy procession. One
poor old woman who was being taken away into captivity passing close by good Brother Jerome, clung to
his clothes, and implored him to save her; but he
could do nothing, and so she was dragged off like a
beast of burden, by the rope round her neck. We had
nothing left to ransom her with. . . . The march past

Bulletin de la Société Anti-Esclavagiste, Dec. 1888, p. 177.

occupied a considerable time—the rear guard was not gone when the rain left off. These detestable vampires have now swooped down upon Ubembé; we can see in the distance the incendiary fires they are making there.

'These horrible expeditions depopulate the country round us; all the villages where only yesterday we went to catechise, are now vast deserts.

'One of the unhappy women whom the Ruga-Ruga had kidnapped has just expired before our eyes. She struggled and screamed when she was taken, and would not submit to be chained, whereupon one of the slave-hunters discharged a pistol at her breast. She fell mortally wounded; she was *enceinte*, and shortly afterwards gave birth to a dead child As she lay on the ground writhing in agony we lifted her up and carried her into our enclosure. She was acquainted to a certain extent with the truths of religion, we spoke to her of heaven, and asked if she would like to be baptized. She assented to this, and accordingly we baptized her; after that her wailings ceased. Now she is dead. O my God! who will put an end to all these horrors! . . .'

We quote again from the letters of the Algerian Missioners :—

'. . . In the evening we witnessed the melancholy spectacle of a slave-raid in the neighbouring country; on all sides we beheld burning villages, and fugitives endeavouring to make good their escape by betaking themselves to the waters of the lake. The Ruga-Ruga returned loaded with chickens, goats, fish, &c., whilst a band of about thirty of these brigands scoured under our very eyes the hills and lower regions of the river Maongolo where the unfortunate fugitives lay hid. In

the evening they came back, bringing with them the
women and children in chains!

'It was a terrible sight. One longs to shoot down
on the spot these infamous robbers who know no law,
human or divine, and thus kidnap their fellow-creatures
in order to enslave both soul and body. We might
succeed in freeing many of the poor captives were we
to allow our people who carry arms to fall on these
incarnate fiends, but that would be open war, and
would infallibly be the destruction of our mission.

'Alas! when will some European power interfere
to put an end to this accursed traffic in slaves, and the
myriad evils that follow in its train? A detachment of
fifty European soldiers, well armed and acclimatised,
would be able in a fortnight to exterminate this troop—
a rabble of some two or three hundred robbers—
which is the terror of all the districts from Tabora to
Manyuema, and the whole of the Tanganyika as far as
the Albert Nyanza. Yet what can we helpless missioners do, except pray to God on behalf of the unhappy
negro, and his worst enemies, the Arabs and the
métis? It is truly horrible to witness these man-hunts!

'In the evening of this sorrowful Sunday, the
recollection of which will never fade from our minds,
the Father Superior sent one of the fathers to the
Arab camp to request that an end might be put to
these persecutions as speedily as possible and the whole
band take their departure without delay, and allow our
Christian negroes to return to their villages, where
almost all the plantations had been destroyed. The
Arab chief, who is utterly unable to enforce obedience
among his followers, promised to go early the next
morning; he allowed us to ransom those of the women
and children, the victims of the day's expedition, whose

ransoms we had the means of paying. We part with everything we can for this purpose. Fancy the delight of the happy individuals who were thus enabled to return to their homes, and on the other hand the hopeless misery of the unfortunate creatures who could not share in the deliverance, and were forcibly dragged away chained to the forks, uttering shrieks of despair. Would that we had the means of setting them all free ! '

' Mzovera, a most useful tool in the hands of the Arab trader who makes it his business to depopulate the Marungu, has found himself this time, in spite of his apprehensions, obliged to pass through our little territory with the pitiful prey he has collected on his expeditions. Happening not long ago to fall in with one of our men, he spoke to him openly of his fears, and his wish to take another route, to avoid displaying his captives before our eyes. His booty consists of ivory and slaves ; the latter amount to about 200 men, women, and children, fastened together with long chains like the beads of a rosary. " The caravan is heavily laden," Mzovera remarked to me, " more so than any I have ever seen." It had halted twelve days at Kyula, nine at Katela, and it ought to have halted three weeks in our neighbourhood considering how worn out the captives were through fatigue, rough usage, and scanty food. In order to shorten his journey and lessen his expenses, he wanted to hire our boats to transport his slaves to Ujiji, thinking that they would suffer from seasickness and thus economise his provisions ; but we indignantly refused to lend ourselves to the cowardly stratagem. He was therefore obliged to give some of his captives up to us, being unable to procure for them the trifling amount of nourishment absolutely necessary to keep them from dying of inanition. Thus we were able to ransom eleven children, two of whom were literally reduced to skeletons and appeared to be at the point of death, so that the sum of seven francs sufficed for their purchase.

'We like talking to the older ones, who give us harrowing details respecting their wretched existence. "Those Wangwana tire us to death," they said in their childish simplicity, "they capture us for the sake of making us die of hunger. We will not drag along over the stones any longer; we should like to stay here with the white men; we are comfortable here; at any rate, we get enough to eat." One poor little creature, who, though nearly three years old, had not been weaned, said to one of his companions : "We must slip away and go back to our mother;" he was seven or eight days' march from home. His comrade came to me directly, saying : "Kabwilé wants to run away." Father Moinet did his best to comfort the poor child. "Wait a little, my child," he said, "it is still the rainy season, the rivers are swollen, and the roads are bad." "Mamma, mamma," sobbed the child, "I want mamma." "It is too late to go to-day," the kind father answered; "besides, if you go away from us, the Wangwana will catch you, and beat you, and you will never see your mother again; but if you stay here with me, you will see her again, and the Wangwana will not hurt you any more." These arguments prevailed, the child was appeased, and left off crying. These children were only given up to us because they were an encumbrance to the caravan ; but for that, we should not have been able to rescue them, as they would have fetched a higher price at Ujiji.'

'Mzovera is on the move with his caravan ; we have

been asking the children whom we ransomed if they would not go with their former master. "*Rawe, rawe*; no, no," they say, " we mean to stay here with you."

' No sooner had Mzovera gone than a second caravan arrived, and a heavily freighted boat. A portion of the slaves were disembarked on the shore, and we have the sight of the forks and chains over again ; but the owners were half afraid to let the children be seen, so the boat was pushed off and now rides at anchor. " The white men are there," the leader of the caravan remarked ; " they see us, we will wait to unship the children till they are gone." We were in fact watching them from a mound overlooking the harbour. These slave-caravans always present the same melancholy aspect; one sees might taking precedence of right, even the right of life itself; suffering in every shape, one more mournful than the other ; the purest feelings of nature set at nought, the family tie severed, the bonds of friendship broken, a death in life.

' In this district, in the heart of Africa, pillaging, slave-hunting, kidnapping goes on worse than ever ; the country round is ruined, and soon will be a complete desert. Manyeuma is being scoured in every direction, the last drop will be squeezed out. At Mtaua, the post of the district, not a day passes without hundreds of slaves being shipped on board the dhows. . . . In the space of two months more than four hundred slaves have been conducted past our station ; the extinction of the race cannot be far off.'

A French Missioner writes from the Mission of Kibanga, Upper Congo :—' This mission is progressing favourably, and every day adds to our flock. The opportunities of freeing slaves are not wanting this year, as the children seized and carried off by the Wangwana are sold at vile prices in and around Ujiji, where many die of starvation because their owners cannot get rid of them. From January 1 to June 1 we have been able to ransom 150 slaves—men, women, and children —so that we have now 300 children in the Orphanage, without counting the elder ones who are established in our Christian villages, and who are also very numerous. The very low price we have had to pay for them has enabled us to ransom so many ; but, unfortunately, our resources being exhausted, we have had to stop.

' Our hospital is filled, principally by old men, slaves ransomed for a few yards of calico, or by old negresses cast adrift by their husbands or their children, to whom, on account of their age, they can no longer be of use. This entirely pagan maxim practised almost all over Africa, viz. :—" When thy father and thy mother, having become old and consequently useless, begin to bend towards the grave, rid them of life, or drive them into the woods," exists here in all its horror. It is on this account that, thanks to the generosity of one of our patrons, we have been able to found an asylum for these poor abandoned creatures, in which we provide for their corporal wants, and for the far more precious requirements of their souls. The aged are a special object of our care, and when we find any of them in the villages near us, we endeavour, by simply giving them their daily bread, to draw them towards us. As these aged people are only a useless burden, their relatives let them come to us without opposition.

' Quite recently, a poor old negress, living at some days' travelling distance from the mission, having heard

of the care we take of old persons like herself, and com-
paring their lot to her own miserable existence, made
up her mind to come to us also. Under the care of
another good old woman, she soon recovered from the
fatigue of her journey; she was happy, she said, and
wished to die near the missioners, in the house of
their children. But alas! it was not to be so, and her
happiness was not to last long, for her owners, hearing
that she had taken refuge with us, came to claim her
and to take her away. They cared little for this poor
creature, but they wanted compensation for what they
said was their loss. Some goods were offered them,
but their conditions were so onerous we could not come
to terms. The poor woman was therefore dragged away
forcibly and obliged to set out for her village. As her
limbs, stiff through age, did not permit her to keep up
with her owners, a man armed with a stick was stationed
behind her to force her on. A truly ferocious beast,
he did not spare the blows on the back of his victim,
and after a few minutes she stopped, her strength failing
her. We then heard the report of firearms in the
direction they had taken. The poor woman had fallen
on the path, shot through the head. Several of our
converts, suspecting the crime, rushed immediately
to the spot, but it was too late, the victim had expired,
and the murderers had escaped.

'Such, not to mention more than this one case, are
the scenes we are often obliged to witness, without
being able to prevent them, all owing to the lack of a
few yards of calico. How the heart of the missioner
bleeds at seeing these atrocities, and with what fervour,
mingled with compassion, he prays to God from the
bottom of his heart: "Thy kingdom come!"'[1]

[1] *Bulletin de la Société Anti-Eslavagiste de Paris*, October 1888, p. 17.

The condition of the captives on board the slave-vessels is notorious.

'The Egyptian Government had, it appeared, been pressed by some of the European Powers to take measures for the suppression of the slave-trade; a steamer had accordingly been ordered to capture all vessels laden with this infamous cargo. Two vessels had been seized and brought to Khartoum, containing eight hundred and fifty human beings! packed together like anchovies, the living and the dying festering together, and the dead lying beneath them. European eye-witnesses assured me that the disembarking of this frightful cargo could not be adequately described. The slaves were in a state of starvation, having had nothing to eat for several days. They were landed at Khartoum; the dead and many of the dying were tied by the ankles and dragged along the ground by donkeys in the streets. The most malignant typhus, or plague, had been engendered among this mass of filth and misery thus closely packed together.' [1]

Mr. Robson, a missionary who left Newcastle a few months ago for Eastern Africa, confirms the account of Sir S. Baker.

'Of course you all know about the blockade of the Zanzibar coast. It is stopping the slave-carrying in dhows off the coast, but not by any means stopping the slave-trade. Greater horrors are perpetrated than ever. The Arabs, not being able to get their slaves taken by sea, are driving them overland, and not one slave in ten reaches the destination. The other day, within sound of the blockading guns, I saw a slave-caravan. A few weeks ago a slave dhow was captured. On boarding, the English officers found half the slaves dead, and the others in a

[1] *The Albert Nyanza*, ii. 324.

most pitiable plight. Twenty of the children were sent to me. I could not attempt to describe their horrible condition—living skeletons, without a shred of clothing, and covered with filth and vermin. They had not tasted water for four days, and were all ill of dysentery. They were all children from six to eight years old. The older ones had not survived their cruel treatment. Since I received them one has died, and two others, I am afraid, will not recover. All the rest have gone on famously. The children have taken a violent fancy to me, and greet me with screams of delight whenever I make my appearance. They know nothing of the Swahili language, their country being Makua, opposite Mozambique. This week I have taken them into school. They seem as if they would take kindly to their work. Oh, the horrors of the slave-trade! I dare not begin a full account of it or I should weary you with horrors. I left England with my mind not fully made up as to my attitude towards it, but I have no hesitation now. We missionaries in the Sultan's dominions are supposed not to interfere with the slave-trade, but the supposition has no weight with me. I shall do everything in my power to help any slave who runs away from his tyrant.'

Can anything be imagined more heartrending than these shocking accounts, eloquent with the eloquence of truth? They are, however, the recitals of eyewitnesses of the harrowing scenes, not of the actors in them. We will now allow one of the kidnapped slaves to tell his own story.

THE SLAVE'S OWN TALE

Farraghit Emmanuel Bienno, twenty years of age, is a rescued slave, ransomed by Cardinal Lavigerie's White

Missioners, and now studying at Lille, in order to become
in his turn a priest and a missioner. We shall let him
tell his own sad tale in his own simple words.

'I was born at Kaffouan, in the Southern Soudan,
in 1869. I was two years old when my father died. I
remained in the tribe with my mother and my younger
sister. One day my mother was going with my sister,
myself, and some other inhabitants of our tribe to a
neighbouring village near Kaffouan, when we suddenly
found ourselves surrounded by Touareg merchants, who
alarmed us by showing us their daggers and sticks. A
negro who was with us unfortunately cried out for help;
he was immediately felled to the ground and killed by
one good blow of a stick. Another old negro endeavoured to defend himself, and shot at the merchants
an arrow which he carried; but it fell harmless and
only excited the rage of the Touaregs, who stabbed the
old man to death. Lastly, having slain those who cried
out and tried to make any defence, these terrible
merchants led us all off to the tribe of the Bamba. Some
Arabs bought those of us who appeared strongest. My
mother, who was considered good and fit for work, was
at once put into service. A cruel Arab tore away our
mother from us without allowing us to say good-bye.
I was left alone with my little sister; but I have often
seen her again in my dreams, and often have I cried in
awaking again. I have never heard speak of my
mother since.

'I was then about six, and my sister four. The
market over, the caravan set off to cross the desert.
Our masters were on camel-back, and we poor slaves
had to drag wearily behind on foot. The Touaregs
very rarely halted. At the halts they ate a sheep or a

kid of their flock, and threw the bones to us, as to dogs.
Those were lucky who could get any. At the end of
two days' march my little sister, worn out with the
burning and painful road over the sand, fell down quite
exhausted in the midst of the desert. I stopped beside
her, whilst the caravan went on. A Touareg saw us;
he came up and began to shout and lash us with his
whip, to make us go on. My little sister cried bitterly,
for she could not walk. Then the merchant, seeing he
could get no profit from this four-year old slave, killed
her with blows of his stick before my eyes. I saw my
little sister die! Then the Touareg threatened to kill
me at once if I did not rejoin the caravan. He kept
striking me with his stick and the whip, until I was
back in the ranks with my fellow slaves.

' After some days more, the caravan reached the end
of its journey. The Touareg merchants took us to the
Bamba. The king bought about one hundred negroes
from the caravan. Of these fifty were destined to be
burnt alive to appease " the spirit of evil " who had
sent a severe fever upon the prince. I was bought with
some others for a horse, and so became the slave of the
King of the Bamba. I remarked before his tent hundreds
of negroes' heads strung upon ropes. These were the
remains of human sacrifices offered by the king to his
gods. I was afraid, and expected every day an order
to have my head cut off for the king's pleasure. But
after some days I was sent to Timbuktu, with four or
five other negro slaves like. myself. Later on I was sold
to some Arabs. They made me suffer greatly. After the
market I had to follow, with dreadful fatigue, the caravan
into the desert. All along the road there was to be
seen nothing but dried or putrefying corpses; they
were those of slaves massacred by their masters. In our

caravan the slaves were divided into bands. We were forty or fifty negroes to each band, of every age and sex, and every tribe of Central Africa. We walked one after the other. As several slaves attempted to escape, a strong iron ring was fastened round the neck of one slave ; to this ring a smaller one was fastened, and to this a long chain fixed which bound all the negroes together, regulated their movements, and prevented their flying. As time was pressing, the masters kept beating us with thongs and whips. How sad it was to see the aged and sick! They clung in desperation to their companions in misery, and when the band halted to gain breath for a moment, there were some who remained hanging like an inert mass to the collar. Dreadful scenes marked these moments of rest. If the poor negro slave was at the end of his strength they still kept lashing him. It required a few minutes for the Arabs to unfasten the chain, but the minutes were too long for these dealers in men. What happened then? Why, they cut the negro's head off, and the band, relieved, resumed its march.

' Every change of master was for me the occasion of fresh torture. The Arab or Touareg who bought me took me after the market away from my tribe, and then, in a forest or an oasis, he had to *mark* his property to distinguish it from that of others. The first time I was sold my master, a Touareg, tied my feet and hands, and with a knife made two tattoo-marks or deep incisions on the right and left cheek. The blood flowed and I suffered very much. I was very little, only six years old. When I fell into the hands of the Arabs they used to mark their slaves in a different manner : when I least expected it an Arab took a bit of sharp marble, and with it made two deep cuts on my right cheek.

The sufferings I endured were terrible, but I had to bear them without uttering a sound. I have been sold six times, and I carry on my face fifteen deep scars, made by my masters, Touaregs and Arabs, six on the right cheek, six on the left, and three on the forehead. I belonged to Aïn Salah, and lived in a tent, because I was too small to work. Once my shackles were taken off my feet, and I was told to follow the caravan to go to Warglah, in order to be exposed for sale at the slave market. We were arranged in order of build, the strongest and stoutest in front, the little ones and the dying behind. I saw many purchasers come up and take away my companions. Nobody would have me; I was too miserable looking. But it was thanks to my sickly appearance, that the White Father, who offered to buy me from my master, got me for one hundred francs. After being ransomed I was sent to Tunis and Algiers to learn French and Italian. For some time past I have been in France.' [1]

Such is the ransomed slave's own story, perhaps the first such story that has been told so fully by one of the actual victims. What can be imagined more touching than this simple, heart-rending narrative!

We cannot here omit some portion of the eloquent speech addressed by his Eminence Cardinal Lavigerie to a meeting of the Anti-slavery Society in London on July 31, 1888, as he states with great force the existing evils.

'England [he said] has now in Africa numerous and immense domains, or vast empires they may more fitly be called, and she cannot be uninterested in the question which is for Africa one of life and death. Slavery in the

[1] *Illustrated Catholic Missions*, Feb. 1889.

proportions that it has now assumed means, in fact, the approaching destruction of the black population of the interior, with the impossibility of penetrating and civilising the heart of the country. I said a moment ago that I came here to plead the cause of the slaves ; I retract those words. That cause has already been pleaded by eloquent tongues—by David Livingstone and others ; but I come to add new facts to those offered already by your own explorers. I shall only speak of what I know through my missioners or through released slaves.

' My missioners, the White Fathers—so called on account of their habit—are established in the Sahara and upon the high table-lands of Central Africa, from the north of Nyanza to the south of Tanganyika. Eleven of them have suffered martyrdom, whilst more than fifty others have died from fatigue and hardships. Such men have the right to be heard and to be believed. Without speaking of other parts of Africa, or dwelling upon the testimony of Commander Cameron, who affirms with truth that half a million slaves at the least are sold every year in the interior of Africa, I will content myself with saying that the testimony of our missioners not only confirms but raises this estimate for those regions where they are established. They have seen with their own eyes, in the course of ten years, whole provinces absolutely depopulated by the massacres of the slave-hunters, and each day they are obliged to witness scenes which point to the rapid extinction of the race. In the last letter which I have received from Tanganyika, dated in March last, they tell me that every day they see caravans of slaves arriving, and that every day they see boats crossing the lake, loaded almost to sinking with their freight of human chattels. They tell me, particularly, of the province of Manyuema, which at the time of the death of Livingstone was the richest in ivory and population, and which the slave-hunters have now reduced to a desert, seizing the ivory, and reducing the inhabitants to slavery in order that they may carry the ivory to the coast, after which their captives would be sold. The contempt for human life engendered by such examples as these, and by the passions of the slave-hunters, is so great that you can imagine nothing more horrible. An excess of cruelty causes them to make use towards men of terms hitherto reserved for wild beasts—it is all of a piece with the custom of Central Africa; for the blacks themselves, when they have slaves, adopt the terms of the slave-hunters and call them by no other name than *my beast, my animal*.

' I have given some examples of these in a letter published a week ago in the French journals. The unfortunate people who are captured for slaves are treated like beasts—men, women, and children; listen to these words, you who are Christians, they are treated like beasts—the horror of their situation passes all imagination; they are hunted like animals, and when they are caught are compelled to bow under a yoke: their heads are forcibly thrust between the space made by a small triangular-shaped piece of bent wood attached to a long pole, and so they are driven. If this state of things continues, Africa as a nation cannot remain; these horrors are incompatible with the existence of Africa, and that country will be absolutely and irredeemably lost. Let me draw your attention to the meaning of these words. Africa is divided really into three zones. First the lowlands, along the seaboards of the Mediterranean, the Atlantic and Indian Oceans. Advancing towards the interior there is a raised plateau of about two thousand feet above the sea, and above this first plateau there is a second immense table-land, about four thousand feet high. It is there that fall every year those abundant rains which form the great lakes, and from these lakes flow the vast rivers of the Nile, the Congo, the Niger, the Zambesi, and their innumerable affluents. The nature of the soil, the heat of the sun, and the abundance of water contribute to make this country one of the richest and most beautiful in the world, truly an earthly paradise. The population also was, and in some provinces still is, very numerous and happy and peaceable. It is this population which Islam is exterminating at this moment by means of her slave-hunters, and by virtue of her doctrine that the blacks are an inferior and cursed race, whom they are at liberty to treat worse than we treat our animals. I say to you, God made the white man, God made the black man, but the devil himself made slavery.

' And now how are we to stop all these evils ? Europe has recently divided Africa, at the Congress of Berlin, where Belgium, England, France, Germany, and Portugal have demanded and acquired rights over this immense country by mutual consent. As if, however, the demon of destruction wished to hinder the happy result of resolutions taken by the Great Powers, the internal slave-trade has acquired the proportions which I have just described. For the last century Islam has seized, little by little, the third part of Africa, and has established new empires in the north. It seems as if she now, being unable to conquer the remainder, wishes to annihilate the people in an outburst of mad rage by means of her slave-hunters. But if the governments of Europe have acquired rights, they have contracted duties. The one does not go without the other, and we may call to mind the words of Montesquieu, that " among so many use-

less treaties they ought to make one of mercy and pity."
And this is why, after a time of silence, now comes the
time to speak out. Know then that for over half a
century, and whilst our gaze was fixed upon other
countries, Mohammedanism was invading, slowly and
silently, with indefatigable perseverance, one half of
Africa. In certain regions, those nearest to us, it
founded empires; the rest were secured for the further-
ance of slavery. May God preserve me from accusing,
without compulsion, any man, and especially any people.
I live, besides, in the midst of Moslems. If they do not
look upon me as their father, I ought, in my capacity of
pastor, to look upon them and love them as my children.

'But I cannot resist saying to-day that, of the errors
so fatal to Africa, the saddest is that which teaches, with
Islam, that humanity is made up of two distinct races
—one, that of believers, destined to command; the
other, that of the cursed, as they style them, destined
to serve. Now, in the latter, they consider the negroes
to constitute the lowest grade—namely, that on a par
with cattle. The negro in their estimation is, as Leo
XIII. forcibly says, a beast destined for the yoke.
Having reached by their conquests the heart of a continent peopled by negroes, the Moslems have therefore
betaken themselves to the work, which is justified by
their doctrines. By degrees slave-trading bands, formed
by them, have advanced into the interior, coming from
Morocco, from the country of the Touaregs, from Tunis
towards Timbuktu and the countries which surround
the Niger, from Egypt and Zanzibar towards the region
of the lakes and even beyond the Upper Congo, and
almost to the frontiers of the British possessions and of
the Cape Colonies. Everywhere they prosecute the
same impious hunts which feed their commerce. Some-

times the marauders, concealing themselves along the paths, in the forests, and in the grain fields, violently carry off the negro women and children who may pass by unattended.

' Things have reached such a pass in the vicinity of the great lakes that now (I quote the words of one of my missioners) " every woman, every child, that strays ten minutes away from their village has no certainty of ever returning to it." The impunity is absolute. No negro chief of the small independent tribes, among whom all the country is divided, has the power of repressing this violence. Whilst the slave-trading bands, composed of Arabs and half-castes, and even of coast negroes, go armed to the teeth, the savage populations of the highlands of Africa have no other weapons than stones, clubs, and, at best, darts and spears. They are, therefore, incapable of coping with the robbers who attack them, and of saving themselves. But it is not only isolated persons they attack. They organise their expeditions as if they were going to war; sometimes they proceed alone, sometimes in company with neighbouring tribes, to whom they offer a share of the pillage, and who on the morrow become the victims in their turn. Thus they fall at night on defenceless villages, setting fire to the straw huts, and firing upon every one they meet. The inhabitants try to escape, seeking safety in the woods, in the heart of impenetrable thickets, in the dry beds of rivers, in the tall grass of the valleys. They are pursued. The aged, the men who offer resistance, all who cannot be sold in the markets of the interior, are killed; the women and children are seized.

' But I have already described these horrors. I am tired of trying to find new epithets for them. Listen to this sad description of the caravans which carry off the slaves. All that are captured—men, women, and children— are hurried off to some market in the interior. Then commences for them a series of unspeakable miseries. The slaves are on foot. The men who appear the strongest, and whose escape is to be feared, have their hands tied (and sometimes their feet) in such a fashion that moving becomes a torture to them; and on their necks are placed yokes, which attach several of them together. They march all day; at night, when they stop to rest, a few handfuls of raw "sorgho" are distributed among the captives. This is all their food. Next morning they must start again. But after the first day or two the fatigue, the sufferings, and the privations have weakened a great many. The women and the aged are the first to halt. Then, in order to strike terror into this miserable mass of human beings, their conductors, armed with a wooden bar to economise powder, approach those who appear to be the most exhausted, and deal them a terrible blow on the nape of the neck. The unfortunate victims utter a cry, and fall to the ground in the convulsions of death. The terrified troop immediately resumes its march. Terror has imbued even the weakest with new strength. Each time some one breaks down the same horrible scene is repeated. At night, on arriving at their halting-place, after the first days of such a life, a not less frightful scene awaits them. The traffickers in human flesh have acquired by experience a knowledge of how much their victims can endure. A glance shows them those who will soon sink from weariness; then, to economise the scanty food which they distribute, they pass behind these wretched beings and fell them with a single blow. Their corpses remain where they fall, when they are not suspended on

the branches of the neighbouring trees ; and it is close
to them that their companions are obliged to eat and
sleep as well as they can.

'Among the young negroes snatched by us from this
hell and restored to liberty there are some who, long
afterwards, wake up every night shrieking fearfully.
They behold again, in their dreams, the abominable
and bloody scenes which they have witnessed. In this
manner the weary tramp continues—sometimes for
months, when the caravan comes from a distance.
Their number diminishes daily. If, goaded by their
cruel sufferings, some attempt to rebel or to escape,
their fierce masters cut them down with their swords,
and leave them as they lie along the road, attached to
one another by their yokes. Therefore it has been
truly said that, if a traveller lost the way leading from
equatorial Africa to the towns where slaves are sold,
he could easily find it again by the skeletons of the
negroes with which it is strewed.

' Is this to be allowed to continue ? To you, ladies,
I address myself especially ; you see how it is the
women who are treated with the chiefest indignities.
In favour of these women, then, I ask you, their sisters,
to plead to your husbands and your brothers ; do not
allow them to weary of the cause. Rouse them to a
fervour which will never sleep before this traffic has
been abolished. But though I appeal to the Christian
charity of all, though I ask for your pity and
compassion for the black slaves, remember this —
charity is much, compassion is much, but *force is
absolutely necessary.* Nor can the opposition be successful merely by hindering the transport of slaves into
Asia by means of cruisers ; it is necessary to strike the
evil at its root, and to destroy the markets of the

interior, or to render them useless by establishing—as your great Gordon wished to do for the basin of the Nile—barriers against slavery composed of natives, led and instructed by Europeans, in order to supplement the maritime barriers formed by your cruisers.

'Let Christians, then, band together. I speak of Christians worthy of the name, for it is necessary to have clean and honest hands for such an enterprise, and not the red hands of pirates, like those which formerly devastated America. We want men who will give all their energy, all their love, and all their life to this object—men like your own Stanley, men like the great Emin Pasha. Already something has been done. I speak of a man, a Frenchman, a Pontifical Zouave, who with three hundred men alone is guarding and protecting villages from this abominable pest. That man is Joubert. We do not want enormous armies. The negroes ought, in reality, to afford the means for their own regeneration. They can, if they are armed and properly led; as we witness at this moment in the case of that heroic man Emin Pasha, who, for more than ten years, has, by the aid of his native troops, kept the whole of his great equatorial province free from the ravages of the slave-hunters. The success of his example might well stimulate similar action in other parts of Africa.

'But what we want is energy, life, and devotion to the cause. This is what civilised governments ought to give to the cause; but if they cannot give this, if their preoccupations are too great—I am no politician, I do not wish to encourage complications—why then, we will appeal to the people. A crusade is to be preached, and the people should know their duty. Something has been done already, but more is needed.

Something must be done for the negroes whom we protect. I myself have brought up young negroes from the interior, and have had them educated as doctors that they may practise the beneficent art of healing among their own people. The first three of these native black doctors set out from Malta for the Great Lakes, on July 18, in one of the steamers of the British India Company. I am happy in being thus able to-day publicly to tender my thanks to the English people for the aid given me in this work.

'And now it is necessary to draw a practical conclusion from this discourse. What I ask from this great assembly, without distinction of persons—for however much some of us may be divided on some subjects we are all of one accord when it becomes a matter of liberty, of humanity, of justice—is that it should, according to the individual strength of each one, join in a generous agitation in favour of a cause so deserving of our sympathy. We need support also of a pecuniary kind for our little army : heroes we may have, and that is much, but heroes must live ; I know that heroes must eat, and heroes must drink, and means sometimes not only support, but make heroes. For this object I appeal to your English generosity, and I entreat you all to join me in the utterance of a loud cry to God first of all, and then to all Christian people. "God save Africa !" May God save her by exciting for her defence men animated by charity and Christian courage ! Where can I better hope to have this prayer heard than in a great assembly like this, where we meet under the auspices of the admirable society founded to fight against slavery and the slave-trade more than half a century ago, supported by the early

liberators, Thomas Clarkson, Sir Fowell Buxton, Joseph
Sturge, and other men of noble character.

'Now, after having carried on the combat, oftentimes to victory, and after having witnessed in later
days, not only the entire extinction of the slave-trade
across the Atlantic, but also the abolition of slavery
itself in Cuba and Brazil, the Anti-slavery Society finds
itself pledged to carry on the gigantic task for the suppression of Mohammedan slavery, which would give the
death-blow to the internal slave-traffic in Africa; and
for this object I appeal to you—for humanity, for your
brethren, for charity, for mercy—to make a response
to my prayer.'

It has already been remarked that it is of the
slave-hunting and slave-trade as carried on by the
Moslems that Cardinal Lavigerie has almost exclusively
spoken.   It is perhaps natural that he should do so,
since he has been living in the midst of Mohammedans
in the North of Africa, and sees how the followers of the
Prophet are advancing rapidly southwards, offering to
the heathen tribes the fatal choice between conversion
to their creed and the miseries of slavery. The domestic
slavery of Africa, which carries with it even worse
evils than exist elsewhere, is thus referred to by the late
Sir James Marshall, who lately took part, while on an
official visit to the Niger, in an actual crusade against
it :—

'It must be borne in mind that there is a horrible
form of slavery prevalent throughout the whole of the
Dark Continent which is not under European control.
This is the slavery which every tribe is ready and
anxious to practise upon other tribes. The very people
who are constantly captured and carried off by the more
powerful Arab tribes are themselves everywhere ad-

dicted to the practice of doing the same to any neighbours they can conquer, and every powerful tribe, like
that of Dahomey, keeps up its prestige by regular raids
upon other and weaker tribes, for the sole purpose
of capturing slaves. And these persons so caught are
not merely subject to the loss of freedom by becoming
the slaves of their conquerors; they also supply the
victims for the ceaseless innumerable murders which
the devilish religion of the heathen negroes demands
for the rites which we know under the name of human
sacrifices. This religion varies in different localities so
far as the names and legends of the evil spirits which
are worshipped are concerned; but there is a horrible
catholicity and unity in the belief which everywhere
prevails, that after death the free man remains free,
and that the slave remains a slave in the service of the
spirit of whatever master he belongs to. It therefore
follows that the free man after death requires slaves in
accordance with his rank and wealth when alive, and
that slaves are sent to him by his family and dependants
as an attention and mark of respect which would bring
down serious punishment and calamity if neglected.
The people of Africa have to be delivered from themselves and from the cruel, bloody tyranny of their own
chiefs and heathen priests, as well as from the attacks
of the slave-hunting Arabs.'[1]

Fetichism of the grossest kind is the religion which
prevails among the numberless tribes of Western Africa,
a religion deemed by many travellers unworthy of the
name, since it is a cultus of cruelty and vice, a barbarous worship, which, instead of elevating, serves only
to debase. The divinities are examples of crime; their
adorers invest them with the tastes, the weaknesses,

[1] *The Missionary Crusade in Africa*, p. 10.

the wants, the vices of humanity; there are adulterous and wicked gods, drunkards, liars, and thieves. There is no crime, debauch, or act of cruelty which the history of the negro's gods and goddesses does not contain.

'It is in Dahomey that fetichism most closely approaches idolatry, as the unsubstantial shadows and apocryphal demons, the good and evil genii of woods and deserts, who protect or persecute mankind, are on the Slave Coast replaced by tangible objects. By the roadside grotesque clay images, roughly fashioned into the human shape in a crouching position, may be seen under a roof of palm leaves; this is Elegba, the genius who urges men to sin, the most dreaded and most wicked of evil spirits. Elegba is not always satisfied with the animals sacrificed to him, but must be appeased with human blood. In wars and public calamities human victims alone propitiate the angry gods.

'Human sacrifices are usually offered in the night. No one is allowed to leave his dwelling. "The night is bad," the blacks say; the sound of the drum and the dismal chant of the fetich-priests alone indicate that human blood is to be shed. The victim is gagged, and the head is cut off so as to allow the blood to stream over the idol; then the body is thrown into a ditch or thicket, or else suspended to a tree in front of the fetich, where it is left to decay. On one occasion a prince, being ill, consulted the fetich-man as to the cause of his illness; the answer given was that it arose from the anger of a spirit, and would not cease until some human victims were immolated. This was accordingly done.

'The negro believes that the dead lead an existence very similar to their past life, except that it is much sadder. Those who were slaves in this world remain slaves in the next; those who are kings here are also

kings hereafter; they have the same pleasures, the same
habits, the same needs they had whilst living. Hence
the kings, chiefs, and persons of wealth must be furnished with a retinue of women and of slaves to keep up
the dignity of their position, and secure to them the
comforts suitable to their rank, and they become enraged
with the living if they do not liberally supply their
wants and desires. Victims are therefore sacrificed
beside the graves of chiefs, a considerable number of
women and slaves being massacred that they may
accompany the dead, and minister to him in another
world; and from time to time messengers are sent to
acquaint the dead with what takes place on the earth.

'These ideas render necessary slave-raids and continual wars in order to procure a supply of victims.
Dahomey has acquired a sad notoriety from the slight
value there attached to human life.

'One day the king of Dahomey had thus despatched
several couriers to his predecessors, when he remembered some insignificant detail of his commission
that had escaped his mind. An old woman was passing,
carrying on her head a pitcher of water. The king
called her, and gave her his message. The poor wretch,
trembling all over, begged and implored mercy.

'"I have done nothing wrong," she said.

'"I know that," replied the king, "but I am sending
you to my father; go at once." Resistance was in vain;
the poor creature knelt down, and the executioner cut
off her head.'[1]

[1] *Fetichism and Fetich-worshippers*, p. 98.

CHAPTER II

MOHAMMEDANISM AND SLAVERY

Is Mohammedanism responsible for slavery in Africa?
Many deny it altogether, and assert that it is no more
just to charge the religion of the Arabs with the
cruelty of the Arab slave-traders than it would be to
blame Christianity for the introduction of drunkenness
and moral corruption into tribes which before the
coming of the Christian Europeans were sober and
virtuous.   Others go so far as to assert that the very
institution of slavery is in no way wrapped up with
Islamism, and that the day will come when the
Mohammedan nations will suppress it throughout their
borders as Christian nations have done.   It is not a
question of religion, they say, but of advancing civilisation and wider experience.   The time has not yet come
for Egypt and the Arab settlements to substitute free
labour for slavery, any more than it had come to
Christian Italy in the early centuries after the Christian
era.   The Koran does not forbid slavery any more than
the Bible, but it inculcates gentleness and kindness to
the slave.   The laws and customs handed down by the
Prophet tend to raise gradually the position of slaves,
and to lead ultimately to their liberation from bondage.

This question is a very important one in its bearing
on African slavery.   It is but part of a wider question—
viz. the influence of Mohammedanism on uncivilised

nations, and its attitude to the religion of Christ. On this wider question there is once more a great divergence of opinion.

The opinion which is traditional among Christians looks upon the religion of the Prophet as the most deadly foe of Christianity, as having fallen like a blight on a large portion of mankind, who, but for it, would have been Christians; and as having substituted for the continuous progress which is the effect of Christianity, and the civilisation it necessarily brings with it, a progress which goes up to a certain point and then stops short and refuses to go further. It moreover prevents any advance to higher things. Its civilisation is but a spurious article, a worthless counterfeit of Christian and European civilisation. Not so many moderns, who represent Islamism as paving the way for Christianity, as an intermediate and almost indispensable stage in the road from barbarism to the higher civilisation, ι. halting-place midway between paganism and the religion of Christ, whence it is far easier to raise the negro to a higher belief than from the degradation and darkness of fetichism and devil-worship and the grosser forms of idolatry. They welcome the conquest of large districts of Central Africa by Mohammedan invaders as not only beneficial in itself, but useful in preparing the way for their conversion to Christianity.

We will banish for the moment the Arab slave-traders whose ill name might prejudice our impartial consideration of the question, and ask ourselves which of the two opinions just put forward is the true one. Does Islamism lead up to Christianity and to the higher civilisation, or does it wherever it prevails present an insuperable bar to its advance?

One thing is certain, that in the continent of Africa,

Moslemism is at the present time steadily advancing. Certain districts on the west coast may have been parcelled out among Christian nations, but the apportionment is little more than nominal, and a Christian protectorate, even where it is permanent and effective, does not mean as a matter of course the spread of Christianity among the native inhabitants. In the heart of the country it is Moslemism, not Christianity, which everywhere is gaining converts and subduing whole tribes to its sway. 'It counts in its ranks,' says Mr. Blyden, ' the most energetic and enterprising tribes. It claims as its adherents the only people who have any form of civil polity or bond of social organisation. It has built and occupies the largest cities in the heart of the continent. Its laws regulate the most powerful kingdoms. It produces and controls the most valuable commerce between Africa and foreign countries ; it is daily gaining converts from the ranks of paganism ; and it commands respect among all Africans wherever it is known, even where the people have not submitted to the sway of the Koran.' [1]

In all human probability Africa is more likely to become a Mohammedan than a Christian continent. Are we to rejoice in its progress or to lament it, on the understanding that it occupies a place which at present Christianity is not prepared to fill, and that the tribes that accept its sway would remain, at least for years to come, in barbarism and for the most part pagans ?

It is undeniable that Islamism is in many respects an advance on the forms of religion, if religion it can be called, that are prevalent in Africa. The native religions are in general some form of devil-worship or fetichism. Travellers tell us that many of them have

[1] Blyden, *Christianity, Islam, and the Negro Race*, p. 7.

no idea of a Supreme Being, and that their only idea is of a malignant spirit who has to be propitiated by human sacrifices or driven away by the noise of tom-toms. Where Islamism prevails the moral atmosphere is entirely different. The mosque takes the place of the hut of the fetich-man, and the prayer five times a day of the gross dances and unwholesome excitement of pagan festivals. Even where the religion of the Koran has not yet taken the place of paganism the Mussulman teacher is looked upon as a superior being, and the general moral tone of the pagan village seems to be raised by his presence. He avails himself of the prevalent customs of the pagans and gradually moulds them into something consistent with Moslemism without in any way compromising his faith by any admixture of paganism in the religion which he teaches them. His charms, consisting of passages from the Koran, appeal to African superstition and are highly esteemed by the natives. His frequent ablutions and silent prayers proclaim him to be a great fetich-man. His very Moslem rosaries are fascinating to the savage mind. He is free from the prejudices of race which render it difficult for the European to hold free intercourse with the negro. The Mohammedan missionary travels about with a freedom altogether unknown to the European. It is quite a mistake to suppose that the conversion of the negro tribes is effected merely by force; on the contrary, the work has been done, and is being done, at least in a great degree, by peaceable words, by the influence of a higher civilisation. It is also a great mistake to suppose that Arabs in general are regarded all over Africa as enemies by the native tribes. In some districts where the traders make their cruel raids it is so, but the Arabs are in many parts looked upon as their patrons and protectors. The Arab missionary comes as a man of peace and settles down in a native village as the friend of the inhabitants. His converts are won by his personal influence and the preaching of the doctrines of the Koran. His personal superiority to the natives soon gives him authority among them. He is the instructor of their children, their counsellor in difficulties, and the savage mind recognises in him one who can avert misfortune and set at defiance the evil eye that they dread, and the evil spirit which is too often their only idea of a Deity. The Mohammedan missionary is also in many cases the physician of the village as well. 'Although the practice of medicine,' writes Captain Allen in his 'Niger Expedition,'[1] 'is in the lowest state of degradation, clouded with all possible superstitions, yet its professors, the mallams, are well provided for, and are even looked up to. The mallams profess to teach Mohammedanism and to practise the healing art. Charms in the form of scraps from the Koran are resorted to in all cases of difficulty. It is through the mallams that I entertain strong hopes of extending vaccination throughout Africa, at all events along the banks of the Niger.'

As the educator of youth the Arab has unlimited opportunities of proselytism. He teaches the boys of the village verses of the Koran, and ties round their necks and wrists slips of paper with the words from the Koran written on them. Mr. Blyden describes the careful training in the sacred books imparted by these Moslem missionaries :—

'The boys under their instruction are first taught the letters and vowel marks ; then they are taught to read the text, without receiving any insight into its

[1] Vol. ii. p. 120.

meaning. When they can read fluently they are taught
the meaning of the words, which they commit carefully
to memory ; after which they are instructed in what
they call the "jalaleyn," a running commentary on the
Koran. While learning the jalaleyn, they have side
studies assigned them in Arabic manuscripts, containing
the mystical traditions, the acts of Mohammed, the duties
of fasting, prayer, alms, corporal purification, &c.'[1]

The villages which adopted the Mussulman creed
under influences like these soon experienced the advantages of their new religion. It was a new power in
their midst, and their neighbours became conscious of
their superiority. The Mussulman villages unite together by reason of the new tie of their common faith
in offensive and defensive alliance. They are able to
defeat the attacks of their pagan foes, and to defend
themselves against the pagan slave-hunters. Their
comparative freedom from the demoralising effect of
the hostile incursions which in former times had destroyed their villages, massacred the men, and carried
off the women and children, begins to manifest its
happy effects in a steady advance in industry and
civilisation. In this way a number of large towns,
the names of which are, however, scarcely known to
Europeans, Kano, Sokoto, Misada, &c., have sprung up
in Central Africa.

It is partly by these means and partly by the sword
that Mohammedanism has won for itself the Western
Soudan, and the whole region which goes by the name of
Nigritia. Mr. Blyden tells us that ' after the first conquest of the Moslems in Northern Africa, their religion
advanced southward into the continent, not by arms,
but by schools and books and mosques, by trade and

---

[1] *Christianity, Islam, and the Negro Race*, p. 205.

intermarriage.' This statement seems to be rather more favourable to the peaceful view of Moslem conquest than the facts of the case justify, but there is nevertheless no doubt that persuasion and gentle influences had a larger share than is generally supposed in the advance of Islam. But whatever be the means adopted, the existence in North Africa of more than sixty millions of Mussulman Africans at the present day is the best proof of the success of the Arabs and of the importance to the future of Africa of the power that they are likely to exert in moulding her religious and political future.

We have therefore to concede that, Christianity apart, Moslemism has hitherto exercised a certain beneficial influence over the negroes. No one can be surprised at it. A religion which teaches the unity of God, the necessity of prayer, and which destroys with unsparing hand the idols of paganism, must necessarily be an advance on the degraded superstition of the idolater, or the still more degraded worship of the devil himself, even though it contains elements of evil which render its permanent effect upon a nation a striking contrast to the purifying and elevating influence exercised by the religion of Jesus Christ. A false religion must always contain this double element, and it is difficult, in some cases almost impossible, to decide whether such a religion is an advantage to mankind or not. But there is a test which we can always apply to any false religion, and by means of which we can pronounce it a source of good or of evil to mankind. As we watch the gradual conquest of the world by Christianity, we find that in some countries the existing religion seems to have paved the way for Christianity, and prepared the hearts of men for its reception. When it came into contact with the teaching of Christian missionaries and apostles, all that was good in it was taken up and absorbed in the new faith, and all that was evil fell away and disappeared. Wherever this is the case, it is a strong evidence that the pre-existing elements of good were stronger than those of evil in a majority of those who lived under its sway ; or at least it had not exercised such a corrupting and debasing influence as to cause those who were its devoted adherents to reject Christianity. This is the reason why Judaism was the natural home of Christianity, and Rome, in spite of the corruptions that had overgrown its primitive belief, still had a religion which in earlier days was a rather pure form of theism, and therefore, in spite of the struggle of a degraded imperialism against Christian beliefs, they ultimately won the day in the city of the Cæsars.

To apply this to Mohammedanism. Some enthusiastic admirers of Mohammedan influence, and, strange to say, some professedly Christian missionaries, would have us believe that Moslemism is the advance guard of Christianity. A certain Mr. Gibson, rector of Trinity Church, Monrovia, in a published letter says :—

' Whatever may have been the influence of Mohammedanism on races in other parts of the world, I think here, upon the African, results will prove it to be merely preparatory to a Christian civilisation. In this country, and almost immediately in our vicinity, it has recovered millions from paganism, without, I think, having such a grasp upon the minds of the masses as to lead them obstinately to cling to it in preference to Christianity, with its superior advantages. The same feelings which led them to abandon their former religion for the Moslem will, no doubt, lead them still further, and induce them to embrace ours when properly presented. I express this opinion the more readily from several interviews I have had lately with prominent parties connected with some of these tribes.'[1]

Mr. Blyden himself seems to concur in this view, and tells us that Mohammedanism would easily be displaced by Christian influence, if Christian organisations would enter with all vigour into the field.

Now, if this is true, we ought to proceed in a very different manner in our warfare against slavery from that which we should adopt if Mohammedanism is to be regarded as an enemy.

When we look at the relations of Islamism to Christianity, wherever the two have been brought into contact, it seems strange that any Christian, conversant with the historical attitude of Mohammedanism to Christianity, can regard it with any feelings except those of hatred and abhorrence. From its earliest days it has not only stood apart from Christianity, but has been its fiercest and most successful opponent. There is something in the Crescent which seems to give it a mysterious power of resisting the influence of the Cross. It admits just enough of Christian or quasi-Christian doctrine to afford an excuse for rejecting all the essential elements of the religion of Jesus Christ. Its false Prophet takes the place of the true Prophet; its spirit of fatalism of Christian resignation. Its promise of a sensual paradise to all who die fighting against the Cross is at the same time a caricature of the promise of Heaven to the Christian martyr, and a most effectual incentive to an eternal hatred of the 'Christian dogs.' The traditional instinct of Christendom arguing an irreconcilable opposition between the kingdom of Christ

[1] *Christianity, Islam, and the Negro Race*, p. 216.

and the kingdom of the false Prophet is founded on the inner contrast which pervades the two religions. Christianity is essentially inclusive : Mohammedanism is essentially exclusive. Christianity is catholic : Mohammedanism disowns any sort of universality. Christianity regards those outside the fold as friends to be won, as it may be in heart though not in outward appearance, perhaps virtually if not consciously, servants of the same Master : Mohammedanism regards all those who do not profess the religion of the Prophet as enemies to be hated and to be forced into submission if they will not willingly submit. Christianity teaches us to conquer, nay to crucify, the flesh with its passions and concupiscences : Mohammedanism flatters the sensual appetite ; its ideal life not only does not exclude, but countenances and approves a free indulgence.

Other religions have a sort of instinctive admiration for the religion of Jesus Christ ; Mohammedanism alone treats it with the utmost contempt and looks down upon the Christian as an inferior being from the very fact of his Christianity. Mohammedanism, so far from being a stepping-stone to Christianity or a stage on the journey from barbarism to Christian civilisation, is the most dangerous rival that Christianity ever encountered, and, what is more, the most dangerous foe of all true civilisation. It has in it the power of raising those who are its adherents up to a certain point, and there it not only stops short, but blights any further power of growth. Its undoubted energy and power of conquest are but a passing phase ; when the struggle is over and the battle has been won, Islamism seems to have exhausted its energy. The fanatical zeal which swept all before it sinks into the feeble apathy of a civilisation half civilised, half barbarous. The devoted courage which led the soldiers of the Prophet to show a reckless daring which seemed to promise great things subsides into a stolid indifferentism paralysing effort, and apparently unable to make any further exertion.

Cardinal Newman has pointed out, in his essay on the Turks, the features of Mohammedanism which render progress beyond a certain point absolutely impossible. The fine arts wither wherever the religion of the Prophet prevails; painting and sculpture are impossible under a system that absolutely forbids any representation of the human form, or indeed of any natural object. Mohammedans carry out the Jewish injunction against the making of graven images with a literal exactness which the most extreme of Puritans would disown, and add to it a fierce denunciation of any sort of representation of any living thing. Hence the ideal faculty is starved. Instead of leading men on to a love of things unseen through the medium of what appeals to sense, Mohammedanism separates the two. Things visible cease to be employed as a means of rising to the invisible. Hence follows not only a perpetual barbarism, but the degradation and coarse sensuality which are the law of all countries where Moslemism has long prevailed. It is the glory of Christianity that it makes the whole world a means of drawing nearer to God. Ever since God Himself appeared in human form and had a human Mother, the curse has passed away from the sensible world, and it is only by its misuse that it drags men down instead of raising them. Christianity not only develops art out of nature; out of a love of art it develops a love and appreciation of religion. Destroy art, and religion loses its hold over man's lower nature and over sense.

A civilisation that despises art is but a veiled barbarism; a religion which forbids the use of art in its
service can never subdue the lower nature and the
faculties of sense to the service of God. Hence the
gross immorality of Turkey and Egypt. The religion
of Mohammed shows itself a sensual religion from the
mere fact of its utter neglect of art. The highest
forms of art are possible only to those who have before
them the pure models which derive their beauty from
their virginal modesty and the divine grace that mani-
fests itself in feature and expression. Where the fine
arts decay morality necessarily decays with them:
where they are practically forbidden, there must
always be found a low morality and a blighted
civilisation.

It may be true that the glories of Italian art
would be thrown away upon the negro, and that he
has no æsthetic perception capable of appreciating a
high type of artistic excellence. But this is no reason
for throwing away one of the most important instruments for raising him in the moral order, or for
neglecting what is an indispensable element in any
religious teaching that is to influence his life, or in any
permanent form of progressive civilisation. It is
because his higher faculties have been so little trained
that it is the more necessary to appeal to him through
the lower.

We must teach him religion and civilisation alike by
external symbols attractive to his eye, by bright colours
and pictures, which are sufficiently simple to make
themselves understood to his untrained intelligence.
The representations employed may be rude and not
such as would accord with European taste; but in the
earliest Christian paintings there was the same primitive

roughness. Some representation the negro must have, if things invisible are to be a reality to him and to exercise a regenerating power, winning him from darkness and degradation and leading him on to the light of Christian and progressive civilisation. Islamism, in denying him this, may raise him to the low level that it has itself attained, but it will, after this point is reached, not only be a complete bar to further progress, but model him in the same corruption and apathy and hopeless debility that gradually settles down on all Mussulman lands.

The neglect of the fine arts is not the only symptom of Moslem barbarism ; the nature of the Koran and the fixity of its code of laws is another necessary bar to any continuous advance in social and moral development. In this respect the Koran is a complete contrast to the Bible. Instead of laying down principles of morality which are in themselves unalterable, but are capable of indefinite modification according to time and place and circumstance, it leaves no room for the mental activity of successive generations to mould it to the existing state of things. Its laws are fixed with an unbending rigour which leaves no room for the legitimate play of human intelligence. It has none of the flexibility of Christian ethics, none of their power of adaptation. Hence Islamism has the very effect on mental and moral development that would be attributed in the physical order to some food that stimulated the growth of children until they were half grown, but thenceforward not only ceased to nourish them but positively stunted their bodies for the rest of their life on account of its being unable to assimilate itself to the more advanced digestion. It never has exhibited, and never can exhibit, a full-grown man in the moral or mental order :

all are pigmies as compared even with the ordinary Christian type. It is a system which, to quote Cardinal Newman's words, ' closes up the possible openings and occasions of internal energy and self-education.' This policy has its root in the nature of the teaching of the Koran just as all Christian progress is founded on the lessons taught in Holy Scripture.

At the same time Islamism, with its semi-barbarism and fatal inactivity, when its period of conquest is over, is quite incapable of learning any lessons from others. It is an exclusive religion, and one, too, which is intensely narrow and blind in its exclusiveness. The idea of its being a stepping-stone to Christianity would be as repulsive to the believer in the religion taught by Mohammed as it is false in itself. The Moslem regards himself as unspeakably superior to all others, and would disdain to learn from them any lesson in matters either secular or religious. Then too it has none of the assimilating power of Christianity which attracts to itself all that is good in art or science from those with-out its fold, acknowledging their superiority wherever such superiority exists, and learning of them the lessons which, outside of its own province, they are continually able to teach. The Christian stands aloof from none, despises none, judges none inferior to himself. He regards his faith indeed as immeasurably superior to all other forms of religion, but in matters which do not concern the faith he is ready to learn from all. He is essentially a man of wide sympathies and universal charity. But the Mohammedan is essentially narrow and national ; he despises and loathes the Christian, and, instead of regarding him as a wanderer to be brought into the true fold, he looks upon him as an enemy to be resisted with implacable hostility. It seems strange that any one who is acquainted with the history of the Moors in Spain can ever believe that the natives of Africa are to find in Islamism a halfway house on the road to Christianity. Any one who maintains such a theory must have a very limited knowledge either of one religion or the other. Between the religion of Mohammed and the religion of Jesus Christ there always has been and always will be war to the death.

The religion of Mohammed is the most powerful, the most determined, the most successful enemy that the religion of Christ has encountered. The one is narrow, exclusive, degrading to soul and body; it crushes out all human energy when it has had time to develop its true character, and effectually bars the road to exalted virtue or heroic sanctity. The other is liberal, inclusive, exalting; it fosters all that is good in human nature, and the more perfectly it is carried out, the higher does it raise both nation and individual; there is no height of perfection, no degree of holiness to which those may not aspire who are obedient to its divine counsels. The one may mitigate the condition of slaves, but at the same time slavery is a necessary element in it wherever it prevails; it mitigates the condition of the slave only in order to perpetuate his slavery: the other first mitigates the condition of the slave, then gradually emancipates him from his slavery until he is a slave no longer, but a free man in Christ Jesus. In dealing with the question of slavery there can be no truce between Christianity and Islamism in countries where Islamism has established its withering influence. The peaceful influence of the Christian missionary may win for slaves their liberty; but where the false Prophet holds sway, moral pressure or physical force, the prevailing power of a superior civilisation and a mightier nation, or else the more violent weapons of material force, will alone induce the Mussulman to give liberty to the captive, and to cease to enslave the barbarous tribes who may minister to his greed of gold and to the indolence and luxury of the debased civilisation of the East.

CHAPTER III

ATTEMPTS TO SUPPRESS SLAVERY

THE mission of which Sir Samuel Baker gives a graphic account in his 'Ismailia' is one which was the first serious effort to put a stop to the slave-trade by an expedition up the country. Hitherto all that had been done was an attempt to blockade the coast and prevent the export of slaves. In this way English cruisers had effected an amount of good for which the whole civilised world has reason to be grateful. But their work was very limited. It was not difficult to run the blockade, and the enormous profit made it worth while to incur a little risk. Even if they could have prevented a single slaver from crossing the sea, they would not have done much towards stopping the traffic ; it was like healing the surface of a cancer the roots of which ran far down into the system. The real work had to be done in the interior of Africa, the disease reached the very heart of the country. Sir Samuel Baker's expedition was an attempt to suppress the slave-trade on the White Nile and the adjoining countries. No limits were assigned to his operations, but from the very nature of things he could not attempt to embrace the whole African continent. It was the stream of emigration which passed from the neighbourhood of the Great Lakes by way of Darfur and Kordofan overland and by water down the White Nile that he undertook to encounter. He started with every advantage, with full powers from the Khedive, and with the moral support of the English Government. His object was to establish a chain of military stations and commercial depôts distant at intervals of three days' march, throughout Central Africa, with Gondokoro as the basis of operations. He had supreme authority, the power of life and death, not only over all members of the expedition, but over all the countries belonging to the Nile basin south of Gondokoro. He hoped to found a new civilisation, to save the population who were being destroyed in the most fertile regions of Central Africa, and to establish a legitimate trade where before shameless plundering, murder, rapine, pillage, had been the methods generally employed, and so (to quote his own words) 'to open the road to a great future where the past had all been darkness and the present mere reckless spoliation.' [1]

There seems little doubt that the Khedive was in earnest in this wish to see his magnificent scheme honestly carried out, but the officials in high quarters had no intention of fulfilling their sovereign's desire. From the first, passive opposition met the enterprise at every step. Judicious procrastination was successful in postponing the start for months, and when the vessels were secured and Sir Samuel Baker was ready to start from Khartoum with the troops furnished to him by the Sultan, and the boats he had with difficulty purchased to convey them, there were no sailors to be had, as the slave-traders had persuaded them to keep out of the way in order that they might not have to take part in the expedition. When at last he succeeded in manning the boats, it was with unwilling crews composed of the worst possible materials. Most of our

[1] *Ismailia*, i. 8.

readers will have read the story of the expedition and its failure; it was quite impossible to succeed where all in authority were determined that it should fail. Even at Fashoda, which one would have thought was within reach of the Central Government, Sir Samuel Baker found the local governor engaged in a razzia on the Shillooks and kidnapping their wives and children to sell to the slave-traders. This very man had only a few weeks before assured Sir S. Baker that the slave-trade was entirely suppressed in that part of the country, and that no trader would venture to pass his station, while all the time he was levying a regular toll on all the slaves who were brought down the river, and was doing his best to encourage the trade which brought him in a large personal revenue.

The way in which the trade was carried on even at the time that Sir Samuel Baker was encamped on the river, will be best understood from his account of his capture of one of these vessels on its way down the White Nile from Fashoda to Khartoum. He had established a military station at Tewfikugah, a little below Fashoda, and kept a sharp look-out for all suspicious craft that should pass that way.

On the 10th of May a strange sail was reported to him. As it neared the station he sent out a boat ordering it to halt, and instructed his aide-de-camp, Colonel Abd-el-Kader, to search the vessel. The captain and agent were astonished at his considering the search necessary. The vessel had on board a quantity of corn stowed in the hold for the crew and soldiers, and a cargo of ivory beneath the corn. There was not a person on board besides the crew and soldiers. Such was the story of the officials. The real state of things Sir Samuel Baker shall tell in his own words.

' Colonel Abd-el-Kader was an excellent officer ; he was one of the exceptions who took a great interest in the expedition, and he always served me faithfully. He was a fine powerful man, upwards of six feet high, and not only active, but extremely determined. He was generally called " the Englishman " by his brother officers as a bitter compliment reflecting on his debased taste for Christian society. This officer was not the man to neglect a search because the agent of Kutchuk Ali protested his innocence, and exhibited the apparently naked character of his vessel. She appeared suspiciously full of corn for a boat homeward bound. There was an awkward smell about the closely boarded forecastle which resembled that of unwashed negroes. Abd-el-Kader drew a steel ram-rod from a soldier's rifle, and probed sharply through the corn.

' A smothered cry from beneath, and a wriggling among the corn, was succeeded by a woolly head, as the strong Abd-el-Kader, having thrust his long arm into the grain, dragged forth by the wrist a negro woman. The corn was at once removed; the planks which boarded up the forecastle and the stern were broken down, and there was a mass of humanity exposed—boys, girls, and women, closely packed like herrings in a barrel, who under the fear of threats had remained perfectly silent until thus discovered. The sail attached to the mainyard of the vessel appeared full and heavy in the lower part; this was examined, and upon unpacking, it yielded a young woman who had thus been sewn up to avoid discovery.

' The case was immediately reported to me. I at once ordered the vessel to be unloaded. We discovered one hundred and fifty slaves stowed away in a most inconceivably small area. The stench was horrible when they began to move. Many were in irons; these were quickly released by the blacksmiths to the astonishment of the captives, who did not appear to understand the proceeding.

'I ordered the rakul, and the reis or captain of the vessel, to be put in irons. The slaves began to comprehend that their captors were now captives. They now began to speak, and many declared that the greater portion of the men of their villages had been killed by the slave-hunters.'[1]

It was no easy matter in this and similar cases to know what to do with the liberated slaves. They had been so often deceived that they could not understand the truth, and, having been accustomed to brutality, kindness was a thing quite incomprehensible, and anything like gratitude was out of the question. Some of the women freed on the occasion just mentioned he had married to the Egyptian soldiers serving under him, but on the first convenient opportunity they ran away, not only with the clothes provided for them by the government, but with whatever they could lay hands upon of the soldiers' kit. There was also considerable difficulty in keeping the soldiers in order; they soon got heartily tired of the expedition and some of them deserted. The tribes, moreover, instead of welcoming them as deliverers, were in many cases hostile; what was worst of all, the officers of the expedition actually took advantage of it to purchase slaves, and when they arrived at Gondokoro, Sir Samuel Baker discovered that one hundred and twenty-six of these slaves had been added to their numbers, and this at a time when food was scarce, and when they were surrounded by enemies. To interfere with the slaves that the officers had before

[1] *Ismailia,* i. 127–8.

starting on the expedition was found to be quite impossible ; the occasional interference of Sir S. Baker to prevent cruelty was very unpopular with the forces. During his absence from Gondokoro two-thirds of his followers returned to Khartoum, and the reinforcements sent occupied thirteen months on the journey, and arrived just as the expedition came to an end.

The fact which gradually dawned on him was that the White Nile was simply rented by the slave-traders, and, though the intentions of the Khedive may have been honest enough, yet those of the Egyptian Government, and of almost all the high officials, were simply to satisfy England by allowing the expedition, and to render it nugatory by such passive and active opposition as would be certain to prevent its producing any permanent effects. The governor-general of the Soudan tolerated and secretly connived at the existing state of things, and Baker's rank and title of governor-general of Central Africa weakened his authority and did not render his position very acceptable. Between the governor of the Soudan and the Sheik Achmet a contract [1] had been entered into which was very seriously imperilled by the expedition of Sir Samuel Baker. The establishment of the station on the White Nile was naturally objected to by him as putting an end to the razzias by which the traders had secured the slaves and cattle that they exchanged for ivory. His objection was not unreasonable, and an arrangement was made in favour of his existing interests. The agent of Achmet was his son-in-law, one Abou Saood, who, like a prudent man, pretended to enter into the views of Sir Samuel Baker, vowed fidelity to him, and contracted for the supply of food to his troops and for the transport of stores, ammunition, &c.

[1] *Ismailia,* i. 156.

This man seems to have been determined from the first that the expedition should fail, or at all events that he would somehow or other turn it to his own profit. If it gave him opportunities for larger profits and a more extended system of plunder, well and good ; if not, he would watch carefully for every opportunity of bringing it to nothing. He was a great friend of the colonel who commanded Baker's troops, and did his best to sow disaffection. Unfortunately, the only opportunity he gave of sending him prisoner to Cairo was lost. On after-reflection Sir Samuel Baker regrets the mistake he made on the side of leniency. ' I should have arrested him,' he says, ' and transported him to Khartoum, when he first arrived at Gondokoro with the cattle stolen from the Shir.' [1] But it would have been a risky piece of justice on account of his friendship with the officers of the expedition and the two thousand five hundred armed men that he had under his command. As time wore on his treachery became more evident, and we find Baker writing in August 1872, not long before his term of service came to an end, ' I ought to hang Abou Saood, but much diplomacy is necessary,' and he came to the conclusion that it would be unwise to get rid of the slave-hunters by physical force, as it would have left his little army, which had dwindled down to one hundred and forty-six men, exposed to considerable danger from the armed natives. Baker afterwards regretted his ill-timed clemency and wished he had run the risk. After swearing fidelity to him, Abou Saood did his best to ruin him at Cairo by spreading about every sort of false report. He represented that his trade had been spoilt by the Englishman's interference, and appealed for protection to the Cairo Government. He was so far success-

---

[1] *Ismailia*, ii. 121.

ful that when Baker's expedition was closed, and he had established at Fatiko a military port which he hoped would be the nucleus of an effective chain of similar stations, it was found that Abou Saood had succeeded in rendering all his work nugatory. He learned from one of Abou Saood's *employés* on his way back to Khartoum, that, during his absence, several cargoes of slaves had passed the government station at Fashoda, and that at that very moment three vessels with seven hundred slaves on board, belonging to Abou Saood, were on their way south to a station below Khartoum, whence they were to march overland and finally to pass to the Red Sea and other markets. On this occasion Sir S. Baker writes :—

'I was most thoroughly disgusted and sick at heart, after all the trouble and difficulties that we had gone through for the suppression of the slave-trade. There could be no question of the fact that Abou Saood, the great slave-hunter of the White Nile, was supported by some high authority behind the scenes upon whom he could depend for protection. This was apparently the last act of the drama in which the villain of the piece could mock and scoff at justice, and ridicule every effort I had made to suppress the slave-trade. His vessels were actually sailing in triumph and defiance before the wind, with flags flying the crescent and the star above a horrible cargo of pest-smitten humanity, in open contempt for my authority. . .

'The slave-hunter *par excellence* of the White Nile, who had rented or farmed from the Government for some thousands sterling per annum the right of trading in countries which did not belong to Egypt, was now on the road to protest against my interference with his trade ; this innocent business being represented by three

vessels with seven hundred slaves that were to pass
unchecked before the government station of Fashoda.' [1]

After this, indeed, there was a gleam of hope. The
three vessels were captured by the governor of Fashoda
acting under Baker's orders. Abou Saood was put in
prison, and the Khedive promised that he should be
punished according to his deserts. Before leaving
Egypt he was able to write :—

' The territory within my rule was purged from the
slave-trade. The natives of the great Shooli tribe,
relieved from their oppressors, clung to the protecting
government. The White Nile, for a distance of sixteen
hundred miles from Khartoum to Central Africa, was
cleansed from a traffic which had hitherto sullied its
waters ; every cloud had passed away, and the term of
my office expired in peace and sunshine.' [2]

Alas for the vanity of human wishes ! No sooner
was Baker gone than Abou Saood was released, and not
only released, but appointed assistant to his successor !
What chance was there of suppressing slavery when
this was the temper of the higher officials of Egypt ?

For many years past the British Government has
done much to suppress the slave-trade along the extensive line of West African coast under its dominion, by
blockading the ports where the slaves were shipped on
board Arab sailing vessels to be transported to other
countries. But stopping the export of slaves has by no
means put an end to slavery in Northern Africa. It
has not even mitigated its horrors, but merely driven it
further inland, out of the sight of Europeans. In the
south and east the slave-trade is said to have increased
fourfold of late years, as if the fear lest their infamous

---

[1] *Ismailia* ii. 482–4.   [2] Ibid. ii. 513.

traffic should be abolished accelerated the efforts of the traders.

The domestic slavery that exists in Africa is not in itself an evil of such magnitude as to call for European interference. In some respects it is a most desirable alternative for worse evils. The continual wars among the tribes of the interior leave in the hands of the victors prisoners in large numbers, who, if they are not sold as slaves, are almost invariably put to death. The recognition of slave labour and the existence of a market for slaves prevents a great deal of butchery. It renders belligerents more active in taking prisoners than in killing. They are generally sent to a distance to be sold, as if they were too near their homes their masters would not be able to prevent their escape. As long as the sale is to some other African tribe, and the slaves are not exported beyond the sea, or sent down to the coast or across the Sahara, their sufferings are not more than are inevitable under the circumstances. They are often like family dependants, and recognise their position and acquiesce in it. It is useless for them to attempt to escape, as any stranger found at large would at once be recaptured and sold unless claimed by his owner. In some parts there are entire villages of slaves who till the soil for their masters and have a sort of practical independence. Their lives and liberties are at the disposal of their masters, and from time to time both one and the other are sacrificed to the barbarous customs and the caprice of their owners, but in other respects they do not differ much from free labourers.

Domestic slavery commences in Western Africa as soon as the boundaries of the Gold Coast and Lagos are passed. Powerful tribes like the Ashanti and Dahomey keep up their prestige by annual expeditions against weaker tribes for the purpose of enslaving them. Their captives are carried back in triumph, and too often are sold to the Arab dealers to be disposed of hundreds of miles away. Weaker tribes fight among themselves and when they make prisoners the prisoners are invariably sold as slaves. The Arabs incite tribe to attack tribe and aid the stronger party in order to obtain material for their nefarious traffic. Almost all the large towns of the interior have slave-markets. There is a continual demand for fresh slaves, and fresh slaves means fresh inter-tribal wars. It is the interest of the chiefs to keep up these wars and of the Arabs to foster them. The chiefs and fetich-men exercise as a rule despotic powers. The Africans are intensely conservative in their habits and their ideas, and regard this power of their chiefs as a sort of divine right with which it is quite hopeless to interfere. For this reason the idea of putting down slavery by one vigorous blow or series of blows is out of the question. It would do far more harm than good. The English Government has always acted with a conviction of this fact. In the Gold Coast protectorate slavery was recognised till 1874. Open slave-markets were not permitted, but private barter existed everywhere. An excellent regulation gave to the slaves the power of summoning their masters if they were treated cruelly, even at the time that the officers of the government assisted in their capture if they ran away.

After 1874 slavery was made illegal on the Gold Coast, but very few of the slaves claimed their liberty. They could not have earned their livelihood if they had done so, and even those who had been in slavery for only a short time were as usual far away from their own homes and could not have reached them. The influence of England did not at first materially alter the state of society except in the towns actually on the coast, and no attempt was made to force any sudden and complete change on the natives. Slavery was interwoven with all their habits, customs, laws, and it would have been a very questionable policy to take violent measures for its suppression. But there is an element in the domestic slavery of Africa which would dye it with a deeper stain than attaches to any other form of slavery all the world over if it were an essential element in it. There exists a belief among the native tribes that after death the happiness of their relations depends on their having a number of slaves to wait upon them as they had during life. It is therefore a duty to the deceased to provide a suitable escort for him in the nether world, and this is to be done by the sacrifice of a number of slaves at his grave. This 'custom' has led to the most hideous butchery, and has prevailed wherever fetichism had not been supplanted by European or Arab influence. The treaty with Ashanti in 1874 contained a clause enacting the abolition of human sacrifices. But, unfortunately, it was never enforced. In Lagos itself and the country round, the evil was put a stop to, but it went on much the same as ever even within the limits of the English protectorate. In the outlying districts no efforts were made to suppress it, and when the colony of Lagos would, if supported by the English Government, have put down the inhuman cruelties perpetrated in the neighbouring territories, the Colonial Office refused to sanction any forcible interference.

Happily of late years England has become more conscious of her responsibilities. Last year a company which exercises the authority of the British Government on both banks of the Niger, sent out a special commission with instructions to take any means in their power to destroy this terrific evil. The task was no easy one, considering the conservatism of the African and his tenacious adherence to the customs. Yet the reader will see from the narrative of Sir James Marshall, who was asked by the company to head the commission and organise a judicial system in the territory subject to them, that public opinion was strongly in favour of the abolition of the murderous custom which it was the object of the company to suppress. It was one of those rare cases in which the use of force was calculated to produce a permanent result. The natives had not the courage to abolish the human sacrifices themselves, on account of their fear of the chiefs and the fetich-men; but they welcomed the judicious compulsion which forced the change upon them. In them there was none of the religious animosity felt by the Mohammedan towards the Christian. Their moral standard, it is true, was not a high one, but it was sufficiently high to recognise the abomination of the wholesale murders practised on the death of a chief, and to rejoice in this abomination disappearing from among them. The object of Sir James Marshall was therefore not the abolition of domestic slavery, but the abolition of its worst and most revolting accompaniment, the massacre of slaves on the occasion of their master's death.

His crusade was a most successful one. It was only on a small scale when compared with the vast expanse of territory in which slave-hunting and slave-murder are carried on, but for all that it was felt throughout the whole district of the Niger, and will not be without considerable effect on the position of slaves in that region.

Over the lower Niger a British protectorate had been established through the energy and enterprise of the National African Company, which first took possession of that river, and carried on vigorous and successful mercantile operations there. Hence at the Berlin Conference the representative of Great Britain was able to claim the Niger countries on behalf of his government; and now, by authority of a royal charter, and in accordance with treaties made with the native tribes, the jurisdiction and sole rule over both banks of the river and its mighty tributary, the Binué, belongs to the Royal Niger Company as it is now called.

From the council of this company Sir James Marshall received, in the latter part of 1887, a request to accept the position of Chief Justice in the Niger territories.

'Having retired from that position in the colonial service on the Gold Coast in 1882, on account of my health being no longer able to bear the climate,' he writes, 'I declined the honour. I was then asked to go out for a short time in order to organise a judicial system suitable to the country. This I did not like to refuse, as the council considered me specially fitted by my experience for a work which I knew was of the greatest importance for the future of this young empire. I therefore accepted, on the understanding that I should not stay longer out there than three months, and should return sooner if I wished.'

Sir James Marshall was accompanied to Africa by Mr. Kane, who was appointed to act as puisne judge in the Niger territories as long as Sir J. Marshall remained there, and to assume the office of Chief Justice on his

departure.   On March 1 they commenced their voyage
up the river in one of the company's steamers, and on
the evening of the 4th they anchored for the night
within a few miles of Asaba, their destination.   We are
enabled, through Sir James Marshall's kindness, to give
in his own words an account of the main incidents
in this episode in the story of African slavery :—

'Judge Kane and I,' he writes about three weeks
after his arrival, 'have been a good deal exercised in
mind at finding that the natives here carry on the
brutalities of killing slaves quite near our house.   There
is no head king with his chiefs, but there is an immense
number of chiefs or headmen, who wear red caps and
carry ivory horns which they blow to let people know
they are coming.   They also smear their faces with
white paint, and have a very revolting look.   Throughout the tribe, which is extensive, there are said to be
some five hundred of these men, who elect a council of
fifty to carry on some sort of government.   This want
of a head will make it easier to break them down if
necessary.   Every man, before he can wear a red cap,
has to kill two slaves ; and when one of them dies, at
least three are killed.   I was thinking yesterday what
could be done to stop this, when I received a message
from the chiefs of Asaba to the effect that they
had heard that a great man had come out and that they
wished to pay me a visit.   We sent for the interpreter,
who knows the people and state of the country well,
and said I should not see them unless I could speak
out about slave-murder.   He said he thought it would
be an excellent opportunity for doing so, and therefore
we arranged to receive them on the next Tuesday.
Before that day came, the interpreter, Mr. Taylor, took
Kane and myself to visit the *Juju* grove, where the

human sacrifices take place. Two of his men went with us, as not a native of the place would dare to do so. We went by a quiet, unfrequented way, having a gun to look as though we were out for sport, and got to the place. There is a cleared space, surrounded by huge trees and bush, which gives it a very weird, superstitious appearance ; but there were not as many traces of murders as I expected to see ; the corpses are thrown into the bush and the animals devour them. But there were two skulls, apparently of children, which had not been carried away. I determined to tell the chiefs of this.

'On the 27th, our room was cleared and prepared for the *Durbar*. Soon there was a constant noise and blowing of horns, tinkling of bells, &c., and the interpreter came to say that the chiefs had assembled in the market place and were ready to come. So we put on our robes, and the commandant came, and one of the officers carried my cane. The chiefs came into the compound one after the other with their attendants ; all the horns blowing together made a terrible noise. When they had all been placed, we went in without procession, and sat on three chairs—I as Chief Justice in the middle, Kane on my right, and Harper (the commandant) on the left, with the staff-bearer alongside. Father Lutz and the Protestant missionary also sat with us by invitation. There were about forty red-cap chiefs, besides the attendants, so that the room and verandah were crowded. They looked so dreadful with the streaks of white paint on their faces, and eagle feathers sticking straight out from their ears, that I began to feel my courage about speaking out about the sacrifice of slaves rather diminishing. The commandant then saluted them, and introduced me as the great judge.

I stood up, and, after the usual salutations, I began by telling them that I had been a judge in Africa for a long time, and was sent out by the great Queen; that I was a great friend with the chiefs and people; that the chiefs sat with me in court and heard *palavers* with me; also of my being at Lagos where I heard of the Niger, and knew many of those who came here for trade. In time I had found my health and strength would not allow of remaining longer, so I had gone home, and told the great Queen I could not go out any more, and sat down in my house with my family to rest and be quiet. But I had kept up great interest in the countries where I had been, and also in the Niger countries, as I belonged to the Niger Company; and, now that it was found necessary to send out judges here, I had been asked to go, as I had been out so much. I said, " No, I am too old, I cannot;" but I would go for a short time and take a younger judge who would stay on. This led to the crucial part. I said I came here hoping to be friends with the chiefs and people as I had been in the other countries, but that when I came here my heart was sad to find that all the chiefs were *murderers*. There was a slight movement of uneasiness, but not a word was said. I then went hot at it, and told them we had been to their Juju grove, and·seen the skulls of two children who had been lately murdered. I also told them I had received information that three persons had been murdered only two days ago at another place close by, at the funeral of a chief, and that this would not be allowed; that the strongest measures would be taken to put it down, and I should let it be known among the slaves that they might look to us for protection, and whenever it was known that a murder was going to be perpetrated the soldiers would

be at once sent, and that chiefs and Juju-men would
be liable to be hanged. I ended by saying it was no
case of palaver, it was a case of peace or war. They
were very uncomfortable and here and there some
of them indulged in a contemptuous laugh, especially
one huge creature, more ornamented than any one, who
doubtless enjoys murder. I then returned to the
friendly strain, and hoped all would be peace and prosperity. When I had finished I introduced Judge Kane
to them, who in a few incisive words told them that he
agreed with every word I had said, and that when I
was gone he would carry out the policy laid before
them.

'We then retired and told them to consult together,
but that they need not give a reply at present to what
I had said about the sacrifices. When we went in again
one of them spoke and said the chiefs saluted and welcomed us, and were glad we did not press for an
immediate reply, as they would consult amongst themselves and with others before giving it. They thanked
us, and with a few friendly words the affair came to an
end, and forthwith there was a burst of talking and
horn-blowing that made us glad when they were gone.
The company has hitherto done nothing to put down
human sacrifices, or mitigate the worst forms of slave-
dealing and slavery. By the terms of the charter it is
pledged not to interfere with any religion, heathen,
Christian, or Moslem, existing in its territories, but this
does not include rites and practices distinctly contrary
to humanity. Weakly children are constantly sold to
the Asabas cheap, and they do for sacrifices.

'Taylor told me that the effect of my speech has
been very great, and there is a strong party in favour
of putting an end to the murders. The natives wanted

very much to know how we got to the Juju grove, but he evaded the question, saying white men go everywhere.'

A great impression had evidently been made upon the natives by the firm attitude and menacing words of the Europeans, but immemorial customs could not easily be abolished. It happened, moreover, that within a few days of the meeting of chiefs described above two important headmen of the neighbourhood died, and usage demanded that three slaves should be sacrificed at the funeral of each chief. The natives found themselves in a difficult position, as they could not prevent knowledge of the matter reaching the English, and they had been plainly informed that, were the barbarous custom conformed to, the chief of each village where the funeral took place would be held responsible for the murder of the slaves. They knew too that there was a strong military garrison in Asaba, and that, if necessary, force would be resorted to. It was thought, therefore, that they would be afraid to observe the accustomed rites; but it was not so, as we learn from Sir James Marshall's narrative.

' About midday on April 6, Mr. Taylor informed us that the funeral ceremonies were commencing, and that three slaves were already placed beside the corpse, who would be sacrificed at night. We at once sent a messenger to demand that the slaves should be brought into the barracks, but without effect. We sent for the commandant, who at once agreed to rescue them, and sent out a force of seventy men, armed with Martini rifles, under the command of an officer. Judge Kane and I walked in the centre of the column. My own expectation was that the Asabas would take to flight as soon as they saw the force advancing. But the further we went the greater the number of armed natives we saw gathering together about the houses and compounds near the road, and some stalwart men swaggered by close to us, armed with as ugly-looking spears as I could wish to see. After having marched about a mile and a half, we arrived at the compound where the funeral was going on, and came upon a scene of intense excitement. We halted and our commander made all preparations for a fight. Inside the compound we saw the chief of the family, armed with a musket, and struggling violently with his attendants, who evidently were horribly afraid lest he should succeed in firing it at us. In another direction a chief was engaged in a similar struggle, and behind the hedges of the compounds were many men ready to fire on us. Mr. Taylor and his men at once advanced into the funeral compound to calm the excitement by gestures and friendly words, and found that the corpse and the slaves had all been removed. It was an intensely anxious time, for it was evident that if a single shot were fired we should immediately be hotly engaged in a fight at close quarters, in which both flint guns and spears could be used with effect. It was therefore a great relief to see three men come forward carrying stools, which meant that they wished to hold a " palaver." We went to where they sat with Mr. Taylor as interpreter. With all the politeness which is invariably to be found in these savage people, the spokesman commenced by thanking us for the honour we had done them in coming to pay them this visit. I knew they would prefer taking our heads, but was glad to hear the sentiment expressed. They then proceeded to promise that if we retired the slaves should not be killed. I proposed to Mr. Taylor that we should carry off one of these men as a hostage, but giving a look round he said we were not strong enough. So having received this promise we marched back again, and saw what made us fully understand that if we had begun to fight we should have encountered hundreds of armed men on all sides as we returned.

'That night at nine o'clock the firing of a big gun announced that the three slaves had been sacrificed. Very possibly the men who promised they should not be slain meant that the promise should be kept, but the angry chief who wished to fire on us, supported by the young warriors, carried all before them, and insisted on the custom of their country being carried out. After all was over they began to collect outside our compounds, thinking we might at once go out to revenge the murder, and extra guards were placed round the premises. The next day some messengers came in from the Asabas wishing to see me and talk over the matter.

'I declined to have anything to say to them, but Mr. Seago, one of the officers of the Company whom we had sent for from the nearest factory, gave them an interview and found them very defiant. They intimated that they were quite ready to fight. This was followed up by numbers collecting in the bush outside and firing off guns, accompanied by defiant shouts and gesticulations to the sentries and any one they could see. At night the entire premises of the Company were fairly besieged by numbers of armed men in the bush just outside a thin and fragile paling, but no attack was made.'

The hostile demonstrations on the part of the natives came to nothing. The second funeral took place, at which human victims were again killed, but about the station all was comparatively quiet. On the 12th a sortie

was made by the military force, and some houses were
fired. This evidently alarmed the enemy. On the
following day a red-cap chief came to sue for peace,
promising there should be no more killing of slaves.
But the judge would not hear of peace till the murderers
were given up, and on this being refused some shells
were fired from the barracks, which made the savages
fly in all directions. A second attack on the villages
of Asaba proved more effectual; the houses and every
Juju temple or image were destroyed, very little resistance being met with. The chief of the village where
the second funeral took place submitted, and gave up
the man who had caused the sacrifice of the slaves.
This culprit was hanged.

' Finally,' Sir J. Marshall writes, ' a message was sent
to the enemy to say that a similar attack would be made
each day until the town was destroyed unless they submitted. This they soon did, and on April 21 a party of
red-cap chiefs eagerly accepted a treaty with the Company, the first article of which was that there should be
no more human sacrifices.

' The results of this treaty were soon seen. A few
days after peace had been made, Mr. Taylor informed
us that two slaves had come in as a deputation from the
slaves of Asaba who wished to thank the white men for
what they had done for them. Mr. Taylor brought
them in, one a young man who acted as spokesman,
and the other a good deal older. They had none of the
hideous white paint on their faces like their masters,
and were much more pleasant to look upon and to listen
to. Having prostrated themselves so that their fore-
heads touched the ground, which is the salutation of
slaves, the spokesman said that at first the slaves could
not believe that the war was made for them; that they

had been kept like fowls and goats by their masters,
who took them out when they pleased to be killed, but
that now they knew they would be protected and the
slaves of Asaba sent them to thank us. I assured them
that the war was made on their account, and that, if
necessary, the white man would fight again for them,
and that it would be their own fault if they submitted
to these cruelties any more. The poor fellows immediately prostrated again, and on leaving the older man
stretched out his arms as wide as they would go, and
said, " My heart feels as big as this."

'Every one felt delighted at such a happy ending to
the war which had freed the slaves from being used as
human sacrifices. It was not only at Asaba that the
blow was felt; it was a lesson which the chiefs and
slave-holders in all the surrounding neighbourhood will
not forget.'

A subsequent letter from Judge Kane gives further
proof of the permanent effect of the work done on behalf
of the slaves. He writes :—

'Mr. Taylor informed me that a deputation of slaves
was coming from all the Asaba villages to give their
thanks for what had been done for them. They came
on the 28th of August to the number of twelve. The
young man whom you will remember again acted as
spokesman. The old man being sick was unable to come.
They said that the Asaba people had not ill-treated them
since, and had not even threatened them in secret, and
that now they felt they were men and not mere beasts.
They brought two goats as a token of thanks. At first
I did not wish to take them, but, finding that they would
be offended if I declined, I did so. I told them it was
true that the palaver was on their account, and that it
was horrible to find that slaves were being killed, not

because they had done any wrong, but just as a man might kill a bullock when he wanted chop (*i.e.* food). I went on to say that the judges had taken it up, and that white men had risked their own lives to save those of the slaves, and that the Asabas had made a book (*i.e.* a written agreement) with the Company not to kill people in this way, and that I believed they would keep it, but that if they did not we should be told about it at once. Also, that as they were now men, they should try to be worthy of that character and work well, for if they lived idle and worthless lives they would get into trouble again.'

The success of this enterprise with the chief abuse of domestic slavery in Africa shows clearly what may be done among the natives who have not come into contact with the Arab traders, and how a judicious admixture of moral influence and of vigorous measures, where there is a hope of their results being permanent, may gradually mitigate the worst features of the slavery that exists among the natives themselves.

CHAPTER IV

SCHEMES FOR THE SUPPRESSION OF SLAVERY

THE futility of all the exertions hitherto made for the general abolition of slavery in Africa has now become plainly apparent, and is recognised by the public opinion of England. Despite the praiseworthy efforts of the British Government, the expenditure of vast sums, and the loss of many valuable lives in the attempt to suppress it, the evil, far from abating, has in late years, we are told, increased alarmingly. The presence of an English squadron has, it is true, virtually put an end to the export of slaves from the West Coast, but the trade in that portion of the continent is not done away with, it is merely driven further inland, where the slave-hunter carries on his raids with redoubled energy. At least half a million black men are bought and sold in the markets of the interior every year. In Eastern and Central Africa the slave-trade not only holds its own, but increases year by year, and whole provinces are half-depopulated. The German and English cruisers blockade the coast, but the Arab *dhows*, with their freight of human merchandise, contrive for the most part to elude their vigilance. This is due, probably, to the short distance they have to run, and the facility wherewith the transport can be made under cover of night. Commercial enterprise has not succeeded in substituting legitimate trade for the nefarious traffic in human chattels, nor in persuading the native chieftains that it is more profitable to carry on pacific barter with the European merchant than to capture slaves and sell them to the Arab dealer. Missionary effort has penetrated into the heart of Africa, but it is almost powerless in presence of the Moslem marauder. For twenty-nine years Cardinal Lavigerie has laboured for the redemption of the negro; he has sent out many bands of missioners. Some have suffered martyrdom, others have died of fever and hardships. The survivors report no improvement; on the contrary, matters are growing worse. Converts have been made, and individual slaves ransomed from their captors; but the moral influence of the missioner has not availed to prevent a single razzia. Where nature has done much for man, and where man himself seems capable of progress, where a numerous and happy population might peacefully dwell, the slave-trader creates desolation. Slave-hunts are carried on in these countries as far as the sources of the Niger; the sale of slaves takes place publicly in all Mohammedan provinces on the same large scale as ever. More than this, in the regions of the Great Lakes a fresh outburst of fanaticism has taken place, resulting in the massacre of the Christians and the expulsion of every white man. Throughout a wide extent of territory the feeble flame of civilisation kindled by the missioners has been utterly extinguished.

Travellers have done good service to the cause of humanity by revealing the atrocities of the slave-trade. They defy description, they are unparalleled in any page of history. It is now an acknowledged fact that slavery is the greatest obstacle to the civilisation, colonisation, and evangelisation of Africa. The voice of public opinion has been raised in indignant protest, but the denuncia-

tions of the civilised world, far from checking, appear
rather to have given a fresh impetus to the iniquitous
traffic. Pope Leo XIII., whose words are generally
full of moderation and gentleness, has condemned it in
the most emphatic terms. He solemnly declares it to
be contrary to the divine law and to the laws of nature.
He denounces as infamous and most villanous this
trade in human beings. He appeals against it to every
Christian in accents of sorrow and authority. He has
endeavoured to stimulate the governments of Europe to
strenuous and united efforts for its suppression, and does
not content himself with exhorting them alone, but, as
the Father of Christendom, he beseeches them to arrest
it, to prohibit it in those regions where their influence
can be felt. Cardinal Lavigerie, commissioned by the
Holy Father, has undertaken to preach a crusade
throughout Europe; not a crusade for the recovery of
the sepulchres of the dead, but a holy war to save the
lives of the living. The reports of his missioners and
his own burning eloquence have been effectual in arousing the conscience of Christian society. Everywhere he
has met with sympathy and co-operation from Catholics
and Protestants, from states and from individuals. He
succeeded in gaining the attention of Prince Bismarck,
and it was owing to his efforts that the German
Reichstag, on the proposition of Dr. Windthorst, committed itself to the policy of putting down the slave-
trade. Societies for that purpose have been formed in
nearly all the chief cities of Europe, and large sums
have been subscribed. The time has now come when
steps must be taken to give practical effect to the resolutions passed at the Congress of Vienna and the
Berlin Conference for the extirpation of the evil. It is

a gigantic evil, and demands a strong remedy. Where is that remedy to be found?

Various proposals have been made, and various schemes suggested, for the suppression of slavery. No one specific can be brought forward with any hope of success. No one nation, no one class of individuals, can be entrusted with the accomplishment of this great mission. The concerted action of all the Powers of Europe, of all classes of society, will be necessary; negotiations are being made to secure it. An international conference to discuss the question has been proposed, and it is to be hoped that the project will shortly be realised.

The first article in the programme of suggestions for any future conference is that the representatives of the various Powers should be urged to declare that the status of slavery shall be no longer recognised by international law, and the slave-trade treated as piracy. This method of repression was successfully adopted by England, both in India and on the Gold Coast of Africa. From the time that the legal status of slavery was abolished by the British Parliament, the slave-trade became extinct as far as this country was concerned. The same method ought to be efficacious on the East African coast. Doubtless if the suggestion received the assent of the Powers, it would imply the exercise of a little wholesome severity, the adoption of stringent measures against all who were detected in the prosecution of the traffic in human beings. If a proclamation were issued that, after a certain date, every vessel suspected of being a slaver would be subjected to sharp scrutiny, the crew tried by court-martial, and, if found guilty, condemned to summary and condign punishment, we should hear no more of slavers mocking the pursuit of English or German cruisers by flying the French colours. Pemba would cease to be a depôt, and the Comoro Islands a basis, for this horrible commerce. The planters in the island of Réunion could not, as they now do, supply, by importing slaves from Madagascar, the lack of sufficient labour for their sugar estates, caused by the fact that the emigration of coolies has ceased. The trade would become too risky to be generally remunerative. If the highway by water were made thoroughly unsafe for the slave-vessels, and at the same time the governors of the Mussulman states could be persuaded to lessen the demand by discouraging the traditional custom of purchasing negroes for household slaves, there seems little doubt that by degrees the export of slaves from the coast of Africa, with all its terrible accessories, would be effectually stopped. The transmarine trade forms, it is true, only a part of the scandalous traffic which is carried on by the Arabs, and which afflicts the conscience of civilised mankind; but the stoppage of it would, at any rate, be a heavy blow to the whole iniquitous system. Had the prohibitory regulations issued at the Berlin Conference been rigorously enforced, the slave-trade would not have attained its present proportions. If slaves were not purchased in Turkey and Western Asia, they would not be captured by thousands in Africa.

Another very necessary measure to be taken is to place further restrictions on the importation of arms and ammunition into the regions where the slave-hunters make their raids. From this trade, it must be confessed, England derives great profits. The amount imported has never been so great as at the present time. In places where, some eight or ten years ago, not one man in a thousand owned a gun, rifles are now seen in the hands of almost every one. Vast quantities of guns and powder are pouring across Africa from Liberia viâ Tanganyika, and even running the coast blockade, English and German traders vying with each other in eagerness to supply the demand. The recent recrudescence of the traffic in slaves is a source of great emolument to the Arab traders, and they employ the money thus gained in the purchase of firearms. This serves to render them increasingly bold and insolent, since they thereby acquire power over the natives, and gain for themselves the prestige which the possession of these murderous weapons gives to the white man in the eyes of the savage.

This point is one on which Cardinal Lavigerie strongly insists.

A slave-dealer, he relates, was once asked how he penetrated into the heart of Africa, and who was the ruler of those remote regions. ' I will tell you the name of the monarch of Central Africa,' he replied, laying his hand on the weapon he carried, ' it is *King Rifle.*' This answer is true enough. Were a law to be passed prohibiting the Arabs, and those merciless marauders, the *Métis,* from carrying firearms and purchasing ammunition, and were every infraction of this regulation made punishable by banishment, it would in a short time have the effect the Cardinal asserts of ridding those provinces of Africa of which Europeans have obtained possession, of the three or four hundred—their numbers do not exceed this figure—human fiends who carry off or destroy millions of helpless victims, in concert with the native chiefs to whom they have taught the creed of Islam and the art of slave-hunting.

This leads us to speak of another essential measure for the suppression of the slave-trade; it is the destruction of the Moslem ascendency throughout the whole interior.

The one thing needed for Africa, Professor Drummond says, is a system of organised protection for the native and the breaking up of Arab dominance. The influence exercised by the slave-dealer over the native chiefs is astonishing. He persuades them that the sale of women and children as slaves is far more profitable than the cultivation of friendly relations with the merchant and the missionary. The fact that some of the missioners have sheltered runaway slaves is even made a handle for representing that the missioners themselves are slave-dealers. He finds it no difficult matter to convince the jealous chieftain that the white man's object is to undermine his authority, that the presence of the missioner will bring calamities on the land. Mwanga, the lately deposed king of Uganda, was the most powerful ruler of Central Africa. His sway extended over ten millions of subjects. He was completely under the dominion of the Mussulmans, who carried on the trade in slaves with him on an extensive scale. The number of negroes whom he kidnapped during his raids in the adjacent provinces, and afterwards sold, is estimated at not less than from sixty to eighty thousand a year. That was his principal source of revenue; by it he obtained the means of purchasing arms and ammunition which were supplied to him by the Arabs of Zanzibar. To this they owed their ascendency over him. Interested motives and the habit of years made him their firm ally; had they succeeded in making a Mussulman of him he would have been a mere tool in their hands. Tippoo-tippoo, the great slave-hunter, and his lieutenants are no less ready to do their bidding.

In the Soudan, the Moslem traders gradually effected the conquest of the whole country from Egypt to the Atlantic Ocean, dividing it into small kingdoms. The negro inhabitants were formerly all heathens ; they are now all Mussulmans. Their conversion has been accomplished principally by forcible means, and has clinched their fetters. Islamism is essentially antagonistic to Christian civilisation, and every negro who bends his neck beneath its iron yoke becomes *ipso facto* the irreconcilable enemy of all Europeans. A similar transformation is what the Moslem traders are desirous of effecting in Eastern Africa, with the design of closing her gates for ever against the invasion of European nations. The wholesale massacre of Christians and the expulsion of the missioners from Uganda proves the whole of the district to be in the hands of the Arabs. They desire to have the entire country around the Great Lakes as a happy hunting ground for the pursuit of human prey, subject to no law, and responsible to no ruler. A few years ago they regarded Saïd-Bargash, the late Sultan of Zanzibar, as their sovereign. Despite the distance they recognised his authority ; his co-operation was besides necessary to carry on the trade in slaves and to procure a supply of firearms. The power of the Sultan in the interior is now simply *nil*. It is much to be regretted that since the unclaimed parts of Africa have been appropriated by the several European Powers, the traditional authority he exercised has been to a great extent done away with. Except within the limits of a narrow strip of land on the sea-coast, the Arabs, finding that he has no longer any power to enforce his authority, and that it is no longer their interest to obey him, have returned to their old fanaticism, and are advancing further into the interior, where they create states for the better prosecution of the slave trade.

It was a great error on the part of European governments in a country where the Mussulmans, although numerically few, exercise a profound and widespread influence, to attempt from the first to assume the sole and direct command. Instead of refusing to recognise the power of the Sultan in the interior, a wiser course would have been to have carefully maintained him in authority, or at least in the semblance of authority, and the prestige it gave him. Through him the Arabs of the interior could have been effectually controlled, at any rate for a time, until a solid footing had been acquired by the new-comers. Then the Mussulman agents might have been gradually superseded by government officials or the agents of the colonial company. At the present moment, if not too late, it would be well to restore to the Sultan the power of which he was so peremptorily and unadvisedly stripped. His former powers might even be added to with advantage, and his relations with the Moslem traders put back on the old footing. In consideration of financial benefits, terms could be dictated to him. This was the method of procedure pursued by France on the occupation of Tunis. The civil list of the Bey was augmented by one-third, and his right of dispensing justice scrupulously maintained. England acted in a similar manner in Egypt; in fact no other course of conduct is open to a Christian power, if it would strike root on African soil. The Mussulman regards it as a kind of apostasy to yield direct obedience to a Christian, while he considers disobedience to the Mohammedan governor as tantamount to a sin against God, whose representative he is. If resistance is impossible, the Mussulman retreats out of reach of a power that his religious tenets and worldly interests alike forbid him to obey.

Some say that the domination of the Arab trader can only be put down gradually by the competing influence of civilised commerce and colonisation. The European merchant must exploit the fields in which the Arab with his gang of armed scoundrels has hitherto collected ivory, sacked villages, and made captives of the inhabitants. Every approach, it is said, towards the settlement of white men as traders in the heart of Africa will drive the slave-hunters from their blood-stained routes ; a pacific policy, the moral influence of sustained missionary effort, will at length secure to the negroes of the once dark continent the blessings of liberty, and put an end to the sale and barter of human beings. Cardinal Lavigerie, on the other hand, advocates the employment of a certain amount of armed intervention. His project comprises the introduction into Africa of a body of armed men, to form a sort of continental blockade against the slave-caravans, and open a line of anti-slavery stations on the lakes. An appeal from the anti-slavery societies which have lately sprung into existence would be responded to by young men in almost all lands, and the rules of these societies place them at the disposal of any government which is willing to organise an expedition of this nature. Cardinal Lavigerie alone received the names of more than a thousand volunteers in the space of not many weeks. He has frequently expressed his conviction that the establishment of anti-slavery stations on the lakes and in the Congo would be practically useless, unless backed up by a considerable amount of physical force. On the arrival of the earliest English Protestant missionaries at Lake Tanganyika, some twelve or fourteen years ago,

their presence placed a check at first on the slave-trade.
After a time, when their mission was discovered to be
of an entirely peaceful nature, it went on as before.
What might then have been done by a mere handful
of men could not now be accomplished by less than
several hundred, or even thousand.

In the address delivered last year in the Church of
St. Sulpice, in Paris, Cardinal Lavigerie expressed his
views upon this subject.

' Charity,' he said, ' however great, will not suffice
to save Africa. It requires a more speedy, more
decided, more efficacious remedy. Our Holy Father
the Pope, after appealing to charity, then appeals to
force, but a pacific force, which would be employed
not for attack, but for defence. He addresses himself
for that purpose to all Christian states. They can
indeed do much by using their moral influence with the
Moslem rulers, and holding them responsible for the
continuation of the infamies committed by the African
slave-traders. Our missioners echo this appeal, and
they declare that the slave-dealers can only be stopped
by force. I quote from a letter of one of the White
Fathers :—

' " Alas! when will some European power interfere
to put an end to this accursed traffic in slaves, and the
myriad evils which follow in its train ? A detachment
of fifty European soldiers, well armed and acclimatised,
would be able in a fortnight to exterminate this troop
—a rabble of some two or three hundred robbers—
which is the terror of all the district from Tabora to
Manyema, throughout the whole length of the Tanganyika up to the Albert Nyanza."

' My own idea quite coincides with this proposal. It
is my belief that five or six hundred European soldiers,

well organised and well officered, would be sufficient to
suppress slave-hunting and slave-selling in the higher
table-lands of the African continent—the district, that
is, which extends from the Albert Nyanza to the south
of Lake Tanganyika. We have already had practical
illustration of the utility of armed intervention in the
work accomplished by a brave man, a true Christian
hero, who formerly held a commission in the Papal
Zouaves, and also took part in the Franco-German
war.[1] At an age when the enthusiasm of youth was
over he offered his services to us, desiring to dedicate
the remainder of his life to the defence of the African
negro. For several years he has been living alone in
the neighbourbood of one of our mission stations, at
Mpala, on Lake Tanganyika, his existence being one
long series of privations and sacrifices. He has constituted himself the protector of the surrounding
villages, and with the arms with which we have
supplied him, he has formed a body of militia consisting of two hundred negroes. These native soldiers
would, it is true, not bear comparison with European
troops, but they are no longer utterly defenceless, and
they are able to strike awe, within a certain radius,
into the slave-hunting *Métis* and their allies the Ruga-
ruga.

'What is really needed is that the European states,
among whom the Congress of Berlin has, to borrow an
expression of its own, parcelled out the unclaimed
districts of Equatorial Africa, should maintain, each in
its own territory, a sufficient military force in every
place where the inhuman traffic prevails. But if these
different states should, on account of financial em-

---

[1] M. Joubert, or Saint Joubert, as he used familiarly to be called when
serving with his regiment in Rome.

barrassments or difficulties of any other kind, insurmountable for the moment, find themselves unable to
do this, why should there not be recalled into existence
in those barbarous countries some one of the military
and religious orders formed for purposes of defence in
the middle ages, when the inhabitants of Spain and
Eastern Europe were, together with the dwellers on
the shores of the Mediterranean, subject to the incursions of the Turkish invader, and, in consequence, too
often carried off into slavery? The names they bore
have been made for ever illustrious by the valour of
the knights and the services they rendered to Christianity. Who has not heard of the Knights of Malta,
of Alcantara, of the Teutonic order? In subordination
to the Church's authority, upheld by the protection of
princes, they sought not conquest, nor such bloodshed
as she cannot approve, but the defence of the weak,
the repression of violence, the accomplishment of a
work which at that period the regularly constituted
states were powerless to perform.

'I appeal to you, the Christian young men of
all the countries of Europe, and I ask what should
hinder you from reviving, on behalf of the barbarous
lands of the interior of Africa, so long closed against
civilising influences, the noble achievements of your
forefathers? Why should we not see, with the sanction
of the Church and of her pastors, a renewal of the
unselfish devotion which was the glory of past ages?

'A different system of organisation would doubtless
be necessary, one more in harmony with the exigencies
of the present day. Heraldic quarterings, a *sine quâ
non* for admission into those ancient orders, would not
now constitute an indispensable requisite; all we
should ask would be courage, self-abnegation, a readi-

ness to suffer and die for the brethren. We should thus have, side by side with the scions of illustrious houses, intrepid priests who would act as chaplains and infirmarians, artisans who had left the workshop and laid down the implements of toil in order to take up the sword, and shed their blood for the liberation and salvation of their fellow-men, for the honour of the Christian name, and to the glory of their respective countries. In the midst of the moral corruption which is creeping in everywhere and degrading everything, is it nothing to find an opportunity of devoting one's life to a worthy cause, of leaving behind one the memory of heroic deeds, of carrying to the judgment seat of God the merit won by a glorious death?'

This appeal made by Cardinal Lavigerie to the secular arm enlists very general sympathy but not universal approval. The scheme of a military expedition into the heart of Africa does not commend itself to the judgment of all who are best qualified to form an opinion on the subject. The deadly influence of the climate, fatal to the European constitution, would speedily thin the ranks of the 'five hundred resolute men' to whom the Cardinal would confide the liberation of Eastern Africa. A pernicious miasma seems to greet the stranger on the threshold of the continent, and before the more salubrious regions could be reached, where the mission stations of the equatorial lakes are situated, the expedition would be more than decimated, its physical energy and strength reduced to the lowest ebb. Captain Hore, who has long been resident at Tanganyika, believes that it would not have the hoped-for effect of putting down the slave-trade, but would merely divert it to another route. He reminds us also that, were the Arab traders banished from their present haunts, the

work of suppressing slavery would not be done. They
have taught the natives their trade, and a great part of
it is carried on by the Africans themselves, one tribe
making raids upon a weaker neighbour ; and this will
probably be the last and most difficult phase to abolish.
It may be and has been, locally and temporarily, put
down by coercive means, but it can never be permanently got rid of except by the gradual process of
civilisation, by substituting the principles of Christianity
for the old pagan ideas, and this will be no easy task.
Sir James Marshall attests that the native is as keen a
slaver as the Arab. An immense proportion of the
slaves annually kidnapped and sold in the markets of
the interior, estimated by Cardinal Lavigerie as—to take
the minimum—five hundred thousand yearly, perish in
Africa, being slain as sacrifices. The practice of offering
human victims to the gods of the heathen prevails in
Central and Eastern Africa to almost if not quite as
great an extent as on the west coast and on the banks
of the Niger. King Mtesa, the late monarch of Uganda,
who received the missioners kindly and treated them
well, massacred his slaves in wholesale fashion.
Although a man of superior mental capacity, who
could understand and enjoy an argument, and could
speak and write Arabic, he was so superstitious that if
he dreamt of any of the gods of the country he believed
it to be an ill omen, and offered human sacrifices to
appease the offended deity. He dreamt of his father,
and in consequence had five hundred people put to
death in one day. He also believed that if he dreamt
of any living persons it was a sign that they meditated
treachery, and he condemned them forthwith to be
executed. Yet he was considered merciful in this
respect, being softened by an illness from which he

suffered. His chiefs often said, 'If Mtesa were well, there would be plenty of executions.'

A more pacific means proposed for the regeneration of Africa is colonisation. In a speech delivered by Victor Hugo at a meeting for the abolition of slavery, held in Paris in 1879, after describing in eloquent language the magnificent scenery, the fertility, the many natural advantages of Central Africa, he exhorted the European nations to occupy this land 'offered them by God,' to build towns, to make roads, to cultivate the earth, to introduce trade and commerce, to preach peace and concord, so that it should no longer be a scene of strife, the theatre of oppression and bloodshed. But experience has proved that European settlements in Africa are not attended with happy results either for the colonists themselves or the aborigines. Besides the physical difficulty of the climate, which affects the colonist so unfavourably, there are moral difficulties which are insurmountable. It is hard for a strong race to do more for a weak race than bestow upon it some of its vices, and the history of European colonisation too often records the melancholy fact that foreign intercourse has only resulted in a spurious civilisation and general demoralisation of the natives. What is wanted in Africa is that the foreign element introduced should have for its object the improvement and education of the negro, that it should teach him to be his own liberator, his own saviour. This the European cannot do, on account of his ignorance of the negro. Foreign slavery on the one hand, and aboriginal barbarism on the other, are the only circumstances in which he has had the opportunity of contemplating his black brother. He simply knows nothing of him, and is consequently unable to sympathise with or guide him. Until quite recently, the greatest ignorance with respect to the continent of Africa prevailed in the civilised world. But since the eyes of Europe have been turned on Africa, the work of exploration has been carried on with enthusiastic energy. Fertile plains and wide lakes have been found to exist in regions formerly supposed to be trackless deserts of shifting sand. Meanwhile very little effort is made to gain information about the inhabitants of the country, their character and capacities. The white man thinks he knows all about the negro. The prominent traits of the Africans who are carried away as slaves into other lands—mostly people of the lowest class, who do not in any wise represent the average moral or intellectual qualities of their fellow-countrymen—are fixed upon the whole nation. One of their own race, born in exile, thus speaks on the subject :—

'Among the evils wrought by the slave-trade, none has been more damaging to Africa and the negro race than the promiscuous manner in which the tribes have been thrown together and confounded in the lands of their exile; and in dealing with the negro question Europeans overlook this fact altogether. There are negroes and negroes. The numerous tribes inhabiting the vast continent of Africa can no more be regarded as equal than the numerous peoples of Asia or Europe can be so regarded. . . . All these, differing in original bent and traditional instincts, have been carried as slaves to foreign lands and classed as one.' [1]

Not only have different races been classed as one, but in the markets no discrimination has been made between the descendants of chieftains and the offspring of slaves. All have been placed on the same level, denominated as 'niggers' from their black skins and woolly hair, and,

---

[1] Blyden, *Christianity, Islam, and the Negro Race*, p. 311.

judged of by the majority—the lowest in the social scale
being the most easy of capture—pronounced to be little
better than the brute creation, ' irredeemable and unim-
provable.'

The impression given by travellers, too, who have the
opportunity of judging of the negro in his own country,
is generally taken from those parts where the people are
harassed and persecuted by slave-hunters, whose ravages
render improvement impossible. Sir Samuel Baker
speaks forcibly of the blighting effect of the slave-trade
on the character of the natives, and their social organisation, the industrial and economic life of the country.
' All idea of commerce, improvement, and the advancement of the African race,' he says, 'must be discarded
until the traffic in slaves shall have, ceased to exist.'
Both Livingstone and Baker mention regions free from
the slave-trade, where the people were superior and
had many of the elements of progress ; but the denizens
of these favoured parts were mostly warlike and powerful tribes, into whose territory the peaceful white man,
as well as the marauding Arab, was afraid to venture.

The conviction that the European has little power
of judging adequately of the negro, of understanding
his character, of ascertaining what influences are required to promote the development of his powers, and
the experience of the physical and moral difficulties
which beset the efforts of Europeans to introduce civilisation into Africa, has led to the attempt to establish
negro colonies from America, to entrust the regeneration of Africa to the African himself.

The idea of negro colonisation is one that at first sight
seems a little utopian. The prejudice existing against
the negro is the belief that he is a mere child who
cannot lead and must needs be led. But the success of
the American Colonisation Society in founding the

republic of Liberia is a sufficient answer, we do not say to the difficulty, but to the alleged impossibility of a negro colony. The obstacles to be surmounted were such as to make the task seem almost a hopeless one. There was nothing but discouragement bestowed on the enterprise in America, and in Africa there were insuperable dangers and hindrances in the way. The pirates had to be dislodged from the neighbourhood of the new settlement. The Portuguese slave-traders had been established for centuries and had demoralised the whole country round. The wars among the native tribes arising out of the slave-trade rendered the position of the colonists a precarious one. Yet they struggled on; enlarged their borders, purchased lands, and in course of time became an independent State recognised as such, for the last forty years, by the various European courts and by the United States. It is gradually making its way into the interior, establishing settlements on the healthy table-land which lies away from the west, and by degrees incorporating many of the aboriginal tribes. It possesses an efficient school system, and a college of higher studies to which influential chiefs of the interior are beginning to send their sons. Agriculture is on the increase, trade is flourishing; there is regular and frequent communication with England and America. There is a prospect of a large influx of coloured men from the States who are beginning to appreciate the possibility, and to feel the attraction of the prospect, of an independent home in the land from which they are exiles. For exiles the American negroes are, and exiles many of them feel themselves to be. They have never taken root there or become part and parcel of the nation. They are a race apart. The distance between them and the whites is too great to allow of their amalgamating. A race does not overleap the intermediate steps from barbarism to advanced civilisation from the mere fact of living in a civilised country. The coloured men, in spite of the boon of freedom, remain much what they were several generations back. Their tastes, habits, customs, ways of thought, and manner of life are still African, and their affections are naturally in Africa also. It may be that the absence of opportunity has prevented the development of any sort of desire in most of them to return to the land whence they sprang, but if once the tide of emigration set in they would return with all the prestige and advantages which would be conferred upon them in the eyes of their fellow-countrymen by their sojourn in America, and which would in reality qualify them to be the guides, and teachers, and law-givers, and educators of their uninstructed natives. One who is himself a coloured man, one of the most highly-educated and large-minded of his race, and who was for some years the Liberian Plenipotentiary at the English Court, tells us that there are in America many negroes who realise their duty to their fatherland, and who have ' a restless sense of homelessness which will never be appeased until they stand on the great land where their forefathers lived ; ' and he quotes the words of a bishop of the African Missionary Episcopal Church, who says with great reason that history has shown that an oppressed or degraded race must emigrate before any material change takes place in their civil, intellectual, or moral status. This craving for the fatherland, this permanent and irrepressible impulse, as the same author tells, though it has never been as yet encouraged by the American Government, must in time lead to emigration on a large scale. If only a tenth part of the coloured men of

America were to return to the land of their fathers, it would be enough and more than enough to change the face of the African continent.

In an address delivered before the American Colonisation Society in 1853 the Hon. Edward Everett, after pointing out how, out of the long sufferings of the negroes the providence of God seems intending ultimately to bring the regeneration of Africa, states a fact which subsequent experience has confirmed.

'When that last noble expedition, which was sent out from England, I think in the year 1841, under the highest auspices, to found an agricultural settlement in the interior of Africa, ascended the Niger, every white man out of one hundred and fifty sickened; all but two or three—if my memory serves me—died; while of their dark-skinned associates, also one hundred and fifty in number, with all the added labour and anxiety that devolved upon them, a few only were sick, and they individuals who had passed years in a temperate climate, and not one died. I say again, sir, you Caucasian, you proud Anglo-Saxon, you self-sufficient, all-attempting white man, you cannot civilise Africa. You have subdued and appropriated Europe; the native races are melting before you in America as the untimely snows of April before a vernal sun; you have possessed yourself of India; you menace China and Japan; the remotest isles of the Pacific are not distant enough to escape your grasp, nor insignificant enough to elude your notice; but *Central Africa confronts you, and bids you defiance.* Your squadrons may range or blockade her coast; but neither on the errands of war nor the errands of peace can you penetrate the interior. The God of nature, no doubt for wise purposes, however inscrutable, has drawn across the chief inlets a cordon you cannot break through. You may hover on the coast, but you dare not set foot on the shore. Death sits porteress at the undefended gateways of her mud-built villages. Yellow fevers, and blue plagues, and intermittent poisons, that you can see as well as feel, await your approach as you ascend the rivers. Pestilence shoots from the mangroves that fringe their noble banks ; and the glorious sun, which kindles all inferior nature into teeming, bursting life, darts disease into your languid systems. No, *you* are not elected for this momentous work. The Great Disposer, in another branch of His family, has chosen out a race, descendants of this torrid region, children of this vertical sun, and fitted them by ages of stern discipline for the gracious achievement.' [1]

The negroes and they alone can live in the African climate and reproduce themselves there. To the white man Africa is an impossible climate. The most important parts, the neighbourhood of the large lakes and the banks of the rivers, are so prejudicial to the health of whites as to render their permanent residence there impossible. Missions have to be given up for this reason, and even in the case of those that struggle on the mortality is disastrous. The African fever decimates them. When once they get away from the coast, they are at a disadvantage which practically closes the country to all save the most robust. Men of iron are needed for the interior of Africa. This is the great obstacle to any system of stations along the great lakes. Here and there spots may be found where Europeans can live, but they are exceptional. The difficulty of acclimatisation is one of the greatest barriers to any system of colonisation by Europeans. In the Congo

[1] Blyden, pp. 406–7.

Free State, out of the six hundred whites who agreed to serve for three years there, only five were able to remain the whole time.

But what is poison to the white man is food to the black. The African prospers where the American or European dies; as the climate of Northern America with its severe cold is fatal to the coloured man, so the warmth and moisture of Africa is fatal to the white. But the negro finds himself quite at home there. The climate suits him perfectly. In the tropical zone he enjoys far better health than in the temperate zone. Thus nature points him out as the future apostle of freedom and civilisation to Central Africa.

It may be that Blyden takes rather too favourable a view of the prospects of African colonisation by Africans, but even if we make large allowances for the influence of his love of his own race, and prepossession in their favour, we cannot afford to slight the views of a man who has a right to speak in behalf of the negroes, and whose wide experience and great ability give weight to his words. In England indeed the question is not a very practical one, but in America it is of the greatest importance. The increase of the negroes in the States, which is considerably greater in proportion to their numbers than that of the white population, will in time present serious difficulties, and affect the general condition of the country. A steady stream of emigration would do a great deal to put an end to what is certainly a false position, unavoidable indeed, and a great advance on the state of things in the days of slavery, but one which is prejudicial to the progress of the negroes themselves, and presents a constant series of almost insuperable problems to the American legislature.

The many disadvantages which surround the negro in America are a negative argument for a large system of emigration, which, when the time for inaugurating it shall come, will tell very much in its favour. As long as he remains in America, he is hampered in mind and body, he is warped by his surroundings, he lives among those who dread deterioration, and believe that their vitality and growth depend on their continual assertion against all alien comers, and therefore can neither give place nor opportunity to their former slaves. He is bound to endless imitation; instead of adapting, he copies. He too often despises himself, and the burden of his song is: 'Glory, honour, dominion, and greatness to the white.' [1] Thus he is cut off from the proposal of Blyden; he has no career worthy of rational ambition. We have no intention of entering upon the field of American politics, or discussing the future of the coloured race in the United States; we will simply quote the words in which Mr. Blyden sums up, in the name of the race of which he is the eloquent spokesman, his own convictions on this subject.

'In the United States, notwithstanding the great progress made in the direction of liberal ideas, the negro is still a stranger. The rights and privileges accorded by constitutional law offer him no security against the decrees of private or social intolerance. He is surrounded by a prosperity—industrial, commercial, and political—in which he is not permitted to share, and is tantalised by social respectabilities from which he is debarred. The future offers no encouragement to him. In the career of courage and virtue, of honour, emolument, and fame, which lies open to his

[1] *Christianity, Islam, and the Negro Race*, p. 401.

white neighbours and to their children, neither he himself, nor his sons and daughters, can have any part. From that high and improving fellowship, which binds together the elements from Europe, however incongruous, the negro child is excommunicated before he is born.'[1]

The reason of this seems to be that the distance between the white and the coloured race is at present too great to allow of the healthy development of the latter. We believe that Mr. Blyden is right when he says that a real independent moral growth, productive of strength of character and self-reliance, is impossible to natures in contact with beings greatly superior to themselves. This is a source of difficulty not in America alone, but wherever races far removed from each other in moral and social development, live in physical contact. It is one of the main difficulties of African colonisation, and one which affords a strong support to the system of emigration from America advocated by the American Colonisation Society.

A somewhat similar scheme is proposed in Captain Allen's report of an expedition sent out by the British Government to the River Niger, published under official sanction. His opinion coincides with Mr. Blyden's statement that the slave-trade can only be effectually and permanently suppressed by enlisting native energy in its own cause. 'The white man,' he says, 'may guide, protect, and instruct the indigenous inhabitants of Africa during their mental minority, but there will come a time when they must be suffered to run alone. This is proved both by the physical obstacles which prevent us from dwelling in their land to hold them in leading strings, and by the palpable

[1] Blyden, *Christianity, Islam, and the Negro Race*, p. 398.

failure of all our well-meant exertions for the suppression of the slave-trade which holds that land in
darkness.'[1] Captain Allen proposes to choose the men
in our colonies most fitted for the task of regenerating
their countrymen, and restore them to their own land.
They should be Africans of pure race if possible;
otherwise, the experiment might be begun with the
mixed race, or Mulattoes, who would possess some
portion of the superiority inherent in the white man.
In this way we should, he says, have an intermediate
agency sympathising with both parties. This scheme
may at the outset appear somewhat bold, but would not
prove difficult to carry out. The means he proposes to
adopt are :—

1. The establishment of a colony at the confluence
of the Niger and the Chedda, and eventually on all
other accessible rivers.

2. The formation of a small native military force.

3. The equipment of an African marine service,
whose operations would be limited to ensuring peaceful intercourse between the nations dwelling on the
banks of the Niger, in order to further lawful commerce,
and to enforce treaties already entered into for the suppression of the slave-trade on the river.

The idea of establishing an African force is a principal feature in this plan. The officers should be natives,
holding commissions. The sons of native chieftains
might be persuaded to enter our army and navy with a
view of being educated for the service. Such a motive
as this for advancing in civilisation has hitherto never
been held out to them. It would not be without great
advantages to ourselves too, since experience has abun-

[1] *A Narrative of the Expedition to the River Niger*, by Capt. William
Allen, R.N., p. 421.

dantly proved that white men cannot serve in Africa without a terrible sacrifice of life and health.

Were the scheme found to work well, its operations might easily be extended and its efficiency increased by planting stations on several rivers, with depôts at their mouths, communications being established between them. Thence the system would gradually extend itself into the interior.

In order to maintain discipline among the coloured officers, and restrain them from falling back into the barbarism of the surrounding tribes, it would be well from time to time to transfer the forces, military as well as naval, from one station to another. Strict surveillance would, as a matter of course, be indispensable, both in the case of the military and naval officers, and also that of the civil officials, who, being likewise natives of Africa, would be equally exposed to relapse into a state of savagery. By having constantly to report their proceedings to superior authorities, a spirit of subordination would be kept up, and they would be prevented from either asserting a premature independence or tyrannising over their underlings.

Many of the existing native laws, customs, and institutions are not destitute of value, and might be modified and assimilated so as to render them practically useful. An error into which we Europeans frequently fall is that of meeting the African with our preconceived notions, and requiring him to adopt our institutions and ideas, instead of inquiring into his with the purpose of discovering whether there may not be in them a sufficient element of good to render them worth retaining. At any rate, unless absolutely objectionable, they will probably be suited to him, as he is to the surroundings in which God has placed him. It is certain that some tribes possess not only institutions but qualities and talents which, if rightly directed and judiciously developed, would aid much in remedying the evils which have been caused by their abuse. The country itself, too, if, in endeavouring to ascertain what materials we have to work upon, we examine into its natural and industrial resources, will be found far more productive and rich in things essential to commerce than is generally imagined.

For the native colony he proposes Captain Allen says that a small extent of territory already purchased by the Government would be enough, as it would suffice to afford space for the experiment of cultivation by free labour, as an example to neighbouring nations. From this territory slavery would be banished, but no attempt would be made to interfere with it among the neighbouring tribes. The colony should contain within itself all the elements of native society, together with the usages and advantages of European civilisation, modified and adapted to the exigencies of another nation and another clime and good customs of native growth. There should be a civil governor, a chaplain, with a certain number of catechists and schoolmasters; judges, who would confer with the lawgivers of the country, with a view to the improvement of their legal code rather than the exclusive exercise of ours; medical officers, merchants, artisans, and agricultural labourers, in addition to the naval and military commanders of whom we have spoken.

For the defence of this settlement, which would be subject to British authority, one hundred well-disciplined men from our African regiments, together with a band of the inhabitants enrolled as militia, and two or three small armed steamers, would be sufficient. Not only would attacks from the neighbouring nations be warded off, but the presence of this force would be a great means of repressing the slave-trade not only on the river but on its banks. The independent chiefs would gladly enter into a defensive alliance with us were they delivered from the influence of the Moslem traders, and the dread which they inspire. Captain Allen relates that the natives regarded the presence of the first expedition as a protection and a means of putting a stop to the terror in which they were held. The High Priest of one town called a meeting of the principal inhabitants on the subject of the slave-trade, at which it was readily agreed to furnish men, money, and provisions to any extent if only the members of the expedition would remain with them and protect them—' clean the road,' as they expressed it, of the cruel slave-dealers. The chief of the district himself dared not openly discuss the question of the abolition of the trade, for fear of the Moslems, many of whom were about his court in disguise as spies, and were, of course, interested in the maintenance of the system. In a private interview, however, he gave ardent expression to his wishes for its abolition.

Captain Allen expresses his opinion, which is confirmed by the testimony of other travellers and residents in Africa, that the prejudices of the natives against colonisation, never very strong, would eventually disappear, and that unsuspected talents and energies would be called forth and developed by the presence among them of a community composed of their own countrymen, rescued from a state of bondage, and trained to enjoy the benefits of Christian civilisation. Among many tribes there exists a traditional idea of justice, and the leading characteristic of all is decidedly a love of commerce. Kings, priests, warriors, all, down to the very slaves, are traders in Africa; and although this active commercial spirit has been perverted to the worst of purposes—the sale of their fellow-men—it may be turned to good account. 'It would be well,' the poor creatures used to say to Captain Allen, 'if the Moslems were persuaded that the slave-trade was bad, for then they would cease to sell us.' Since the conquest of the country, a yearly tribute of a large sum of cowries is exacted from the people. If they cannot pay the tax they are not only robbed of their goods but their children are taken away and sold. Allen relates that a boy was on one occasion carried off by the Arabs and taken to Egga, where he was exposed in the market-place for sale. His parents, poor, miserable, and heart-broken, resolved to make an attempt to redeem their child, and for this purpose parted with everything they possessed. With the cowries raised in this way the father hurried off to Egga, hoping to be able to purchase his own child. He had not enough to content his rapacious foes. 'Go back,' said the Arab: 'you must get more cowries. ' Yes,' answered the man, 'I will try to get more.' Upon that the Arab rejoined, 'You had better not come here again; if you do we will sell *you*.' He was thus obliged to return and tell his wife that their child was not to be ransomed at any price.

The frequency with which slaves sometimes change hands is illustrated by the history of a man named Macauley, who acted as Captain Allen's interpreter. Whilst accompanying the expedition he happened to pass through the town where he had once lived as a slave. Almost the first person he met there was the very woman who had sold him—a stout little creature, with some fearful gashes in her face. She laughed heartily, and seemed delighted at seeing her former slave, and wished to present him with a fowl if he could stop a little. She said she had not been aware that it was wrong to sell slaves, and that she had never wished to part with Macauley ; her husband had insisted on it, and, acting on the doctrine of obedience, she had done his will. When a boy, Macauley was kidnapped by the Moslems and taken by them to Egga, where he had been sold to a Mallam, who sold him again to the woman in question. She disposed of him to King Obi, who in his turn sent him with a canoe-load of other slaves to another chief, by whom he was sold to a Spanish slave-ship, which was taken by a British cruiser, and thus he had been set at liberty.

Were the trading propensities of the Arabs and the native population diverted into other channels, the benefit would indeed be great. The Arabs have for a long time had the trade of the country, legitimate and illegitimate, in their hands ; now European enterprise is opening out a market for the export of native products and the import of manufactured goods. By encouraging the native chieftains to employ their domestic slaves in the cultivation of cotton, sugar, &c., a remunerative trade might be established, since the same local advantages— the ready means of communication with the coast, which have facilitated the export of slaves from all parts of the interior—can be utilised for the carrying on of lawful commerce. All undertakings of a commercial nature must, if they are to succeed, be under the immediate protection and authority of Government.

It seems very doubtful whether slavery can be starved out by turning the energies of traders into other and legitimate channels. The profits of the slave-trade are greater than those of any other regular commercial speculation. The slave is an article which is in constant demand. The state of European markets and the caprice of fashion have no influence upon it. It has at the same time the attractive feature of a large element of uncertainty; it is a form of gambling in which there is a chance of an enormous profit if the slaves can be brought down safely to the coast. The risks now enhance the value of the slave, and they are not as a rule such as seriously to interfere with the average profits, but they raise the prices in the market. The judicious trader who lays his plans well and conducts his caravan with due precautions against the capture of his slaves, or their death on the march, knows he will gain a large sum of money on every drove that he can sell. This has a sort of fascination for the enterprising slave-merchant. As a rule he is utterly indifferent to the life or happiness of the slaves. They are to him what a drove of oxen is to the cattle-dealer; the only difference being that every slave who reaches his destination in fairly good condition fetches what would be a fancy price in the case of beasts or other ordinary merchandise.

For this reason the slave-trade can never be supplanted by ordinary traffic on merely commercial grounds. The only means of effecting the change is by rendering the slave-trade so dangerous or practically impossible as to render its profits on an average less than those of lawful commerce. If once the tide can be turned, and other trade substituted for the trade in slaves, the advance in every sort of commerce is 'by leaps and bounds.' This has been the case both on the eastern and western coast. After Sir Bartle Frere's visit to Zanzibar in 1872 the trade between that port and British India has increased fourfold. At Lagos, on the western coast, the advance has been still more rapid since slavery was abolished there. The trade of the Free Republic of Liberia has made steady progress ever since it established itself as an independent Government: the Liberian coffee-plantations are supplying the chief markets in the world. Palm-oil, ivory, india-rubber, beeswax, hides, gum, copal, are being largely exported. Africa has unlimited capacities of production, if once the paralysing influence of the trade in human flesh is removed.

Another scheme for the suppression of slavery and the civilisation of Africa is the establishment in Africa itself of a series of centres under the management of Europeans, where native communities may be formed whose members will become champions of their oppressed fellow-countrymen against the oppressor. The experiment has been tried at Sierra Leone, and with a certain, though very limited, amount of success. It is being tried now in various parts of the continent, and must constitute at least one of the chief elements of any effective scheme for the regeneration of Africa, and the stamping out of the inhuman traffic which is at present fatal to all hopes of lasting improvement. It is what the late General Gordon proposed to himself when he had arranged to go out to the Congo and penetrate into the country lying between that river and the Nile. It is what Captain Joubert, the ex-Pontifical Zouave mentioned by Cardinal Lavigerie, is now doing. He is training a band of negroes to form a corps of militia, and teaching them the use of firearms, in order that they may defend their wives and families, their house and home, from the piratical attacks of the cruel slaver; thus inspiring them with a feeling of self-respect and self-reliance. The presence of Europeans as commanders would have the desired effect of counteracting the influence of the Arabs, who are now the scourge of Equatorial Africa. They have lately made themselves masters of the vast plateau lying between Tanganyika and Lake Nyassa, and have supplied the native tribes with guns and powder and every necessary to carry on the work of devastation. Several lesser tribes now have ceased to cultivate the soil, and live on plunder.

Emin Pasha, who for twelve years has been governor of the Equatorial Province, has been most successful in banishing from his province the slave-dealers who infested it. This was a difficult and a dangerous undertaking, for they had rooted themselves firmly in the soil, and most of the officials in Emin's employ were in full sympathy with them. The petty satraps kept in their employ a number of armed slaves, who were sent about to hunt slaves for their masters, and who did business at the same time on their own account. Whole convoys of slaves used to be sent thence to the markets like beasts for slaughter, children being stolen from their parents to be sold for a bottle of brandy or a pair of old trousers. Emin Pasha relates how, when on journeys of inspection, he used to set free and send to their homes hundreds of slaves at a time, of all ages, many of whom belonged to the governor of the district. In his letters he strongly advocates the system of stations as a means of ensuring the safety and improvement of the country. These were military stations or forts. The following is the description given of them :—

'Each station is fortified, either by earthworks or strong stockades, and each possesses several gates, which remain open from 6 A.M. until 8 P.M., and at which sentries are mounted night and day. From sunset to sunrise no gun may be fired off in or near a station, except as a signal of alarm. At 5.30 A.M. the *réveille*

is sounded, and soon after, the signal " Light your fires!"
At 6 A.M. the roll is called and the gates opened, the
soldiers drill, and the women begin to sweep the streets.
At 8.30 all excepting the sentries turn out to work
in the fields, to draw water, or to fetch wood; the
dew being by that time dried up, the cattle are sent out
to graze. Work lasts till 11.30, when there is an
interval for rest until 2.30 P.M. It then continues till
5 P.M., when all return inside the fort. At 8 P.M. the
roll is called, the gates are shut; and at 9 P.M. all fires
are extinguished, an officer going the rounds to see that
this regulation is obeyed. The orders are most strict
with regard to fire. Should a strong wind arise during
the day, the bugle sounds " Fires out! " and any one not
promptly conforming to the rule is severely punished.
This is a very necessary precaution, as, if a hut catches
fire, it is with difficulty that the whole station is saved
from destruction.' [1]

It was by means of a well-armed and efficient native
force, maintained at these stations, that Emin Pasha
was enabled to suppress the slave raids in the district
under his command. But the force at his disposal was
very small, and repeated applications for reinforcements
of men and arms met with no answer, or at best a very
tardy one. In one of his letters he says :—

'Much to my sorrow, I have had to give up all but
the absolutely necessary stations, and have completely
evacuated the Fauvera, Fadibek, and Latuka districts.
Some of the soldiers thus set free have been employed
to strengthen the stations situated on the river. If
ever a steamer comes and brings arms and ammunition,
I shall be in a position to re-occupy every fort that
may seem necessary. These repeated evacuations do

[1] *Emin Pasha in Central Africa*, p. 521.

not tend, of course, to raise the prestige of the Government among the negroes. If the proper course had been taken from the first, we should not be where we are now. The mischievous prohibitive system, the half-measures, the trifling with the slave-question, the hollow phrases about the equal rights of the Sudânese— all these are bearing fruit now.' [1]

As far back as 1883 he wrote thus to Dr. Schweinfurth :—' If the Government, besides the exploitation of Africa for pecuniary ends, which seems to have been the case latterly, is really bent on carrying on a humanitarian mission there—and that was certainly Ismail Pasha's intention—it can, in my opinion, only be done by uniting the negro districts, the Bahr-el-Ghazal and the Equatorial Provinces, and separating them entirely from the Arab portions of the Sudân. Then a capable European governor must be found for them, who has a love for the work, and will take an interest in the country—not one who does not care whether "blue men or green live by the Albert Lake." He should have three to four steamers at his disposal, and should be commissioned to work out the details of the organisation, of the exploitation of the country, of the disposal of the products, and of matters affecting the slave-trade in conjunction with us the local governors. A commission in Khartúm for slavery affairs, consisting of the governor of the Sudân or his representative, and the consuls, as well as five to six trustworthy natives, Mohammedans and Christians, should be in direct communication with the governor of the negro districts, whose residence should be at Sobat. Fashoda would of course be given up as a *mudirië* (district over which there is a governor).

[1] Ibid. p. 467.

'You have heard of the negro revolts on the Bahr-el-Ghazal? It seems that the negroes there have had enough of being regarded only as "things" from which every possible service is to be extorted, and which are then to be maltreated in return for the work they have done. After many years' experience of the negroes, and intimacy with them, I have really no hopes at all of a regeneration of negroes by negroes. I know my own men too well for that; nor have I yet been able to bring myself to believe in the hazy sentimentalism which attempts the conversion and blessing of the negroes by translations of the New Testament, and by "moral pocket-handkerchiefs" alone; but I do not on that account despair of the accomplishment of our task, viz. the opening up and consequent civilisation of the African Continent. It will be, no doubt, a work of time; and whoever devotes himself to the task must from the first give up all thoughts of fame and of his services being acknowledged.

'But Europe possesses energy for anything, and if one man dies another will take his place and carry on his work. It is strange that Europeans have left our country quite out of sight, and prefer to pour money into the interior by the somewhat worn-out route from Zanzibar, and to enhance the greatness of Sultan Mirambo and heroes of his stamp by tribute. If only a thousandth part of the sums expended on those expeditions, which were, however, intended to form stations, had been employed on fitting out a small expedition—of Germans, of course, I should prefer—and sending it here, I would have sent it forward into the still unoccupied country to the south of Makraká, a real paradise. The men would have been within a few days' march of us, and in constant contact with the world, in a healthy mountain region, and would have been a protection and a blessing to the surrounding negroes. Small stations would in a very short time have been thrown forward to the Congo through the entirely unknown district extending from the western shore of the Albert Nyanza to Nyangwe, or an advance might have been made to the Beatrice Gulf, and finally to the Tanganyika. Has the King of the Belgians no means of forming such a station? And would it be quite impossible for you to start something of the sort? Of course you must not mention me in connection with it, but you may be sure that the men who come may depend on my complete and most zealous support. I must, however, make one remark: I am not speaking of an exploring party, but of the founding of a station—a centre, in fact, for future explorations. The station should maintain itself by hunting, tillage, gardening, &c. (ivory!!) The staff should be chosen with a view to this—men who are not only able to command, and to take the altitude of a star, but who know how to work occasionally, and do not disdain to take a look into the cooking-pot. As an experienced traveller, you will certainly admit that a man who ever has to live and work here would also do better to leave the spirit-bottle behind in Europe. What boundless advantages the country itself would derive from such beginnings! Much more effective support to our struggles against slavery would be afforded by the presence of several Europeans than by that of ten consuls in Khartúm, or by enlarged and emended editions of Anglo-Egyptian slave-conventions. But if Europeans have no money for such purposes, or prefer to waste men and means from Zanzibar, we have at any rate the missionaries.

'I took a great deal of pains during my stay in

Khartûm to prevail on the mission there to undertkae the establishment of stations in this country, not in the foolish manner of past times, but after the model of the French station in Bagamoyo, though perhaps with rather less religious ballast and less psalm-singing. Whether they were alarmed by Mgr. Comboni's death, or what it was, I do not know; but there was so much talk of getting permission from Rome, temporary difficulties, want of money, &c., that there is nothing to be hoped for in that direction. The C. M. S. do not see their way to send a mission here; the other Societies may think differently, but I have no connection with them; and the Germans—do you suppose they have money for the purpose? There remains only Mgr. Lavigerie, with his Turcos and Zouaves—what do you think of my opening a correspondence with him? From what I see and hear, he would be just the man to take an interest in this kind of thing, and he seems to have means enough at command to go to work at once, which is just what I want; for I should like before my death to have a better guarantee for the preservation of the work I have done than could be afforded by the prospect of seeing a highly respectable Bey step into my place, who would neither understand nor love the country and its inhabitants.' [1]

Had the reinforcements and supplies so urgently needed by Emin Pasha been sent out without delay, he would probably have extended his influence, and not only checked but prevented the slave-raids in the ad-joining provinces, whereby large districts have been half-depopulated. But his appeals were unheeded, and meanwhile the sad tidings reached him of Gordon's death, the retreat of the English, and the loss of the

[1] *Emin Pasha in Central Africa*, pp. 425-8.

Soudan. Crippled by the non-arrival of the men and ammunition he asked for, he was unable to prevent the Arabs from gradually increasing their power, and asserting themselves in the regions around the Great Lakes, by causing the expulsion of all Europeans from Uganda.

In the autumn of 1886 he again complains of the want of support, in consequence of which the relapse of the country into barbarism and the slave-trade is to be dreaded. He reiterates his determination to hold his position as long as possible, and not to give up his hopes and plans for the future of the land. 'I am still waiting and hoping for help,' he writes, ' and that from England, whose philanthropic spirit will, I hope, keep her true to her ancient traditions, notwithstanding the rise and fall of Governments. I still believe that, whether Liberals or Conservatives are at the helm, the immense importance of aiding us will not be lost sight of, nor the importance of crushing the slave-trade and keeping my people free. One or two caravans are all that is necessary, and I believe they could easily reach me from the East Coast direct, or from the north-east corner of the Victoria Nyanza. There remains, too, the route through the Usóga and the Lango district. I am of opinion, however, that a good present would smooth all difficulties there ; and it must not be forgotten that if I knew that help was coming to me from that direction, I could easily push forward one or more stations towards the east, and thus stretch out a helping hand to any caravan coming to my relief.'[1]

In a letter of later date he again expresses the hope of receiving assistance from England :—

'If England wishes really to help us, she must try,

[1] Ibid. p. 503.

in the first place, to conclude some treaty with Ugánda and Unyóro, by which the condition of those countries may be improved both morally and politically. A safe road to the coast must be opened up, and one which shall not be at the mercy of the moods of childish kings or disreputable Arabs. This is all we want, and it is the only thing necessary to permit of the steady development of these countries. If we possessed it' we could look the future hopefully in the face. May the near future bring the realisation of these certainly modest wishes, and may we be permitted, after all the trials which God has seen fit to bring us through, to see a time of peace and prosperity in Central Africa!''[1]

The value of an open route through Nyassa land to the coast as a means for putting an end to the slave-trade was first pointed out by Dr. Livingstone. Vessels built for river navigation can steam from the mouth of the Zambesi to its junction with the Shiré, and thence to the foot of the cataracts. A road has been made from the foot of the cataracts to where the river is again navigable. Another road connects Lake Nyassa with Tanganyika, and a steamer on this lake can convey goods more than four hundred miles further into the heart of Africa. For the purposes of commerce this route is an easier road into Central Africa than either the Congo or the Niger. For humanitarian purposes it is the most important road into the centre of the continent, for it crosses all the principal routes of the slave caravans from the interior to the eastern coast. If this route were held the slave-trade would be cut in two and paralysed. This is what Dr. Livingstone insisted on when he asked his countrymen to occupy it, and heal what he called 'the open sore of Africa.' In re-

[1] *Emin Pasha in Central Africa*, p. 509.

sponse to his invitation, several missionary stations were made on the shores of Lake Nyassa, in the table-land above it, and on Lake Tanganyika. These missions carry on industrial as well as evangelical work. The African Lakes Company, started with the primary object of assisting the missions in those regions, and introducing legitimate commerce, has established flourishing plantations there of coffee and sugar, besides cultivating indigo, cocoa, tea, &c.

It possesses four steamers, two plying on the Zambesi, and two on the Upper Shiré and Lake Nyassa; a staff of twenty-seven Europeans, and twelve trading-stations.

Another enterprise the Lakes Company aim at accomplishing is that of buying ivory all along the route at higher terms than the Arabs—who are ivory merchants as well as slave-dealers—can afford to give, and thus diminishing the slave-trade. For every tusk of ivory purchased by the Arabs a negro must be captured or bought to carry it to the coast; or rather not one, but six, as the probability is that, if the march is long, five out of six will die before the coast is reached. On their arrival there both goods and carriers are sold, and a double profit realised by the merchant.

The late attacks upon the mission and trading stations in the region of the Equatorial Lakes indicates a feeling of apprehension among the Arab traders. Finding themselves hemmed in on every side, and anxious to secure a portion of territory for themselves, they have acquired the mastery in Uganda, and are now threatening the existence of the work begun by Livingstone, and so ably carried on by his countrymen on Lake Nyassa. There is little doubt that the aban-

donment of the Soudan has strengthened the Moslem
in his defiance of European power. A crisis is
now approaching which will decide the fate of Arab
ascendency in Central Africa. For years the Arab
traders have been preparing the way for an outburst of
violence, by supplying the native tribes with arms and
ammunition, and stirring them up against the foreign
invader. And now, unless prompt measures are taken,
and succour speedily sent to the handful of isolated
Europeans in the neighbourhood of the Great Lakes,
the Mohammedan power, which has the resources of
the country at its command, will carry all before it ;
missioners and traders will be massacred, or forced to
leave the country ; and the commencement of civilisation and Christianity in Central Africa will be completely swept away.

There seems to be a consensus of opinion as to the
necessity of the employment of military force for the
abolition of the slave-trade and the destruction of the
Arab dominion throughout Africa. Cardinal Lavigerie
has spoken with full knowledge of his subject. He is a
missionary bishop, and yet he asserts that it will not do
to trust solely to pacific weapons. ' Slavery such as it
is to-day,' he says, ' can only be stopped by force. It
is not merely by stopping the transport of slaves into
Asia that this can be done ; it is necessary to strike the
evil at its root.' The object of the proposed conference is to deliberate on the method to be adopted
for this object, and, above all, to ensure united action.
One great reason why the Moslem has hitherto been
able in Africa to bid defiance to Europe is, that it
is one, whereas the European Powers are divided.
Hitherto the nations of the civilised world have not
been induced to take common action against the slave-

trade. It is to be hoped that ere long they will co-operate for this desired end, and that all the Powers who have dependencies in Africa will, by means of a well-armed native force, under the command of Europeans who, like Emin Pasha, 'understand and love the country and its inhabitants,' suppress alto-gether both slave-hunts and slave-markets throughout the territory under their control.

The deadly effects of the climate of certain districts may render impossible the employment of a large European force in any part where the presence of armed men is necessary for the suppression of slavery; but the same objection does not hold against the employment of a native force armed with European weapons and led by European officers. By careful selection of men already inured to African life the loss from fever and other maladies might be reduced to a minimum. We have seen many Europeans often spend long years in Africa, and in the most unhealthy localities, without falling victims to the climate. If among those who volunteer for such service some sacrifice their lives to the task they have undertaken, they will perish in a good cause, martyrs to Christian civilisation and the claims of oppressed humanity.

The following description of the reliquary mentioned in the brief addressed by Pope Leo XIII. to Cardinal Lavigerie in November 1887, was published in the *Tablet* of June 15, 1889 :—'The ancient reliquary presented to the Pope by Cardinal Lavigerie has been placed in the Museum which forms part of the Vatican Library, and as a work of art it is considered a gem. It was found under an altar in the ruins of an ancient basilica not far from Ain-Beida, in Numidia. The basilica itself is in a good state of preservation, and dates about the fifth or sixth century. The reliquary is of solid silver, of an oval shape, and is adorned with symbolic images beautifully chiselled in bas-relief. It has on one side the symbol of Christ on the mystic rock, from which issue the four rivers of Eden, to each of which a thirsty stag is approaching. Two palm trees, one on each side of the rock, signify, the one Palestine, and the other the Promised Land. Continuing round to the other side are eight sheep in the act of coming towards the Divine Lamb, who is in the middle, raised on a sort of little platform, and who is carrying on his back a Latin cross. On the lid is the figure of a martyr with a wreath of laurels on his head, while on each side of the figure are two candelabra. Signor de Rossi, the eminent Professor of Christian Archæology, has observed that in all the monuments which have been discovered in Byzantium and Numidia the saints and the faithful are always represented as being in Paradise by a candelabra as a symbol of light. He is of opinion that the relics of some martyr must have been enclosed in this reliquary, as is represented by the figure on the lid, who bears the crown of eternal life. He considers also the reliquary to be of the same date as the basilica, the Christian symbols especially coinciding with those generally used during the fifth and sixth centuries. The artistic style of the work is altogether Byzantine.'

INDEX.

CEM

Cemetery at Carthage, ancient, 219
— in Tunis closed, 224
Ceremony of kissing the feet of missioners, 152
Christian villages founded, 49
— — success of, 52
Climate of Africa fatal to Europeans, 157, 348
— — salubrious in some parts, 158
Colonisation of Africa, 84
— — by Europeans, 343
— — by American negroes, 345
Colonists, opposition of, in Algeria, 64
Consecration of the cathedral of Carthage, 221
Conspiracy in Uganda revealed by native Christians, 167

Deguerry, Fr., 94, 105
Deniaud, Fr., death of, 154
Difficulties of the missioners' journey, 133
Districts, missionary, formed, 165
Doctors, native, trained in Malta, 283
Domestic slavery, 245, 247, 249
— — a plea for, 313

Egypt, slavery in, 247
Emin Pasha, 361
— — his appeals to England, 367
Emir of Damascus, 18
Emperor Napoleon III., letter to, 66
— — second letter to, 67
— — offers preferment to Mgr. Lavigerie, 71
Employment of native soldiers, 355, 360
Episcopal jubilee of Cardinal Lavigerie, 234
Epitaph composed by Cardinal Lavigerie, 224
Equatorial Lakes, journey of missioners to, 153
Escape of Europeans from Uganda, 189
Expedition, military, proposed by Cardinal Lavigerie, 337

JER

Expeditions, missionary, to Equatorial Africa, 133, 147, 153
Expulsion of religious orders from Algeria threatened, 208

Faith, progress of, in Uganda, 166
Fakis, conduct of, towards slaves, 258
Famine in Algeria, 38
Farewell address to missioners, 148
Fetichism, 258
— 'custom' of, 315
Fever, African, 136, 157
Franco-German war, sympathy with, 86
French Government in Algeria opposed to the Archbishop's plans, 54
Fund for sick and aged priests, 23

Gueydon, Admiral, 73, 79

Hore, Captain, kindness of, 141
Hospital for Arabs, 114
House of Studies, *Les Carmes*, 6, 25
Human sacrifices in the Niger territory, 284, 315
— — crusade to abolish, 317
— — in Central Africa, 342

Importation of firearms into Africa, 332
Indifference of the negro to religion, 158
International Association for the Abolition of Slavery, 129
— conference proposed, 331
Inundations in Italy, subscriptions for, 205
Islamism, inroads of, 253
Italian Capuchin Fathers in Tunis, 195, 200, 226
— Jews in Africa, hostility of, 224

Jansenism, lectures on, 8
Jerusalem, sanctuary in, served by Algerian Fathers, 125

PRINTED BY
SPOTTISWOODE AND CO., NEW-STREET SQUARE
LONDON